dBASE FOR PROFESSIONALS, WITH dBASE IV

dBASE FOR PROFESSIONALS, WITH dBASE IV

NEIL DUNLOP

VNR VAN NOSTRAND REINHOLD
New York

Library of Congress Catalog Card Number 89-16519
ISBN 0-442-20741-7

Printed in the United States of America

Van Nostrand Reinhold
115 Fifth Avenue
New York, New York 10003

Van Nostrand Reinhold International Company Limited
11 New Fetter Lane
London EC4P 4EE, England

Van Nostrand Reinhold
480 La Trobe Street
Melbourne, Victoria 3000, Australia

Nelson Canada
1120 Birchmount Road
Scarborough, Ontario M1K 5G4, Canada

16 15 14 13 12 11 10 9 8 7 6 5 4 3 2 1

Library of Congress Cataloging-in-Publication Data

Dunlop, Neil.
dBASE for professionals / Neil Dunlop.
p. cm.
Includes Index.
ISBN 0-442-20741-7
1. Data base management. 2. dBase III (Computer program)
3. dBase IV (Computer program) I. Title.
QA76.9.D3D854 1989
005.75'65—dc20 89-16519
CIP

CONTENTS

PREFACE

This book is for power users—people who have programmed in another language and who want to learn dBASE as a programming language. It is also for dBASE users who want to learn more about dBASE as a programming language. It is suitable for a text for an intermediate-to-advanced dBASE programming course.

This book focuses on what the programmer needs to know in order to write programs in dBASE. Each chapter covers a separate step in the program development process and provides examples of how to tap the power of dBASE as a programming language in order to solve real-world problems. The beginning of each chapter covers programming principles that are common to both dBASE III and IV. The end of each chapter covers topics specific to dBASE IV.

dBASE IV is an evolutionary product. This book analyzes each dBASE IV enhancement from the programmer's standpoint to see whether it is useful or really adds anything new to the language. This book cuts through the "marketing hype" to analyze what is really new about dBASE IV from a programmer's perspective.

This book takes a nuts-and-bolts approach to programming in dBASE, based on the belief that the power of dBASE is best tapped by understanding the functions and limitations of each built-in command.

This book stresses the essentials of programming in dBASE, many of which are not covered in other books. Contrary to popular opinion, the principles of programming in dBASE have not changed much through the various iterations of the dBASE language. Although various extensions and front ends have been added, the fundamentals of programming in the language remain basically unchanged.

This book discusses each aspect of the design process, focusing on tapping the power of dBASE through gaining an intimate understanding of how it works.

While this book is written specifically for Ashton-Tate's dBASE III PLUS and dBASE IV, most of the programming principles apply to other implementations of the dBASE language such as FoxBASE and Clipper. The program examples use the most general syntaxes across all implementations of dBASE. This book covers the principles underlying all implementations of the dBASE language and addresses the subjects that any dBASE program designer must consider in developing a real-world application in dBASE.

Chapter 1 gives an overview of the development of the dBASE language.

Chapter 2 summarizes the principles of data base design.

Chapter 3 reviews the material that should be known by the reader. It summarizes how dBASE creates and manipulates files from a programmer's perspective. If any of the material in Chapter 3 is confusing to the reader, a beginning book on dBASE should be consulted.

Chapter 4 shows the utility of dBASE functions for manipulating strings, numbers, or dates.

Chapter 5 shows how to use built-in dBASE commands for the most efficient output. Examples are shown of using the LIST command, which often provides the fastest output, to its maximum capability. Output enhancements in dBASE IV are discussed.

Chapter 6 gives a detailed treatment of inputting under program control and describes how input validation can take place using the tools provided by dBASE III PLUS and dBASE IV.

Chapter 7 describes how indexes work so that they can be used for maximum benefit. It includes a section showing how to access records in the most efficient manner possible. Understanding the principles in this chapter is the basis for achieving maximum speed of execution for programs written in any version of dBASE.

Chapter 8 describes how to use indexes and dBASE commands such as SUM, AVERAGE, and TOTAL to extract data from files of any size in the most efficient manner possible. The dBASE IV CALCULATE command is also discussed.

Chapter 9 describes how transaction processing can be used for maximum efficiency of program design.

Chapter 10 removes some of the mystery from SET RELATION TO, which is perhaps the most misunderstood command in the dBASE language, and discusses how to relate files by explaining what is going on when files are related.

Chapter 11 discusses program structure and compares various menuing options including the "old-fashioned" dBASE III menu vs. the new pull-down and pop-up menus in dBASE IV.

Chapter 12 presents the tools available for debugging programs in both dBASE III PLUS and dBASE IV.

Chapter 13 covers SQL and its implementation in dBASE IV. Emphasis is on moving between SQL mode and native dBASE.

Chapter 14 discusses the structure of dBASE .dbf files and how to interchange data in .dbf files with other popular formats such as Lotus or ASCII files.

Chapter 15 covers selected topics such as interfacing with DOS and networking.

Chapter 16 covers some of the more useful features of dBASE IV, including arrays, and some of the more innovative possibilities for using dBASE IV menuing options.

The Appendix consists of two parts: a dBASE III PLUS reference and a dBASE IV reference. The dBASE III PLUS reference covers the commands that are essential to programming in dBASE III PLUS and to most other implementations of the dBASE language. Commands and functions are covered from a programming point of view with tips for the most effective way to use each. The dBASE IV sections cover the new and enhanced features in dBASE IV. For users considering switching from dBASE III PLUS to dBASE IV, browsing through this section will highlight some of the changes in dBASE IV.

This book is about both dBASE III PLUS and dBASE IV. Since dBASE IV is an evolutionary product, chapters start with a discussion of the principles that are common to both dBASE III PLUS and dBASE IV. The end of the chapter then discusses and analyzes the enhancements in dBASE IV to see if they really provide any new functionality. Chapters 13 and 16 and the dBASE IV Appendix are exclusively about dBASE IV.

Conventions Used in This Book

Longer program listings in this book are printed with line numbers for ease of reference. When entering the program, do not type the line numbers.

In program listings, dBASE commands and functions are listed in upper case. Field and memory variable names are listed in lower case.

In some cases the dBASE convention of simply using the first four letters of a command is used. For instance, REPL can be used for REPLACE.

When indexes or tags are used, it is assumed that they have been created previously based on the correct key fields.

In other cases, when a command line is too long for a single printed line, the dBASE convention of using a semicolon to extend the command is used.

Note the following conventions for entering dBASE command lines in different modes.

1. When entering long commands at the dot prompt simply keep typing up to a maximum of 254 characters. In dBASE IV, to enter a command line longer than 254 characters at the dot prompt, press Ctrl-Home to invoke the editor.

2. In MODIFY COMMAND, dBASE III PLUS automatically inserts a soft carriage return character for long command lines. In dBASE IV, MODIFY COMMAND lines up to 1024 characters long can be entered or split using semicolons as described below.

3. When working in an ASCII text editor, including dBASE IV MODIFY COMMAND, put a semicolon at the end of a line to tell dBASE to look on the next line for the remainder of the command.

Chapter 1

THE HISTORY OF dBASE AND ITS PLACE IN THE MARKET

Change is certain. Progress is not.
—*E. H. Carr,* From Napoleon to Stalin and Other Essays

dBASE: THE HISTORY

dBASE grew out of a mainframe data base management system called JPL Data-Management and Information-Retrieval System (JPLDIS) that was developed at the Jet Propulsion Laboratory (JPL) in Pasadena, California by Jeb Long. JPLDIS was used for storing and retrieving information about unmanned planetary missions. The program allowed astronomers easy access to the data using simple one line commands. Wayne Ratliffe, a systems designer at JPL, wrote a similar system for use on microcomputers. In 1979, Ratliffe began selling the program under the name of VULCAN, the home planet of *Star Trek*'s Mr. Spock who was known for his power of total recall.

The first version of VULCAN lacked report generation and indexing capabilities. However, these deficiencies were remedied in a subsequent release.

In 1980, a software distributor named George Tate heard about the program. He tried VULCAN and liked it. Tate took over the distribution of the product, renaming it dBASE II. There never was a dBASE I.

Ashton-Tate was formed by George Tate and others in 1980. There was no Ashton. In 1983, the company went public. From the capital that was raised, about $3.25 million was paid for the rights to dBASE.

User Acceptance

In 1983, ads such as this were appearing in computer magazines:

> dBASE II is a powerful, easy-to-use data management tool for constructing and manipulating numeric and character information files. A special feature of dBASE II is its own English-style program-building-language. You may SORT, EDIT, or DISPLAY a data-base directly from the keyboard, or write menus and programs to support your specific applications (from an Osborne ad listing software available for the Osborne 1 from the July 1983 issue of *The Portable Companion* magazine).

However, many users who bought the product disagreed with the statement that it was easy to use. They found that the "English-like commands" had very strict and sometimes quirky syntaxes. In response to this problem, a cadre of programmers saw the potential in using dBASE as a programming language. Most users preferred hiring a programmer to write a program for them rather than investing hundreds of hours of their own time in learning how to use it. Programmers pushed dBASE further than its originators ever dreamed of.

Many end-user applications were written by programmers in dBASE II. In a sense, the independent programmers did more to promote dBASE II than did the marketing efforts of Ashton-Tate. Users bought dBASE II to run the applications written by programmers.

The dBASE II manual written by Wayne Ratliffe validated the principle that programmers should not write manuals. It was notoriously hard to understand. In 1984, books began appearing that explained how to use the product. User groups sprang up where programmers shared their tips for using dBASE.

In 1984, George Tate, chairman of Ashton-Tate, died unexpectedly. Resultant management changes found Ed Esber elevated first to the CEO role, then to chairman of Ashton-Tate.

dBASE III

While dBASE II, which originally ran on CP/M systems, was ported to the IBM-PC and MS-DOS, Ashton-Tate later made a decision to separate the CP/M version of dBASE from the MS-DOS version.

In mid-1984, Ashton-Tate released dBASE III, which was touted as solving user problems by providing a menu-driven front end as well as enhanced programming features. After working with it, many programmers elected to stay with dBASE II until the advent of the developer's release that later became dBASE III PLUS. The dBASE III menu-driven front end was considered by most programmers to be a joke because of its lack of power. Most serious programmers also scorned the attempts at ease of use, such as views and catalogs.

dBASE III took the original dBASE language and changed some of the command syntax and added additional commands. Some of the syntax changes proved annoying. For instance, in dBASE II the CLEAR command would close all .dbf files and release all memory variables, but in dBASE III it simply cleared the screen.

Many developers were hesitant to embrace dBASE III and to convert their dBASE II applications. The program included a conversion utility that supposedly converted dBASE II code into dBASE III code, but it worked only some of the time. In addition, dBASE III supported local and global memory variables, but the debugging features made it difficult to check the values of local memory variables when a program aborted abnormally. The program debugging features of dBASE III were actually less powerful than those of dBASE II, making program debugging much more difficult.

To correct these problems, Ashton-Tate produced a developer's release of dBASE III, which corrected many of the problems of the first version of dBASE III. This developer's release was later to become dBASE III PLUS.

The 1986 release of dBASE III PLUS made dBASE III useful as a programming language. The Assist front end was somewhat improved, though scorned by serious users. As one end user who took a course in dBASE III PLUS using the Assist mode said after working with a consultant in designing a dBASE application, "I know dBASE can do more than this."

Ashton-Tate did not address the issue of compiling dBASE code, leaving a window of opportunity a mile wide for its competitors to walk through. Into this gap came several software companies who developed compilers that were mostly dBASE-compatible while adding extensions to the language. Since each compiler maker added different extensions, programmers had to make trade-offs between programming in *plain vanilla* dBASE or making use of the extensions.

In addition, Ashton-Tate was attacked on the ease-of-use front by such competitors as Paradox, who provided an easier but powerful way of accessing data.

Ashton-Tate has been criticized often for being more marketing oriented than technically oriented; all versions of dBASE have had long lists of bugs, referred to as *anomalies* by Ashton-Tate.

The dBASE IV Strategy

Ashton-Tate's dBASE IV strategy seems to be to try to include every function offered by its competitors in its bloated new package. They have thrown in a pseudo compiler, saving a true compiler as a carrot for the future, and topped it with a dash of SQL and QBE. Unfortunately, in Ashton-Tate's zeal to incorporate the features of its competitors, not all of the enhancements were implemented well. Ashton-Tate, which was once the market leader, is now in the position of playing catch-up with its competitors and not doing a very good job of it.

The Dichotomy Continues

dBASE is two things: a programming language and an end-user package. Serious programmers admit that it takes a programmer, even one who has programmed in another language, about six months of working with the dBASE language in order to fully tap its power. Ashton-Tate has always tried to downplay the degree of complexity of the language.

On the other hand, end users can start using the menu-driven interface very quickly. However, they often find that they cannot do things as easily as expected through the menus.

The idea of an object-oriented end-user interface is that the user can, with little training, tap the underlying power of the program without doing any procedural programming. An object-oriented front end, such as that of dBASE IV, enables users to work with objects such as screens and views rather than with files and records. It must be evaluated by how much power it gives the end user and how easily that power can be tapped. Ashton-Tate has always exaggerated the power of the end-user interface and downplayed the time required to learn the programming language.

The dBASE IV Control Center

The Control Center is the new front end that claims to allow users to access the power of dBASE through menus. Though some features, such as the screen generators, are fairly well implemented, there are some significant problems with the implementation of other features.

The Control Center consists of a Screen Painter, a Report Writer, a Label Generator, and an Applications Generator. However, the Applications Generator only generates menus—it does not generate the code to implement the menu options unless simplistic built-in dBASE commands like EDIT or APPEND are used. This means that the combination of the Applications Generator and the Screen Generator is probably adequate for an application such as a simple mailing list when there is no sophisticated manipulation of the data. A more sophisticated application could still require a great deal of programming.

Some of the screen generating features are borrowed from Ashton-Tate's single-file manager, RAPID FILE. RAPID FILE is an excellent program for single-file management, but it has not been widely accepted by the market.

The Control Center includes a Query by Example (QBE) mode that allows users to query multiple files based on entering the desired field values on the screen. However, the QBE mode uses sequential access in retrieving data. It does not check to see whether indexes exist. This means that queries are quite slow on large files.

If the Assist mode in dBASE III PLUS taps 10% of the program's power, then the Control Center may get up to 15% or even 20%. But most of the power of dBASE still comes from its use as a programming language. Most complex applications involve more sophisticated manipulation than generating simple screens and queries.

dBASE IV as a Programming Language

Virtually all dBASE III PLUS programs will run unchanged in dBASE IV. However, some additional programming features have been added.

1. SQL—SQL code can now be used in conjunction with dBASE commands.
2. Somewhat improved network capabilities, including automatic record locking.
3. Numerous extensions to the language, many of which are similar to extensions developed by the compilers. The significant enhancements are analyzed in this book. Some of the major ones include arrays, better handling of memo fields, and options for creating menus.
4. A full screen debugger.

PROGRAM DEVELOPMENT

dBASE IV operates in a pseudo compiled mode rather than in an interpreted mode. While it is avowedly not as fast as some of its competitors, there may be a certain method in Ashton-Tate's madness.

The ideal program development environment is one in which the code can be written and debugged; where, each time a syntax error occurs, the program can be stopped, the error corrected immediately, and the program re-executed without recompiling and linking the program. Thus, the ideal program development environment would be one with an interpreter and a compiler that both use exactly the same syntax of commands. Once the program is debugged, it could be compiled for source code protection and speed of execution.

Unfortunately, this has not occurred, for the most part, in the dBASE world. Most of the dBASE compilers have added extensions to overcome the perceived limits of the dBASE environment. Each time an extension is added, some degree of incompatibility is added. Programmers have developed work-arounds such as embedded program control statements that test for which environment is being used and then adjust the command syntax accordingly.

Another oddity of dBASE compilers is that they have been written typically to link in the whole library whether or not specified library routines are needed. Thus the minimum size .exe file generated is approximately 130K, even for a single-line program.

Ashton-Tate has the market position, if not the resources, to develop a real development environment with both an interpreter and compiler that use the same syntax. dBASE IV is a pseudo compiler that does not create a stand-alone .exe file. Rather, it generates a .dbo file that requires either dBASE or a run-time version of dBASE to execute.

Ashton-Tate has announced a true compiler called the Professional Compiler. It will produce a stand-alone .exe file and will link in only those routines from the library that are used in the program. However, Ashton-Tate, like its competitors, plans to include extensions in the Professional Compiler that are not found in dBASE itself.

Speed

Compilers are often compared to dBASE in terms of speed. However, some of those comparisons are illusory. Much of the "slowness" associated with dBASE can be attributed to poor programming rather than to dBASE itself. Very often, by optimizing the code within dBASE, a severalfold increase in speed is noted. Compilers speed up some functions, such as screen I/O and the execution of DO WHILE loops, once the code has been optimized.

However, comparing the overall speed of one compiler with another is often pointless. The functions to measure speed against include the following:

1. creating an index
2. updating an index
3. finding an indexed record (should be instantaneous)
4. painting a screen

They are the functions that most often affect the response time of a program.

End-User Product vs. Programming Language

A high-level programming language is a programmer productivity tool. Typically, programmers make a trade-off between shortening development time and lengthening execution time by selecting a high-level language over a low-level language.

In the last few years, vendors have tried to supply fourth-generation interfaces that allow the user to tap the underlying power of a program without doing any programming. The dBASE Control Center is a fourth-generation environment. The programming language is a third-generation procedural language.

End-user computer magazines often criticize dBASE for being difficult to use and for its so-called limitations. Programmers often snicker when they see such comments in magazines, because they believe that dBASE is best viewed as a programming language. Given the ability to program, dBASE can be made to do almost anything.

Much of the confusion about dBASE in the popular computer press has arisen from the attempt to view it as an end-user data base management environment rather than as a programming language. However, dBASE is better viewed as a programming language that provides the programmer with a powerful set of programming commands rather than as an end-user environment.

A data base management system is a productivity tool—it should make accessing data easy. dBASE has been successful because it provides an easier means of accessing data than writing programs in assembly language, C, or most high-level languages.

Porting dBASE to Other Environments

Ashton-Tate has released products or announced plans to release products to port dBASE to the following environments

Unix
System 36
OS/2

Intent of This Book

This book differs from other books in that it shows the subjects that must be addressed in designing a real-world application. Many other books cover the so-called ease-of-use features of dBASE. This book covers the subjects that a programmer must understand to really tap dBASE's power.

Whether the market accepts one version of dBASE or another, the principles underlying programming in dBASE remain essentially the same. It is these principles that are the focus of this book.

Chapter 2

DATA BASE DESIGN

All the data in a row must be about the primary key: the whole primary key, and nothing but the primary key so help me Codd.
—*Quote found on the wall of an unidentified DBA*

Before you write a single line of code, it is helpful to turn off the computer and think through the steps involved in designing a data base application. Particularly critical is designing the data base files themselves in order to avoid redundancy of data. This chapter will present several simple systems analysis techniques for accomplishing these objectives.

Users often have difficulty describing their needs. This process is useful for first planning the system and later for generating user documentation. As these systems analysis steps are followed, the concept of what the system is to do will be clarified. As each step is performed, it may be necessary to go back and refine previous steps.

COMMUNICATION BETWEEN THE USER AND THE PROGRAMMER

Designing a program is a two-way communication process between the user and the programmer. The programmer must learn the nuances of the user's activities, and the user must learn from the programmer how to use the computer. The techniques discussed in this chapter can facilitate this two-way communication process. In a high-level language like dBASE it is possible to write part of the program, show it to the user, and then make minor changes based on the interview with the user.

When users actually see an input screen or report screen, they can be more specific about how the screen needs to be modified in order to meet their needs.

DESIGNING A SIMPLE MAILING LIST SYSTEM

In the early chapters of this book, a simple mailing list example will be used to illustrate certain basic points. We will assume that the mailing list system is used to store not only names and addresses but also a contribution amount.

Black Box

One simple technique involves thinking of the system as a black box and viewing only the inputs and outputs as shown in Figure 2-1. In this approach, we defer any consideration of what goes on inside the black box until a later time and focus on what goes into and what comes out of the black box.

Thinking Through the Functions to Be Performed

In thinking through the functions that must be performed, it is helpful to list the functions that will later become menu options. These functions might include such things as

1. Add names and addresses
2. Edit existing names
3. Record current contribution
4. Generate mailing labels by zip code
   a. Select certain zip codes
   b. Select certain cities
   c. Select by contribution date
5. Generate alphabetical listing by name
6. Generate contribution analysis by zip code
7. Generate contribution analysis by city
8. Generate contribution analysis by state
9. Purge old records
10. Look at when names were added to the list

For designing menus, these functions could be grouped into subcategories of input and output.

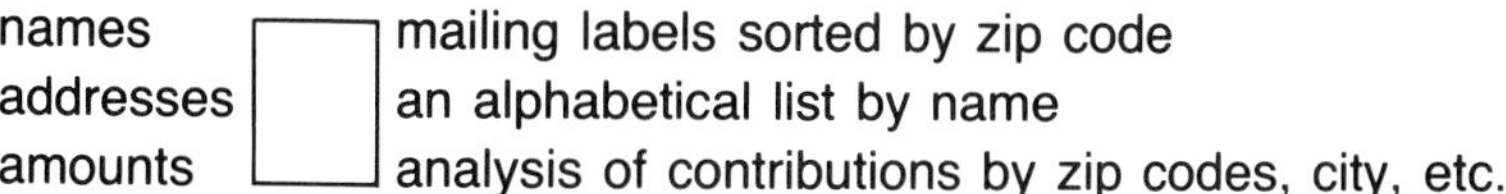

Figure 2-1. Black box showing inputs and outputs of maillist system.

Input Menu

1. Add names and addresses
2. Edit existing names
3. Record current contribution

Output Menu

4. Generate mailing labels by zip code
   a. Select certain zip codes
   b. Select certain cities
   c. Select by contribution date
5. Generate alphabetical listing by name
6. Generate contribution analysis by zip code
7. Generate contribution analysis by city
8. Generate contribution analysis by state

The purge function, which is needed to conserve disk space, might be added to the input menu.

The output menu might be broken down further into a label menu and a report menu.

Expanding on the Functions to Be Performed

For documentation and planning purposes, each function could be expanded upon.

Input Functions

1. Add names and addresses
   —Allow users to enter new addresses into the system
2. Edit existing names
   —Edit existing addresses to reflect change of address
3. Record current contribution
   —Record date and amount of most recent contribution

Output Functions

Labels

4. Generate mailing labels by zip code
   —Generate four-across labels sorted by zip code
   —Generate one-up labels sorted by zip code
   —Generate labels by a specific subcategory or group of subcategories such as the following:
      a. Zip codes
      b. Cities
      c. Contribution dates
      d. Contribution amounts

Reports

5. Generate alphabetical listing
   —Generate a listing sorted by last name and showing amount and date of contribution
6. Generate contribution analysis by zip code
   —Generate a contribution analysis for each zip code. Give options to list by ascending or descending order of contributions within each zip code or to list alphabetically by name within each zip code
7. Generate contribution analysis by city
   —Generate a contribution analysis for each city. Give options to list by ascending or descending order of contributions within each city or to list alphabetically by name within each city
8. Generate contribution analysis by state
   —Generate a contribution analysis for each state. Give options to list by ascending or descending order of contributions within each state or to list alphabetically by name within each city

Other functions may be added as system planning continues.

Designing the Files

In relational data base terminology, we must identify the entities that we will track with the system and then identify the attributes of each entity. The entity here is the contributor, so we must identify the attributes or fields for each contributor. Making a list of the attributes of each contributor is helpful:

last name
first name
street address
city
state
zip code
phone number
date

Further consideration might yield additional attributes:

company
title

Slightly more complicated is how to treat contributions. People make different contributions at different times. Therefore, for each contribution, we must track

contributor
amount of contribution
date of contribution

The question then becomes whether to include the amount of contribution as a field in the contributor file. Such an approach would limit the number of recorded contributions to the number of contribution fields in each record. A more flexible approach would be to have two separate files: one that maintains contributor information and one that maintains contribution information. A one-to-many relation would exist between the contributor file and the contribution file: each single contributor might make many contributions. The file structure might look like this:

Contributor	*Contribution*
ssn	ssn
lname	contributor
fname	date
title	amount
company	
straddress	

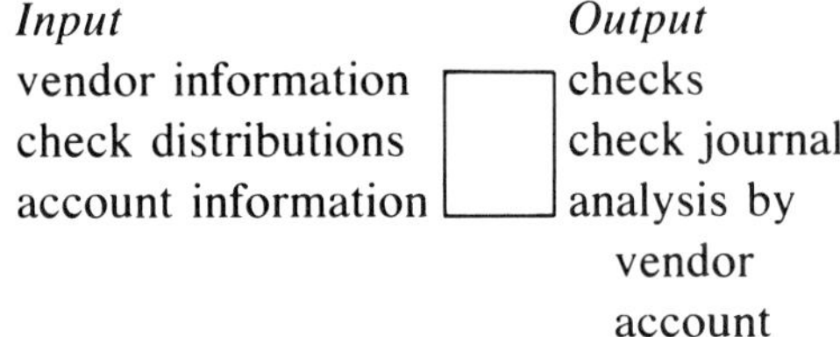

Figure 2-2. Black box showing inputs and outputs of accounts payable program.

city
state
zip
phone

The two files would be linked by a field that would identify the contributor. The social security number usually represents the most reliable key field for uniquely identifying a person. However, for privacy reasons, contributors might not always be willing to volunteer their social security numbers. We will assume in this case that the social security number is available. Thus, social security number becomes the common key field between these two files.

While the above application would properly be designed with a separate file to record each contribution, examples in this book show a simplified method with a single amt field in the main file.

DESIGNING AN ACCOUNTS PAYABLE SYSTEM

A more complex application is a simplified accounts payable system that allows paying bills and allocating each check to multiple accounts. The black box might look like Figure 2-2.

Analysis of Functions to Be Performed

To generate the desired outputs from the inputs, it will be necessary to perform these functions:

Vendors
- Add new vendors
- Edit existing vendors
- Generate a listing of vendors

- Accounts
    - Add new accounts
    - Edit existing accounts
    - Generate a listing of accounts
- Checks
    - Enter check information
    - Edit checks
    - Print checks
        - Print address on stub
        - Print amount on stub
- Reports Generated
    - Check register
    - Analysis by account
    - Analysis by vendor

Designing the Files

To support these functions, these files must be maintained:

- Vendor
    - Vendor code
    - Vendor name
    - Vendor address
    - Periodic amount
- Account
    - Account name
    - Account code
    - Amount
- Checks
    - Check number
    - Vendor code
    - Date
    - Amt
- Distribution
    - Check number
    - Account code
    - Amount

One problem to be solved in a check-writing system is that the amount distributed for each check must be allocated to one or more accounts. If each

Figure 2-3. Relationship among files in accounts payable example.

check was allocated to only one account, an account field could be maintained as part of the record for each check. However, allowing the ability to allocate each check to more than one account requires a separate distribution file where the primary key is *check number + account code*.

Identifying Key Fields

For each file it is important to identify key fields. The main files and the primary key—the field or fields that uniquely identify each record—are listed below.

Vendor file—vendor code
Account file—account code
Check file—check number
Distribution file—check number + account code

Figure 2-3 may serve to help visualize the relationship among files.

The following relations exist. Each vendor has many checks, but each check has only one vendor. Each check has many distributions, but each distribution has only one check. Each distribution has one account, but each account has many distributions.

Secondary keys—key values that are not unique but that may be the basis for retrieving records—for each file would be the following:

Vendor file—state, city
Checks file—vendor code, date
Distribution file—either check number or account number

The questions to be asked might be these.

1. How much did we pay in the first quarter to our vendor ABC, Inc., and from which accounts did we pay them?

2. Which vendors did we pay out of our office supplies account during October?

3. Who was check number 43134 written to, and what was the amount?

Our file design allows us to answer each of these questions.

PRINCIPLES OF DATA BASE DESIGN

These principles should be followed in designing files:

1. Avoid repeating fields—avoid storing duplicate information except for key fields that link files.

2. Avoid multiple dependencies—avoid fields in files that depend on anything other than the primary key.

Avoid Data Redundancy

The basic principle for designing files is that every field that is not a key field is functionally dependent on the whole primary key and is not dependent on any nonkey field.

For instance, if a file were being maintained to track course information, one way to design the file would be the following:

Course file
- Course number
- Course name
- Department
- Faculty ID
- Faculty name
- Faculty address

In this example, which shows the wrong way to design a file, course and faculty ID are dependent on the key field: course number. However, faculty name and address are dependent on faculty ID, which is not a key field. If this design were implemented, then each time a faculty member taught a course, the name and address would have to be stored in the course record. Each time the address was changed for a faculty member, the address in each course record would have to be changed. This approach would result in a tremendous amount of data redundancy. The correct way to design the file is

Course file
- Course number
- Course name
- Department
- Faculty ID

Faculty file
- Faculty ID
- Faculty name
- Faculty address

In this approach, two files are created: one that lists course data and one that lists faculty data. In the course file, the course number is the key field. Faculty ID is a foreign key that can be used to point to the proper faculty record in the faculty file. The mechanism for relating files like this will be discussed in the SET RELATION TO chapter. This approach insures that there will be one unique record in the course file for each course offered and one unique record in the faculty file for each faculty member.

Identifying the Primary Key

Each file should have a single field or group of fields that uniquely identifies each record in the file. Characteristics of an ideal primary key are

1. It should uniquely identify the record. There should be no possibility of duplicates.

2. It should not change. Editing primary keys presents problems.

Examples of Primary Keys

These are examples of primary keys:

1. People data. For information about people, the best primary key is the social security number if it is available. A social security number is presumably unique; it uniquely identifies an individual and does not change over time. However, social security numbers are not always readily available. People may be more willing to give their social security numbers when registering at a college than when subscribing to a magazine, for example.

2. Accounting data. In our accounts payable example, the check number uniquely identifies each record in the check file. The process of assigning the check number must be considered. Due to the possibility of a printer "eating" a check, the number should not be assigned until the check is actually printed.

In the distribution file, the primary key is check number plus account number. This concatenation of fields uniquely identifies each record in the file.

Sometimes it is not practical to have a unique key. In a simple mailing list where social security numbers are not available, there may be no primary key. Access methods such as entering a last name and displaying all records for that last name can be used. Sometimes algorithms are developed to take part of the last name, part of the zip code, part of the address, etc., to attempt to construct a primary key.

Chapter 3

THE BASICS OF CREATING AND MANAGING FILES

A journey of a thousand miles must begin with a single step.
—*Lao-Tzu,* Tao Te Ching

The commands discussed in this chapter are

CREATE <*file name*>
INDEX ON <*key expression*> TO <*file name*>
USE <*file name*> INDEX ind1,ind2,...ind7
MODIFY STRUCTURE
DISPLAY STRUCTURE

CREATING FILES

Data files are created in dBASE by specifying their field structure. In designing the field structure, you must specify the type and length of each field using a full screen editing procedure.

When the following command is executed

```
CREATE file1
```

a screen appears on which the names, types, and lengths of the fields must be entered. As a result of this operation, a file with the name file1.dbf is created. .dbf is the default extension for data files.

This chapter will show how to create a dBASE data file and how to do simple manipulations on the file by entering commands at the dot prompt.

Field Types

dBASE III PLUS supports these field types:

1. Character fields allow the entry of any valid ASCII characters into the field.

2. Numeric fields are used for storing numeric data that will be manipulated as numbers. In specifying the field width, both the total width and the number of places to the right of the decimal point must be specified. The total width includes the decimal point and the places to the right of the point. Once a field is identified as numeric, only numbers, a minus sign, and a decimal point may be entered into the field. Numeric data that are not added and subtracted, such as zip codes or telephone numbers, are best stored in character fields.

3. Date fields allow the storage of dates. The default format is *mm/dd/yy*, although this default format can be changed for display purposes. Only valid dates may be entered into date fields. dBASE will not allow users to enter invalid dates such as 01/32/87. dBASE knows how many days are in each month and which years are leap years, and it makes sure that only valid dates are entered.

4. Logical fields can hold a value of True or False. True is represented by either .T. or .Y. while False is represented as .F. or .N. The main limitation of a logical field is that it can have only two values. For conditions that may have more than two values, using a one-character character field is more effective.

5. Memo fields hold large chunks of text. The advantage of a memo field is that it only takes up space when a record actually has a memo field. The contents of a memo field are contained in a separate file with a .dbt extension. The .dbf file only maintains a ten-character long pointer to the location of the memo field in the .dbt file. In the above example, if a file named file1 is created and if the file contains a memo field, two separate files will be created: file1.dbf and file1.dbt. The contents of the memo fields will be stored in the file with the .dbt extension while all the other data in the file will be stored in the file with the .dbf extension.

In dBASE III PLUS, memo fields have several very significant limitations:

1. A memo field is not searchable for a character string.

2. The contents of a memo field can not be input with a GET statement except under very limited circumstances.

3. It is not possible to REPLACE a memo field with a character type memory variable.

4. When a memo field is edited, the contents of the old memo field is left in the .dbt file, and a new block of data is added. This means that the .dbt file can get very large as fields are edited.

5. There is no memo type memory variable.

All data in dBASE .dbf files, including numbers and dates, are stored in ASCII format, so a user could get along with just character-type fields. However, having numeric-type fields prevents the need to convert character fields containing numbers into numbers before manipulating them. Date type fields facilitate manipulating dates.

Creating a File

To create a simple name-and-address file type the command

CREATE Addrlist

File names are restricted to the DOS limit of eight characters. A file creation screen that allows typing in the names of the fields, the types of fields, and their width is shown in Figure 3-1.

```
                                                     Bytes remaining: 3913
  Field Name  Type       Width  Dec    Field Name  Type       Width  Dec
  ---------------------------------    ---------------------------------
1 LNAME       Character  15
2 FNAME       Character  12
3 STRADDR     Character  2Ø
4 CITY        Character  15
5 STATE       Character   2
6 ZIP         Character   5
7 AMT         Numeric    1Ø     2
8 DATE        Date        8
9             Character



CREATE          ||<C:>||ADDRLIST          ||Field: 9/9          ||  || Caps
```

Figure 3-1. File creation screen showing creation of file addrlist.

Note that all the fields are character types except for the amt field, which is a numeric type, and the date field, which is a date type. The zip code field will contain numbers, but since zip codes are not added and subtracted, it makes sense to define the field as a character type in order to avoid the suppression of leading zeros. The amt field will be used to record contribution amounts and will be 10 characters wide, including the decimal point. There will be two places to the right of the decimal point.

The three field types used in this example—character, numeric, and date—are the most commonly used field types.

Field names may be up to ten characters long; the underline is the only punctuation allowed in a field name.

To terminate the file creation mode, simply press Ctrl-End. In response to the prompt *Press ENTER to confirm. Any other key to resume*, press the Enter key to terminate the file creation. In response to the prompt, *Input data records now? (Y/N)*, enter *N* for *no*.

A file named addrlist.dbf has now been created.

DISPLAYING THE STRUCTURE OF THE FILE

After a file has been created, it remains open. To see the structure of the file, type:

```
DISPLAY STRUCTURE
```

This command causes the following display:

```
Structure for database: C:\db3\addrlist.dbf
Number of data records:        4
Date of last update    : 12/28/88
Field     Field Name     Type         Width     Dec
    1     LNAME          Character       15
    2     FNAME          Character       12
    3     STRADDR        Character       20
    4     CITY           Character       15
    5     STATE          Character        2
    6     ZIP            Character        5
    7     AMT            Numeric         10       2
    8     DATE           Date             8
** Total **                              88
```

This display shows the name, type, and width of each field as entered. It shows the number of records in the file and the date of the last update. The display also shows the total width of each record, which is the sum of the field widths plus one byte that is used for the deletion flag.

OPENING FILES

After a file is created in dBASE III, it remains open. However, if the file were not open, it could be opened by typing

```
USE addrlist
```

When all desired manipulations have been performed on the file, it can be closed by typing

```
USE
```

To close the file and leave dBASE, type

```
QUIT
```

ADDING RECORDS TO THE FILE

When using dBASE, records can be added to a file at the dot prompt by typing

```
APPEND
```

As will be discussed in chapter 6, it is normally preferable for the programmer to write an input routine rather than use dBASE's built-in APPEND command. This bit of programming allows greater control over data entry and insures that only valid data can be entered into the fields.

Using our simple mailing list example, we will add several records to the file with the APPEND command.

With the addrlist file open, type

```
APPEND
```

The APPEND screen is illustrated in Figure 3-2. Data can be entered into each field as shown. dBASE does a minimum of input validation: it insures that

```
LNAME        Howard
FNAME        John
STRADDR      981 Center Street
CITY         Berkeley
STATE        CA
ZIP          947Ø4
AMT              66.ØØ
DATE         Ø1/31/88



APPEND         ||<C:>||ADDRLIST         ||Rec: 4/4        ||   || Caps
```

Figure 3-2. APPEND screen for adding records to addrlist.

only numbers can be entered into numeric fields and that only valid dates can be entered into date fields. The arrow keys can be used to move between fields.

Note that the contents of character fields are left-justified, while the contents of numeric fields are right-justified. When the contents of the last field in a record are entered, a blank APPEND screen appears, allowing entry of the next record. To exit the APPEND mode, press Enter when the cursor is positioned at the first character in the first field.

Additional records can be added, using the APPEND command.

VIEWING RECORDS

The contents of a file can be viewed by typing

```
LIST
```

The LIST command defaults to displaying all the fields in all the records in the file, as shown in Figure 3-3.

Note several things:

1. When the contents of the record are too long to be displayed on one line, they are wrapped around to the next line.

2. The record number appears at the beginning of each record, and the field headings appear at the top.

```
Record#  LNAME              FNAME  STRADDR            CITY      STATE
 ZIP         AMT   DATE
       1  Smith              John   123 Main           Berkeley  CA
 947Ø4    123.12  Ø1/31/88
       2  Jones              Frank  234 Third Street   Oakland   CA
 947ØØ     9Ø.ØØ    /  /
       3  Anderson           Mary   5678 Third Street  Berkeley  CA
 947Ø6     75.ØØ    /  /
       4  Howard             John   981 Center Street  Berkeley  CA
 947Ø4     66.ØØ    /  /
```

Figure 3-3. Default LIST display, showing all fields for all records.

VIEWING SELECTED FIELDS

Sometimes it is desirable to view only selected fields, as in this case where we want each record to fit on one line. This is accomplished by using the SET FIELDS TO command, which has the syntax

SET FIELDS TO <*field list*>

In this case we will enter the command

```
SET FIELDS TO lname,fname,city,state,zip,amt
```

When the LIST command is executed, the results will appear as shown in Figure 3-4.

ORDERING THE DATA BASE

Notice that the records were entered in no particular order with regard to names, cities, zip codes, or amounts. dBASE can make the file appear to be ordered by indexing on a field or a group of fields. Multiple indexes can be maintained for a given data file. The file can be made to appear in different orders by changing indexes. Each index is maintained in a separate DOS file with an .ndx extension. Indexing is discussed in more detail in chapter 7.

Record#	LNAME	FNAME	CITY	STATE	ZIP	AMT
1	Smith	John	Berkeley	CA	94704	123.12
2	Jones	Frank	Oakland	CA	94700	90.00
3	Anderson	Mary	Berkeley	CA	94706	75.00
4	Howard	John	Berkeley	CA	94704	66.00

Figure 3-4. LIST display with only certain fields selected.

To make our simple address file appear to be in name order, the following command can be executed to create an index named *name* that is based on ordering the file according to last name plus first name.

INDEX ON *lname + fname* TO *name*

The syntax of the INDEX command is

INDEX ON <*field expression*> TO <*file name*>

The index file name can be up to eight characters long, meeting DOS file name criteria. Using the eight characters to give a descriptive file name keyed to the index key is most helpful; each index file is stored in a separate file with an .ndx extension.

When the LIST command is executed now, the results are as shown in Figure 3-5.

Note that while the index makes the records *appear* to be in name order, the physical record numbers remain unchanged.

CREATING ADDITIONAL INDEXES

Additional indexes can be created by typing another index command such as

INDEX ON *city* TO *city*

In this case we arbitrarily assign the file name of the index to the name of the field, based on which the index is created.

With the city index invoked, the LIST command will yield the results shown in Figure 3-6.

Now the records are listed in city order.

Record#	LNAME	FNAME	CITY	STATE	ZIP	AMT
3	Anderson	Mary	Berkeley	CA	94706	75.00
4	Howard	John	Berkeley	CA	94704	66.00
2	Jones	Frank	Oakland	CA	94700	90.00
1	Smith	John	Berkeley	CA	94704	123.12

Figure 3-5. LIST of records in index order by lname+fname.

INDEXING ON MULTIPLE FIELDS

It is possible to alphabetize names within a city. To list names alphabetically within each city and to list the cities in alphabetical order, the following index command could be invoked:

```
INDEX ON city+lname+fname TO cityname
```

The listing will now appear as shown in Figure 3-7. Note that the names are now alphabetized within each city.

INVOKING INDEXES

Normally, indexes need be created only once with an INDEX ON command as long as the index is opened each time records are added to the file so that the indexes can be updated. The syntax for opening a file with indexes is

```
USE addrlist INDEX cityname,name,city
```

Up to seven indexes may be opened with a .dbf file. In this case three are opened. The first index listed, cityname, is the master index that is used as the basis for ordering the records. The other two indexes, name and city, are opened so that if a record is added, those indexes are updated. If a record is added without an index being open, that index will no longer be valid.

Record#	LNAME	FNAME	CITY	STATE	ZIP	AMT
1	Smith	John	Berkeley	CA	94704	123.12
3	Anderson	Mary	Berkeley	CA	94706	75.00
4	Howard	John	Berkeley	CA	94704	66.00
2	Jones	Frank	Oakland	CA	94700	90.00

Figure 3-6. LIST of records in index order by city.

Record#	LNAME	FNAME	CITY	STATE	ZIP	AMT
3	Anderson	Mary	Berkeley	CA	94706	75.00
4	Howard	John	Berkeley	CA	94704	66.00
1	Smith	John	Berkeley	CA	94704	123.12
2	Jones	Frank	Oakland	CA	94700	90.00

Figure 3-7. LIST of records alphabetized by name within city.

Note that the more indexes that are used with a file the longer will be the time required to update the indexes when a record is added to the file.

THE RECORD POINTER

dBASE maintains a record pointer that always points to a given record in the file. Thus, when operations are to be performed on a record, they will be performed on the record on which the pointer is positioned.

Different commands have different effects on the record pointer. When a file is USEd without an index, the record pointer points to the first physical record in the file, record number 1. When a file is USEd with an index, the record pointer points to the first logical record—the record with the lowest value of the index key. For instance, when the file is opened with the cityname index, the record pointer points to record number 3, which has the lowest ASCII value of lname+fname for records where the city is Berkeley.

If a file is opened with no index, the record pointer always points to the first physical record.

The LIST command moves the record pointer to the end of the file. If a LIST command is executed and then DISPLAY is executed, a blank record will be shown because dBASE assumes that there is a blank record at the end of file.

DETERMINING THE POSITION OF THE RECORD POINTER

The DISPLAY command displays one record only—the current record to which the record pointer is pointing.

? RECNO() displays the record number of the record to which the record pointer is pointing.

SKIPPING TO THE NEXT RECORD

The SKIP command moves the record pointer to the next record in the file. If no index is invoked, it moves the record pointer to the next physical record until end of file is reached. If an index is invoked, SKIP moves the record pointer to the next logical record, based on the values of the index key.

TESTING FOR EOF()

When skipping through a file, it is important to test for EOF(). EOF() is only true when an attempt is made to skip past the last record, not when the record pointer is positioned at the last record.

MOVING TO THE FIRST AND LAST RECORDS

The GO TOP command will move the record pointer to the first physical record in the file if no index is invoked. The GO BOTTOM command will move the record pointer to the last physical record in the file if no index is invoked.

If an index is in effect, the GO TOP command will move the record pointer to the first logical record; the GO BOTTOM command will move the record pointer to the last logical record.

EXAMPLES OF MOVING THE RECORD POINTER

Assume that the addrlist file has been opened with no index. These commands move the record pointer to the record indicated:

Command	*Record Pointer*
USE addrlist	1
GO TOP	1
GO BOTTOM	4
LIST	5 (dBASE assumes a blank record at the end)
DISPLAY	no effect on record pointer
SKIP	moves to next physical record if end of file not encountered

If the addrlist file was opened with the index cityname, then the commands shown will move the record pointer to the physical records shown:

USE addrlist INDEX cityname	3
GO TOP	3
GO BOTTOM	2
LIST	5 (dBASE assumes a blank record at the end)

DISPLAY	no effect on record pointer
SKIP	moves to next logical record if end of file not encountered

The physical record numbers do not change based on the existence of an index, but the behavior of certain record positioning commands does.

LOOKING AT SELECTED RECORDS

Sometimes it is desirable to look at only certain records in a file. One approach is to use the SET FILTER TO command. Using the SET FILTER TO a condition could be specified to restrict records to a certain condition. If we enter the commands

```
USE addrlist
SET FIELDS TO lname,fname,city,state,zip,amt
SET FILTER TO zip='94704'
LIST
```

the result will be as shown in Figure 3-8. Only the two records that have 94704 in the zip field will be shown.

The same results can be achieved with this sequence of commands:

```
USE addrlist
SET FIELDS TO lname,fname,city,state,zip,amt
LIST FOR zip='94704'
```

The SET FILTER TO syntax is useful if the filter is to be used several times in succession. Saying LIST FOR <*for condition*> is useful when the filter is to be used only once.

To cancel a filter that is in effect, type SET FILTER TO or type USE to close the file and cancel the filter.

WARNING: After setting a filter, a record-positioning command such as SKIP or GO TOP must be issued to properly position the record pointer to

Record#	LNAME	FNAME	CITY	STATE	ZIP	AMT
4	Howard	John	Berkeley	CA	94704	66.00
1	Smith	John	Berkeley	CA	94704	123.12

Figure 3-8. LIST of records filtered for zip='94704'.

reflect the new filter. For instance, a filter might be set while the record pointer is pointing to a record that does not match the filter. A DISPLAY command would display a record not matching the filter, since DISPLAY does not move the record pointer. However, a record positioning command such as SKIP or GO TOP will move the record pointer to a record matching the filter.

ANATOMY OF A FOR CLAUSE

A FOR clause can be used to modify commands such as LIST or DISPLAY. A FOR clause can contain either a single condition, such as FOR zip ='94704', or it can contain multiple conditions separated by the logical operators .OR. or .AND. An example of a FOR clause using multiple conditions is

```
LIST FOR zip ='94704' .AND. lname='Smith'
```

The equivalent construction using SET FILTER TO would be

```
SET FILTER TO zip ='94704' .AND. lname='Smith'
LIST
```

SET FILTER TO remembers the FOR clause.

GETTING RID OF RECORDS

Sometimes it is desirable to get rid of records that have been entered. Deletion is a two-step process in dBASE.

1. Flagging a record for deletion
2. Eliminating the deleted record

To flag a record for deletion, these steps can be taken:

1. Use a positioning command such as GOTO 3 to move the record pointer to the record to be deleted.
2. Type *DISPLAY*, to ensure that the proper record is being accessed.
3. Type *DELETE*, to flag the record for deletion.
4. Type *DISPLAY* again. This time, an asterisk(*) will appear in front of the record, indicating that it is flagged for deletion.
5. To change your mind at this point, type *RECALL*, to remove the deletion flag.

```
. LIST
Record#   LNAME      FNAME   CITY      STATE  ZIP      AMT
      1   Smith      John    Berkeley  CA     94704  123.12
      2   Jones      Frank   Oakland   CA     94700   90.00
      3  *Anderson   Mary    Berkeley  CA     94706   75.00
      4   Howard     John    Berkeley  CA     94704   66.00

. SET DELETED ON
. LIST
Record#   LNAME      FNAME   CITY      STATE  ZIP      AMT
      1   Smith      John    Berkeley  CA     94704  123.12
      2   Jones      Frank   Oakland   CA     94700   90.00
      4   Howard     John    Berkeley  CA     94704   66.00
```

Figure 3-9. LIST of records showing flagging of deleted records.

Making Deleted Records Disappear

To make dBASE think that deleted records do not exist, the command SET DELETED ON can be used. When deleted is set on, records that are flagged for deletion appear not to exist.

For instance, if record 3 is deleted in our sample file, typing LIST will show record 3 with * in front of it as shown at the top of Figure 3-9. If we type *SET DELETED ON* and then *LIST*, the listing will act as if record 3 does not exist, as shown.

To permanently get rid of records that are flagged for deletion, the PACK command can be used. If we PACK a file, the records are renumbered and the deleted records permanently removed.

Another approach to handling deleted records without the PACK command is the following:

1. Copy the deleted records to a purge file.
2. Copy the nondeleted records to a new file.

This sequence of commands would accomplish these results:

```
USE addrlist
COPY TO purges FOR DELETED()
COPY TO new FOR .NOT. DELETED()
```

```
USE
RENAME addrlist.dbf TO old.dbf
RENAME new.dbf TO addrlist.dbf
```

The instruction USE addrlist opens the original file. Next, the instruction COPY TO purges FOR DELETED() uses the DELETED() function to copy only the deleted records to a file called purges. COPY TO new FOR .NOT. DELETED() copies the nondeleted records to a file named new. USE closes the file addrlist. The RENAME command renames the original addrlist file to a file called old that can later be deleted. Next, the file new is renamed to addrlist. So the file new, which contains only the nondeleted records, becomes the new addrlist file, and it is only as large as the records that it contains. At the end of the execution of this program, these .dbf files exist:

1. old.dbf, which is the original file
2. purges.dbf, which contains only deleted records from the original file
3. addrlist.dbf, which contains only the nondeleted records

CHANGING YOUR MIND—MODIFYING STRUCTURE

After a file is created, it is often desirable to modify the structure of the file to change the field structure. This can be accomplished through the MODIFY STRUCTURE command in dBASE. However, there are certain caveats that must be observed when using this command or data will be lost.

When USE file1, MODIFY STRUCTURE is executed in dBASE, these steps are performed automatically:

1. A temporary copy is made of the structure of the file to be modified.
2. The file containing the data is saved in a file called file1.bak.
3. The create screen appears so that field names, types, and lengths can be changed, and additional fields can be added.
4. dBASE uses its APPEND FROM command to append the data from the original file to the new file.

Because of the way in which the APPEND FROM command works, there are certain cases in which data can be lost. When dBASE appends one file from another file, it looks first at the field names to see which fields in the original file match with fields in the file being appended from. Thus, if the field names are changed in one of the files, the data will not be appended to the other file. dBASE is smart enough to know that if field names are changed, it must use another form of the APPEND FROM command so that data will not be lost. This form of the APPEND FROM command relies on the lengths of fields to make sure that data is saved properly.

However, if a MODIFY STRUCTURE operation is executed in which both field names and field lengths are changed in a single operation, some data will be lost.

To minimize the chance of data loss never change both field names and field lengths in a single modify structure operation.

CAUTION: Before attempting a modify structure, always have a backup copy of the file. If the backup copy is in the same directory of the hard disk, make sure that it does NOT have a .bak extension because that is what dBASE uses.

FIELDS TO MEMORY VARIABLES AND BACK

Often the contents of fields are stored to memory variables for manipulation and then transferred back to the fields. The syntax

<*memory variable name*> = <*field name*>

creates a memory variable to contain the field contents. The type of the memory variable is the same as the field type. For example,

```
mzip=zip
```

This code would create a memory variable named *mzip* and store the contents of the zip field from the record to which the record pointer is pointing.

After the data is manipulated, it can be returned to the fields. This operation is performed with the syntax

REPLACE <*field name*> WITH <*memory variable name*>

After the contents of the memory variable *mzip* are edited, they can be transferred back to the zip field with the syntax.

```
REPLACE zip WITH mzip
```

OPENING MULTIPLE FILES

dBASE III PLUS allows opening up to 10 .dbf files at once, subject to the limit of having a total of 15 files open. Since each index is stored in a separate file, if ten .dbf files are open, there can only be a total of five other files open, including index files, report files, program files, etc.

Reasons for Having Multiple Files Open

There are several reasons why it might be necessary to have more than one .dbf file open at once.

1. Posting the contents of one file to another—see chapter 9.
2. Input validating a value against the contents of a file—see chapter 6.
3. Linking two or more files, based on a common key field to generate reports—see chapter 10.

Syntax for Opening Multiple Files

Each .dbf file is opened in a separate work area. A work area can be thought of as a memory buffer for storing the file header of each file. In a more colloquial sense, each work area can be thought of as a stage for opening up a file. Each separate work area is accessed with a SELECT statement. The syntax for opening up three separate .dbf files is

```
SELECT A
USE file1
SELECT B
USE file2
SELECT C
USE file3
```

Each work area has its own separate record pointer. At the conclusion of the above commands, area C is selected so that any record positioning commands entered will apply only to work area C. To move the record pointer in area A, a SELECT A command must be executed first.

Using Aliases

When a field is referenced, it is assumed to refer to a field in the currently selected work area unless an *alias* is used. An alias allows the user to refer to a field in a nonselected work area. The alias can be either the letter of the work area or the name of the open .dbf file in that work area. Thus, assuming that field1 is a field in file1, that field can be referenced from any other work area by using either of the following forms of syntax:

```
? a->field1
? file1->field1
```

The latter syntax is more descriptive for programming purposes. The file name and field name are separated by a pointer symbol that consists of a hyphen (-) and a greater-than sign (>).

For instance, if the contents of a temporary file opened in A were being transferred to the master file open in B, the syntax would be

```
SELECT B
REPLACE zip WITH A->zip
```

These instructions would cause the contents of the zip field from the file open in A to the zip field in the file open in B. Note that record pointer positioning commands must be used to position the record pointer properly in each work area.

CHANGES IN dBASE IV

dBASE IV does not significantly change the process of creating files and doing basic manipulations. However, there are some changes that are worthy of note.

dBASE IV retains the limit of ten .dbf files open at once; however, the limit of total files that can be opened is increased to 99. This means that opening 10 .dbf files with associated indexes would not be likely to cause a problem, as it would in dBASE III PLUS, by exceeding the limitation of a maximum of 15 total files open.

A new float field type has been added that is most appropriate for scientific applications. It allows up to 20 digits of precision. The type N field and all numeric memory variables from dBASE III PLUS are fixed point. Numbers can be converted between the fixed and float type by using the functions FIXED() and FLOAT().

When an expression includes both fixed and floating point numbers, all fixed point numbers are automatically converted to floating point for the calculation. For output purposes, all floating point numbers are converted to fixed point.

The maximum width of both type N and type F fields is 20 including the decimal point and sign. The SET PRECISION TO command must be used to increase the precision from the default of 16 to the maximum of 20 to take advantage of the full 20 digits of precision.

Memo Fields

Functions have been added for handling memo fields that make a memo field type a more viable option than in dBASE III PLUS. Memo fields are more like expanded character fields and string handling functions such as LEN() and AT() can now apply to memo fields. These functions are discussed in chapter 4. The contents of memo fields can now be stored in character type memory variables.

New functions such as MEMLINES() and MLINE() have been added to allow accessing memo fields line by line. MEMLINES() returns the number of lines that the memo field would take up based on the line length established with the SET MEMOWIDTH TO <*n*> command. The MLINE(*n*) function allows retrieving the *n*th line from the memo field. These functions are discussed in chapter 4.

Data can now easily be moved between memo fields and memory variables. While there is still no memo type memory variable, the contents of memo fields can now be stored in character type memory variables.

The command

```
mvar = memo
```

where memo is a memo type field, results in the creation of a character type memory variable named *mvar* that contains the contents of the memo field.

Conversely, after the contents of the memory variable are manipulated, they can be transferred back to the memo field with the command

```
REPLACE memo WITH mvar ADDITIVE
```

The ADDITIVE switch can be used at the end of the REPLACE statement to add the contents of the memory variable *mvar* to whatever is already stored in the memo field.

The APPEND MEMO <*memo field name*> FROM <*filename*> OVERWRITE command has been added. This form of the APPEND command can now be used to append a text file into a memo field. If the OVERWRITE switch is used, the current contents of the memo field are overwritten. Otherwise, the new file is added to the end of the memo field.

CAUTION: While .dbf files *without* memo fields can be moved back and forth between dBASE III PLUS and dBASE IV, problems can arise when .dbf files *with* memo fields are moved from dBASE IV to dBASE III PLUS.

Indexes

In dBASE IV, indexes can be handled as in dBASE III PLUS with a single .ndx file for each index, or a multiple index file can be used. The default is having a single .mdx file with the same name as the .dbf file associated with each .dbf file. The .mdx file can hold up to 47 logical indexes, called TAGS. This .mdx file, called the production .mdx file, is automatically created when the .dbf file is created if any fields are flagged as being index fields. Otherwise, it is created when an INDEX ON *<field expression>* TAG *<tag name>* is executed. Whenever the .dbf file is opened, the .mdx file is automatically opened so that indexes can be updated automatically. However, even though the .mdx file is open, the records are still physically in the order in which they were entered into the file until a TAG is selected. To select an index tag, the command is

SET ORDER TO TAG *<tag name>*

To create a new TAG based on zip code, the command is

```
INDEX ON zipcode TAG zip
```

To turn off all the TAGS and have the .dbf in "natural order," the order in which the records were physically added to the file, the command is

```
SET ORDER TO
```

When the CREATE command is used, the file creation screen now asks if each field is to be an index key field. If it is flagged as *Yes*, an index TAG is automatically created in the production .mdx file based on that field. However, this approach does not handle index keys based on concatenated keys. For instance, if separate fields are maintained for first and last name and both fields are flagged as key fields, a separate index will be built on the first and the last name fields. Such an approach is obviously inappropriate. To build indexes based on concatenated fields, the INDEX ON command must be used to explicitly build the TAG:

```
INDEX ON lname+fname TAG name
```

To select among various TAGS for a file that is already open, the syntax is

SET ORDER TO TAG <*tag name*>

To open a file with a specific TAG from the production .mdx file as the master index, the command is

USE <*file name*> ORDER <*tag name*>

Separate .ndx files can be used optionally, as in dBASE III PLUS. The advantage of the .mdx file is that up to 47 index TAGS can be maintained while only incurring the overhead of opening one DOS file. The other purported advantage of the .mdx file is that, since the production .mdx file is automatically opened when the .dbf file is opened, indexes are automatically updated when records are added. Issues about updating indexes are discussed in the chapter on indexing and on transaction processing.

CAUTION: When copying .dbf files using DOS, it is important to copy both the .dbt files (if memo fields are present) and the production .mdx file. In DOS, this result can be accomplished using

COPY filename.* <*drive specifier*>:

This DOS command will copy the .dbf file as well as the production .mdx file and .dbt file, if they exist.

DISPLAY STRUCTURE now shows an additional column indicating whether a field was designated as an index key when the file was created. If, after the file was created, an INDEX ON command is executed to create a new .ndx file, the new key field is not so flagged in the DISPLAY STRUCTURE table. However, if, after the file is created, an INDEX ON <*key expression*> TAG <*tag name*> is executed to add a TAG to the .mdx file, the field is flagged as a key field.

Alias Support

Commands that open files and move the record pointer now can be made to work in a nonselected area by using the IN switch. For example,

SELECT A
USE file1

```
USE file2 IN B
USE file3 IN C
USE file4 IN D
```

Commands such as the following, that move the record pointer or check the position of the record pointer, now support the IN switch:

```
GO TOP
GO BOTTOM
GOTO
SKIP
? EOF()
```

Examples of using these commands to move the record pointer in a nonselected work area would be the following:

```
GO TOP IN 1
SKIP IN 2
? EOF(1)
? EOF('A')
```

The argument of the IN modifier can be any valid alias expression, including the letter (*A-J*) of the work area, the number (*1–10*) of the work area, or the alias name.

In the above examples, GO TOP IN 1 would go to the top record in the .dbf file that is open in work area 1. SKIP IN 2 would move the record pointer to the next record in the .dbf file that is open in work area 2. ? EOF(1) or ? EOF('A') would return a logical True or False based on whether or not EOF() was true in the .dbf file open in work area 1.

Autosave

In dBASE III PLUS, it is up to the programmer to determine when changes in files are written back to disk. When a file is closed by using one of these forms of syntax, the changes are written to disk:

USE	Closes .dbf file in current work area
CLOSE DATA	Closes all open .dbf files
CLEAR ALL	Closes all open .dbf files and releases memory variables

SET AUTOSAVE ON in dBASE IV automatically writes changes to disk to avoid data loss. SET AUTOSAVE ON is basically for end users who may lose data when they forget to close .dbf files. If proper programming is done, it will be unnecessary, generally, to use SET AUTOSAVE, which will cause time delays in saving the data. Using the approaches described in this book, the programmer can control when the time delays required to write data to disk will occur.

Chapter 4

FUNCTIONS IN dBASE: MANIPULATING STRINGS, NUMBERS, AND DATES

Given enough time, I can program anything in dBASE.
—Anonymous dBASE programmer

Functions provide some of the programmer's most useful tools. dBASE provides functions for working with strings, numbers, and dates. It also provides functions for performing type conversions and for finding out information about .dbf files.

Variables in dBASE are of two types: fields in a .dbf file and memory variables. Fields are created by specifying their type and length, using the CREATE command. Memory variables are created with an assignment statement in one of these forms:

```
memvar=1.0
STORE 1.0 TO memvar
```

The STORE syntax was retained in dBASE III for compatibility with dBASE II. With the STORE syntax, a single value can be assigned to multiple memory variables with one line of code:

```
STORE 0.00 TO memvar1,memvar2,memvar3
STORE ' ' TO mchoice1,mchoice2,mchoice3
```

Memory variable names, like field names, can contain up to 10 characters, with the underline (_) being the only punctuation symbol allowed. Either memory variables or fields can be used as the arguments for dBASE functions. The argument is the entity that the function operates on. Arguments can be combinations of fields, memory variables, and literal values.

The type of a memory variable is determined by the value assigned to it. If a numeric value is assigned to it, it is numeric; if a character value is assigned, it is a character; etc.

Note that dBASE functions are not stand-alone commands. They must be used in conjunction with a dBASE command verb.

STRING HANDLING FUNCTIONS

Some of the most useful functions in dBASE are for handling character memory variables or fields. Virtually any kind of string manipulation can be accomplished by using these functions.

LEN()

The LEN function returns the length of a string. It can be used in several ways:

```
. string='Merry christmas'
. ? LEN(string)
   15
. ? LEN('Hi there')
   8
. ? LEN(string+'Hi there')
   23
```

As shown, the argument of the LEN function can be either a variable, a literal expression, or a combination of the two. In either case, the LEN function returns the length of the string, including all characters and blanks.

SUBSTR()

Perhaps the most useful string handling function is the SUBSTR function. This function allows extracting a portion of a string. The syntax is

```
SUBSTR(<string name>,<start position>,<length>)
```

The first character of a character variable called *str1* can be obtained with the syntax

```
firstchar=SUBSTR(str1,1,1)
```

This syntax says start with the first character of *str1* and take only one character and store it to a memory variable called *firstchar*.

Similarly, the syntax to extract the first two characters of a string would be

```
firsttwo=SUBSTR(str1,1,2)
```

This command says to begin with the first character of *str1* and take the first two characters and put them in a memory variable called *firsttwo*.

A variable can be used as the start position or the length parameter in the function expression. For instance, this program will generate the output shown.

```
SET TALK OFF
string='This is a string'
n=1
DO WHILE n<=LEN(string)
    ? SUBSTR(string,n,1)
    n=n+1
ENDDO
```

```
T
h
i
s

i
s

a

s
t
r
i
n
g
```

What This Program Does

SET TALK OFF turns off dBASE's talk feature that would show on the screen such information as the value of *n* each time it is changed in the program. The talk feature is useful when debugging a program, but in this case it would only clutter the screen.

The command *string='This is a string'* initializes a memory variable named *string* with a string of data.

n=1 initializes a memory variable named *n* to the value of 1. *n* will be a pointer to the character position in the string.

DO WHILE *n* <=LEN(*string*). This DO WHILE condition means that the DO WHILE loop will execute until *n* is equal to the length of the memory variable *string*.

? SUBSTR(*string*,*n*,1) will output the one character starting at position *n* in the memory variable string.

n=*n*+1 increments the memory variable *n* so that it points to the next character position in the string.

The ENDDO terminates the DO WHILE loop and sends program control back to the DO WHILE instruction so that the condition can be verified as true or false. If the DO WHILE condition is true, the loop is re-executed. If the DO WHILE condition is false, dBASE executes the instruction after the ENDDO.

LEFT() and RIGHT()

The LEFT() and RIGHT() functions are special cases of the SUBSTR() function. LEFT() can be used to extract the *n* leftmost characters from a string by using the syntax

```
? LEFT(<string name>,<n>)
```

RIGHT() extracts the *n* rightmost characters from a string if the syntax is used

```
? RIGHT(<string name>,<n>)
```

```
. string='Happy birthday'
Happy birthday
. ? LEFT(string,5)
Happy
. ? RIGHT(string,5)
thday
```

UPPER() and LOWER()

The UPPER() and LOWER() functions convert all the characters in a string to upper case or lower case, respectively. For instance, after a last name is input into a memory variable named mlname, this syntax could be used to force the first character to be upper case and the remaining characters to be lower case.

```
REPLACE lname WITH UPPER(SUBSTR(mlname,1,1))+;
    LOWER(SUBSTR(mlname,2))
```

Note that in the second use of the SUBSTR function, the length argument is omitted. In this case SUBSTR defaults to returning everything from the second character to the end of the string.

TRIMming a String—Removing Trailing Blanks

Sometimes it is useful to remove the trailing blanks from a string. This task is accomplished with the TRIM() function.

```
. string='Hi there
. ? TRIM(string)
Hi there
. ? LEN(string)
    12
. ? LEN(TRIM(string))
    8
```

First, a memory variable named *string* is initialized to be equal to the characters 'Hi there' followed by four blanks. The TRIM() function trims off trailing blanks. Note that the LEN of the string is 12 characters, including the four blanks, while the LEN of the TRIMmed value of string is eight because the four blanks are removed by the TRIM function. Note also that functions can be nested. In the last example, we take the LEN of the TRIMmed value of the string.

Joining Two Strings Together—Concatenation

Joining two strings together is called *concatenation*. dBASE offers two string concatenation operators

- \+ Plus joins two strings together exactly as they are
- – Minus joins two strings together while putting the trailing blanks from both at the end of the final string

An example of using these string concatenation operators is

```
. str1 = ' Hi  '
. str2 = ' there '
. ? str1 + str2
Hi   there
. ? str1 - str2
Hi there
```

In this sequence of commands, *str1* is initialized as ' Hi ' with one leading blank and two trailing blanks. *str2* is initialized as ' there ' with one leading blank and one trailing blank.

The expression ? *str1* + *str2* outputs the combination of the two memory variables. Note the three blanks between *Hi* and *there*. These three blanks consist of the two trailing blanks from *str1* and the one leading blank from *str2*. The + operator joins the two strings, including all of the blanks.

The expression ? *str1* – *str2* returns a slightly different result. There is only one blank between *Hi* and *there*. This is because the two trailing blanks from *str1* are moved to the end of the final string. So, the blank between *Hi* and *there* is the leading blank from *str2*. The – operator moves the trailing blanks to the end of the final string, but it has no effect on leading blanks.

LTRIM()—Removing Leading Blanks

dBASE provides an LTRIM() function for removing the leading, or leftmost, blanks from a string:

```
. ? LTRIM(str1)
Hi
. ? LTRIM(str2)
there
. ? LTRIM(str1) + LTRIM(str2)
Hi  there
. ? LTRIM(str1) - LTRIM(str2)
Hithere
```

The expression ? LTRIM(*str1*) + LTRIM(*str2*) leaves two blanks between the *Hi* and the *there*. These two blanks are the trailing blanks from str1.

The expression ? LTRIM(str1) – LTRIM(str2) removes both the leading and trailing spaces so that there are no spaces between the two words. The

LTRIM() function removes the leading blanks and the – concatenation operator moves the trailing blanks to the end of the final string.

Removing Both Leading and Trailing Blanks

Both leading and trailing blanks can be removed by combining the TRIM() and LTRIM() functions:

```
. ? TRIM(LTRIM(str1+str2))
Hi     there
. ? TRIM(LTRIM(str1-str2))
Hi there
```

? TRIM(LTRIM(str1+str2)) removes the leading and trailing blanks from the string created by using the + concatenation operator to join str1 and str2.

. ? TRIM(LTRIM(str1–str2)) removes the leading and trailing blanks from the string created by using the – concatenation operator to join str1 and str2. Note that the blank between *Hi* and *there* is the leading blank in *str2*.

Padding a Field with Leading Zeroes

Suppose that a serial number field is eight characters long and has leading zeroes. The nonzero elements can be any numbers. The user will enter the nonzero part of the serial number, and the program will automatically pad it with leading zeroes by using

```
mserial=SPACE(8)
@ 2,1 SAY 'Enter Serial Number ' GET mserial
READ
mserial=LTRIM(mserial)
DO WHILE LEN(TRIM(mserial)) < 8
    mserial='0'+mserial
ENDDO
mserial=TRIM(mserial)
```

What This Program Does

First the memory variable *mserial* is initialized as being equal to eight blank spaces. Next the user is prompted to enter the serial number by using @... SAY.../GET and READ. Then *mserial* is LTRIMmed. The DO WHILE loop executes so long as the length of the TRIM of *mserial* is less than eight. With each pass through the loop, a leading zero is added. As soon as the length of the TRIM of *mserial* is eight, the loop is exited and *mserial* is set equal to the TRIM of *mserial*.

With this approach, a serial number entered as *123* would become *00000123*. This approach is often necessary when seeking the serial number by using an index.

Locating Strings within Other Strings

Input validation is one example of when it might be useful to see whether or not one string is contained in another string. dBASE provides several functions for doing this:

1. The "contained in" function is

<*str1*> $ <*str2*>

This function returns a logical True if *string1* is contained in *string2*, and a logical False if it is not.

```
?  ' ' $ 'Hi'
```

would return a logical False because there is no space in the string 'Hi'.

2. The "where is" or AT function returns the starting position of one string within another string.

AT(<*str1*>,<*str2*>)

This function returns the starting position of *string1* within *string2*, or a zero if *string1* is not contained within *string2*.

```
? AT('mile','smiles')
```

This expression returns a 2 because the string 'mile' starts at position 2 within the string 'smiles'.

Using These Functions

These functions can be quite useful for converting input from one form to another. When importing data in which both the last name and first name are contained in one field, so long as the format is consistent, you can use an approach such as this.

Assume that the data are in the form

```
lastname, firstname
```

in a field named *name*. If a new .dbf file is created containing fields called *lname* and *fname* as well as the *name* field, the last and first names could be stripped out in the following manner:

```
REPL ALL lname WITH SUBSTR(name,1,AT(',',name)-1)
REPL ALL fname with LTRIM(SUBSTR(name,AT(',',name)+1))
```

How This Works

In the first case, the *lname* field is replaced with the contents of the *name* field, starting with position one and up to and including the position before the comma. The AT function is used to compute the position of the comma, which is used as the length argument for the SUBSTR function.

In the second case, the LTRIM of the SUBSTR of name starting at the position after the comma is taken and placed in the *fname* field. The AT function is used to compute the starting position of the substring. The length parameter of the SUBSTR() function can be omitted, in which case the SUBSTR() function defaults to returning everything from the starting position to the end of the string.

CAUTION: If SUBSTR is used in an index key, then the length parameter of the SUBSTRING function must be specified to prevent problems.

The REPLACE ALL command goes through and performs this operation for each record in the file.

Writing an LTRIM Function

Earlier versions of dBASE and some compilers did not provide an LTRIM function. However, using the principles discussed in this chapter, users can write their own program to ltrim a memory variable called *memvar*:

```
n=1
DO WHILE n<LEN(memvar) .AND. SUBSTR(memvar,n,1) = ' '
    n=n+1
ENDDO
ltrim=SUBSTR(memvar,n)
```

TYPE CONVERSION FUNCTIONS

Frequently it is necessary to convert between data types. Following are some examples of when such conversion might be necessary:

1. Including fields of different data types in an index key—all fields in an index key must be converted to the same type.

2. Using a single output statement to output multiple fields. With both ? and @... SAY, fields output with the same statement must be converted to the same type.

Conversion from Numbers to Characters

The command

? 'The answer is '+*mnum*

will generate a syntax error because an attempt is being made to output both a number and a character type variable with the same ? statement. To make the statement valid, use the syntax:

? 'The answer is '+STR(*mnum*,10,2)

This syntax converts the numeric memory variable *mnum* to a string. The syntax of the STR function is

STR(<*string name*>,length,decimals)

The length parameter specifies the total length of the string, including the decimal point and any places to the right of the decimal point. The decimals parameter specifies the number of places to the right of the point.

Converting from Strings to Numbers

Sometimes numeric values are stored in a character type variable.

```
mrankno='8'
? VAL(mrankno)
8
```

The memory variable *mrankno* contains an 8 stored as a character. The VAL function converts numbers stored in character variables to numbers that can be manipulated as numbers. If nonnumeric values are stored in character variables, VAL returns a zero.

```
memvar='A'
? VAL(memvar)
0
```

Converting Strings to Dates

To enter a literal date value in dBASE III PLUS, it is necessary to enter it as a character string and to use the CTOD function to convert from mm/dd/yy format to a date value.

```
mdate=CTOD('04/01/86')
```

This clumsy syntax is simplified in dBASE IV by allowing curly braces as delimiters for literal date values:

```
mdate = {04/01/86}
```

Converting Dates to Strings

Sometimes it is necessary to convert dates to strings. For instance, this code will generate a syntax error if *mdate* is a date type variable:

```
? 'The date is '+mdate
```

Again, an attempt is made to output a character and a date variable with a single ? statement. The correct syntax is

```
? 'The date is '+DTOC(mdate)
```

The DTOC function converts a date value to a character value.

USING SUBSTRINGS TO CHANGE PART OF A STRING

Increasing the fiscal year. A fiscal year memory variable is stored in the following string format:

```
mfyr='1986/87'
```

The following code can be used to increment the fiscal year.

```
hfyr=SUBSTR(mfyr,1,2)+STR(VAL(SUBSTR(mfyr,3,2))+1,2)+'/'+;
STR(VAL(SUBSTR(mfyr,6,2))+1,2)
```

DETERMINING THE FISCAL YEAR

If an organization has a fiscal year that runs from July 1 of one year to June 30 of the next year, it is possible to write a function to which a date is passed and the fiscal year is returned

```
*fyr.prg
PARAMETERS date,mfyr
IF MONTH(date) <=6
    mfyr=STR(YEAR(date)-1,4)+'/'+SUBSTR(STR(YEAR(date),4),3,2)
ELSE
    mfyr=STR(YEAR(date),4)+'/'+SUBSTR(STR(YEAR(date)+1,4),3,2)
ENDIF
```

What This Program Does

This program makes use of these functions:

MONTH(*date*). This function takes a date variable and returns the two-digit month as a number.

YEAR(*date*). This function takes a date variable and returns the four-digit year as a number.

STR(*number,length*). The STR converts a number to a string value of specified length.

SUBSTR(*string,start,length*). This function extracts a portion of a string value.

This program is written in the dBASE III PLUS mode with parameters. The memory variable *mfyr* must be initialized as a string variable prior to calling the program. The result will be returned in that variable.

The PARAMETERS statement tells dBASE how to interpret the parameters that are passed to the program. The first parameter must be a date: either a memory variable containing a date or a literal date that is passed by using the CTOD function. The second variable must be a string variable.

The IF statement determines whether the month of the passed date is less than or equal to June. If the IF condition is true, then the fiscal year is constructed as the previous year plus the current year.

If the month is greater than June, the fiscal year is constructed as the current year plus the following year.

WORKING WITH ASCII VALUES

dBASE allows returning the decimal ASCII values of a character by using the ASC function. For instance,

```
? ASC('A')
65
```

The inverse function is CHR.

```
? CHR(65)
A
```

Screen output can be generated with the REPLICATE function. For example, to generate a row of 80 dashes across the screen, use

```
@ 2,0 SAY REPLICATE('-',80)
```

This approach can also be used to generate the IBM graphic set characters on the screen. The following expression, using CHR(177), would generate a row of 80 shaded rectangles across the screen:

```
@ 2,0 SAY REPLICATE(CHR(177),80)
```

FUNCTIONS THAT OPERATE ON FILES

Various functions exist that give information about the open file in the currently selected area.

? DBF() returns the name of the .dbf file.
? RECCOUNT() returns the number of records in the file.

? RECSIZE() returns the length of each record.
? NDX(n) returns the name of the nth index open in the currently selected area.
? LUPDATE() returns the date of the latest update of the .dbf file in the current work area.

DATE FUNCTIONS

dBASE provides various functions for working with dates. Dates can be viewed in various ways, based on the SET DATE setting. Regardless of the way in which they are viewed, however, dates are stored in date fields as yyyy/mm/dd. Several SET commands effect how they are viewed for output.

Dates are commonly represented in the mm/dd/yy format. However, to store a date in this format to a date type variable, the CTOD function must be used, as in

```
mdate=CTOD('01/01/88')
```

SET CENTURY ON/OFF determines whether the first two digits of the year will be displayed. It determines the difference between a display of 01/01/88 and one of 01/01/1988. If CENTURY is on, the first two digits of the year can be edited with a GET.

The ordering of month, date, and year for output purposes is determined by using the SET DATE function. The two most useful settings for programmers in the U.S. are the following:

```
SET DATE AMERICAN    mm/dd/yy
SET DATE ANSI        yy.mm.dd
```

The SET DATE functions only determine how the data is output. Dates in fields are stored as yyyy/mm/dd, the necessary order for indexing purposes.

Extracting Day, Month, and Year

The following functions take a date variable as an argument and return the numeric values of the month, day, and year.

```
MONTH(<date>)
DAY(<date>)
YEAR(<date>)
```

In some cases it is desirable to return the character values of the month or the day of the week. The following functions are useful for that purpose.

```
CDOW(<date>)
CMONTH(<date>)
```

```
. ? CDOW(CTOD('01/01/88'))
Friday
. ? CMONTH(CTOD('01/01/88'))
January
```

The day of the week function, DOW(), allows extracting the numeric day of the week with Sunday having a value of 1.

```
. ? DOW(CTOD('01/01/88'))
6
```

These functions can be combined to spell out the month and day for a given date:

```
. mdate=CTOD('01/01/88')
01/01/88
. ? CDOW(mdate)+', '+CMONTH(mdate)+' '+;
STR(DAY(mdate),2)+', '+STR(YEAR(mdate),4)

Friday, January 1, 1988
```

Date Arithmetic

Dates can be subtracted, or a number of days can be added to, or subtracted from, a date variable. For instance, to set up a memory variable called *duedate* that is 30 days from the current date, the following syntax can be used:

```
duedate=DATE()+30
```

DATE() returns the computer system date in date format. Thus the memory variable *duedate* would be equal to a date 30 days after the system date.

The number of days between two dates can be determined thusly:

```
. mdate=CTOD('01/01/88')
01/01/88
```

```
. mdate1=CTOD('01/01/88')
01/01/88
. mdate2=CTOD('04/15/88')
04/15/88
. ? mdate2-mdate1
    105
```

Examples of Working with Date Functions

dBASE allows the creation of new functions in order to fill in gaps in the language.

1. Function to increment month

   The following can be used to increment the month of a date stored in a memory variable, mdate:

```
? mdate
02/08/88
mdate =CTOD(STR(MONTH(mdate)+1,2)+'/'+STR(DAY(mdate),2);
'/'+SUBSTR(STR(YEAR(mdate),4),3,2))
? mdate
03/08/88
```

   Note: If mdate represents the thirty-first day of a month followed by a month with less than thirty-one days, the month will be incremented to two months in advance.

2. Function to find number of days in month

   This program can be used to find the number of days in any month. The approach used is

   a. go to first day of next month
   b. subtract 1 and take the DAY() function

```
*numdays.prg
PARAMETER mmonth
lastday=CTOD(STR(mmonth+1,2)+'/01/'+STR(YEAR(DATE()),4))-1
? CMONTH(lastday) +' has '+STR(DAY(lastday),2)+' days'
```

This program can be called using this syntax

```
DO numdays with 3
```

to find the number of days in March.

First, the memory variable *lastday* is set equal to the last day of the month passed as a parameter. This is accomplished by going to the first day of the following month and subtracting 1. The year is assumed to be equal to the year of the system date.

The last line of the program then uses the CMONTH() function to extract the name of the month and the DAY() function to extract the number of the day of the last day of the month.

WORKING WITH NUMBERS

dBASE provides various functions for working with numbers. dBASE III PLUS defaults to providing 10 digits of precision, but more precision can be forced by appropriately defining a number. To test for the number of digits of precision, start typing in numbers as shown:

```
. mnum=12345678901234567890
.1234567890123E+20
```

In this case the number is converted to floating point, and 13 digits of precision are retained.

These functions are available for working with numbers:

ABS(<*n*>) returns the absolute value of a number.
EXP(<*n*>) returns *e* to the power specified.
INT(<*n*>) returns the integer portion of *n*, truncating all values to the right of the point.
LOG(<*n*>) returns the natural log of *n*.
MAX(<*n1*>,<*n2*>) returns the greater of two numbers.
MIN(<*n1*>,<*n2*>) returns the lesser of two numbers.
MOD(<*n1*>,<*n2*>) returns the remainder from *n1*/*n2*.
ROUND(<*n*>,<decimals>) rounds off *n* to the specified number of decimals.
SQRT(<*n*>) returns the square root of *n*.

There are subtle distinctions between INT() and ROUND() functions as this example shows.

```
. mnum=1234.567
1234.567
. ? INT(mnum)
    1234
. ? ROUND(mnum,0)
    1235.000
```

INT() chops off the decimal portion of the number, ROUND() rounds off and pads out the rest of the number with zeroes, which may give misleading results by implying a degree of precision that is not present.

dBASE IV

dBASE IV adds a number of new functions to the language.

Date Functions

dBASE IV enhances the way in which dates are handled. A date memory variable can be created and set equal to a literal date without the awkward CTOD syntax. In dBASE IV curly braces can be used as date delimiters:

```
mtoday={11/15/88}
```

This syntax is simpler than the awkward dBASE III PLUS CTOD syntax:

```
mtoday=CTOD('11/15/88')
```

In addition, these new date functions have been added:

DMY() spells out date dd month yy
DTOS() converts date to index key
MDY() spells out date October 27, 1988

For example:

```
. mdate={11/10/88}
11/10/88
```

```
. ? DMY(mdate)
10 November 88
. ? DTOS(mdate)
19881110
. ? MDY(mdate)
November 10, 88
. SET CENTURY ON
. ? MDY(mdate)
November 10, 1988
```

SET CENTURY ON must be executed in order for the MDY() function to spell out the date in the expected format with the year expressed as four digits.

Memo Field Functions

Memo fields have been expanded to be more like large character fields, and they can be searched now for the occurrence of a specified string value. The following functions, which were discussed previously in regard to character fields, now also apply to memo fields:

AT()
LEFT()
LEN()
RIGHT()
SUBSTR()

These functions that have been added allow addressing each line of a memo field:

MEMLINES(<*memo field name*>—returns the number of lines in the memo field
MLINE(<*memo field name*>,*n*)—returns the text in the *n*th line of the specified memo field

For example, for a file with a memo field named m1, the command ? m1 would display the memo field in the following manner with the default memowidth of 50.

```
. ? m1
This is the time for all good men to come to the aid of their party.
```

If the command SET MEMOWIDTH TO 15 is executed, the memo field is now displayed as

```
. ? m1
This is the
time for all
good men to
come to the aid
of their party.
```

in response to the command ? *m1*. Blanks are inserted at the end of the line to wrap words around to the next line.

The MEMLINES() function returns the number of lines that are required to display the memo field based on the line length defined by SET MEMO-WIDTH. The memo field name is *not* enclosed in quotes.

```
. ? MEMLINES(m1)
   5
```

To extract the third line from the memo field based on the current memo-width of 15, the command is

```
. ? MLINE(m1,3)
good men to
```

The string searching features of memo fields can be invoked by using functions such as AT(), which indicates that the word *time* begins in the thirteenth character position in the memo field.

```
. ? AT('time',m1)
   13
```

Conversely, the word *time* can be extracted from the memo field by using the SUBSTR() function:

```
. ? SUBSTR(m1,13,4)
time
```

The character positions are the absolute character positions in the field and do not take into consideration the trailing blanks inserted at the end of each line for word wrap.

Financial Functions

Several financial functions have been added:

```
FV(<payment>,<rate>,<periods>)
PAYMENT(<principal>,<rate>,<payments>)
PV(<principal>,<rate>,<periods>)
```

dBASE can be used now to compute mortgage payments:

```
? PAYMENT(200000,.10/12,360)
    1755.14
```

In this example the annual rate of 10% is divided by 12 to calculate the monthly rate. The total number of payments is 30 years × 12 months = 360.

Math Functions

dBASE IV supports additional precision although it is somewhat inconsistent.

```
. mnum=12345678901234567890
12345678901234567890
. mnum1=123456789012345678901234567890
.12345678901234E+30
```

In the first case, 20 digits of precision are retained. In the second case, floating point format is used with only 14 digits of precision plus 2 digits for the exponents, which equals the default 16 digits of precision. SET PRECISION TO 20, which is the maximum value, seems to have no real effect on the maximum precision allowed when a number is defined.

These math functions have been added.

ACOS(*n*)	Arccosine
ASIN(*n*)	Arcsine
ATAN(*n*)	Arctangent
CEILING(*n*)	Smallest integer greater than or equal to *n*
COS(*n*)	Cosine
DTOR(*n*)	Degrees to radians
FLOOR(*n*)	Largest integer less than or equal to *n*
LOG10(*n*)	Log base 10
PI()	Pi with precision specified with SET DECIMALS TO

RAND(*n*)	Random number between 0 and 1. *n* is the seed value
RTOD(*n*)	Radians to degrees
SIGN(*n*)	1 if *n* positive, 0 if 0, −1 if negative
TAN(*n*)	Tangent

Type Conversion

Two functions to convert between the fixed and float numeric types are FIXED(), which converts float to fixed, and FLOAT(), which converts fixed to float.

Write Your Own Functions

If you don't like the functions provided by dBASE, you now can write your own user-defined functions (UDF's). UDF's are similar to procedures discussed in chapter 11. The procedure to determine the fiscal year from a date can be rewritten as a function:

```
FUNCTION fyr
* udf to determine fiscal year from date
PARAMETERS date
IF MONTH(date) <=6
    mfyr=STR(YEAR(date)-1,4)+'/'+SUBSTR(STR(YEAR(date),4),3,2)
ELSE
    mfyr=STR(YEAR(date),4)+'/'+SUBSTR(STR(YEAR(date)+1,4),3,2)
ENDIF
RETURN mfyr
```

The code above would define a function named *fyr*. It can be accessed in the following manner to calculate the fiscal year for the given system date:

```
? fyr(DATE())
```

The function will be evaluated and return the value of the calculated fiscal year. The value to be returned appears after the RETURN command and is not enclosed in parentheses.

CAUTION: dBASE IV user-defined functions have significant limitations. The manual lists many commands, including LIST and DISPLAY, that cannot be included in a UDF. Because of these limitations, UDF's have limited utility in dBASE IV.

Chapter 5

OUTPUT

Communication has proven as elusive as the Unicorn. . . . There is clearly less and less communicating. . . . In the meantime, there is an information explosion. Every professional and every executive . . . suddenly has access to data in inexhaustible abundance. . . . We get a great many answers. But the one thing clear so far is that no one really has an answer.
—*Peter F. Drucker,* Management: Tasks, Responsibilities, Practices

You gotta figure out what you want to get out of it before you decide what to put into it . . .
—*Former chef turned dBASE programmer*

It is the job of the programmer to work with the end user to determine which information must be extracted from the data base to facilitate the decision-making process. From a great mass of data, selected summary statistics can be calculated, records can be viewed, and reports or other output can be generated.

dBASE provides flexibility in designing output. Screen displays can be designed in almost any way imaginable. Certain records or fields can be selected as needed. The commands discussed in this chapter, in the order of their complexity, are

?
LIST/DISPLAY
@...SAY

THE ? COMMAND

The ? command is used to display the value of a memory variable or field name or to test whether a logical expression is True or False.

```
? lname
? mlname
? lname='Smith'
```

The main convention to observe when using the ? command is that variable types cannot be combined into a single ? command. For instance, this will generate a syntax error due to mismatched field types:

```
? 'The answer is '+mnum
```

The correct syntax for this expression is

```
? 'The answer is '+ STR(mnum)
```

In this corrected expression, both types are converted to character.

The ? command outputs a carriage return and linefeed sequence before outputting the desired text. To suppress the carriage return and linefeed, a double question mark (??) can be used. The following syntax will print *Hello world* on the same line.

```
? 'Hello '
?? 'world'
```

THE AMAZING LIST COMMAND

LIST is an amazingly versatile and quick command for generating output. Before attempting to use more complex output commands, see if the task can be accomplished more easily with LIST. Many users underrate the power of this command.

The full syntax of the LIST command is

```
LIST [<scope>] <field expression> FOR <logical expression>
    WHILE <logical expression> [TO PRINT] [OFF]
```

When the LIST command is entered, all fields for all records in the file are displayed without pausing. The DISPLAY command is similar to LIST, but it defaults to displaying all fields of only one record—the record to which the record pointer is positioned. DISPLAY ALL lists all records but pauses after each screenful. LIST is used most often for printed output, while DISPLAY is used most often for screen output.

Why Use LIST vs. Other Commands

Why use LIST for output when other commands are available? LIST can be used for performing functions handled also by commands such as REPORT FORM and LABEL FORM. In some cases there are advantages to using LIST:

1. LIST is faster, as discussed in chapter 7.

2. Using LIST can make code more readable and easier to maintain and change.

Generating Mailing Labels with LIST

While complex mailing labels can be generated with the Label Generator, this program will print one-up mailing labels by using the LIST command:

```
USE <file name>
crlf=CHR(13)+CHR(10)
SET PRINT ON
LIST OFF crlf+TRIM(fname)+' '+lname+crlf+straddr+crlf+;
    TRIM(city)+', '+state+' '+zip+crlf
SET PRINT OFF
```

The *crlf* memory variable contains a carriage return and a linefeed. Additional *crlf*s can be added to the LIST expression in order to generate the necessary number of blank lines for the label: i.e., if a seven-line label is used with three lines of text, four *crlf*s can be added for proper spacing.

This example illustrates that any valid dBASE expression can be used in the field clause of a LIST statement—not only a field list.

Generate a Print Out of One Record per Page

Sometimes it might be desirable to generate a printout showing each record in the file on a separate page. The following short program will accomplish that result for a simple address file.

```
USE <file name>
crlf=CHR(13)+CHR(10)
peject=CHR(12)
SET PRINT ON
LIST crlf+fname+' '+lname+crlf+straddr+crlf+city;
    +crlf+state+crlf+zip+peject
SET PRINT OFF
```

In this program, at the end of each record, a page eject is sent to the printer. To modify this program for other file structures, the appropriate fields must be listed separated by crlf.

Generating Simple Graphs

Simple graphs can be generated with the LIST command. For example, if we had a .dbf file with the fields

```
lname,c,20
yrs_of_svc,n,5
```

a graph can be generated that lists the last name and an asterisk (*) for each year of service:

```
LIST OFF lname + REPLICATE('*',yrs_of_svc)
```

In this case, the contents of the *yrs_of_service* field is used as the argument to indicate the number of times that the * is to be repeated. The output will be

```
lname + REPLICATE('*',yrs_of_svc)
SMITH          **********
JONES          ************
ANDERSON       ***************
HOWARD         ********
HAMILTON       *****
```

The column headings can be turned off with SET HEADING OFF.

Paging with LIST

Paged output can be generated with LIST by using the approach

```
USE <file name>
pagelen=65
DO WHILE .NOT. EOF()
    LIST OFF NEXT pagelen TO PRINT
    EJECT
    SKIP
ENDDO
```

The value of the *pagelen* memory variable can be changed to reflect the various page lengths associated with different types of printer's paper.

This example assumes that the total widths of the fields are less than the width of a line. If this is not the case, the SET FIELDS TO statement can be used to select certain fields so that the output of each record will fit on a single line.

Paging Output on the Screen

The following short program can be used to enable users to page through records on the screen and to abort at the end of each screen. It is an enhanced use of the DISPLAY command.

```
USE <file name>
SET FIELDS TO <field list>
CLEAR
DO WHILE .NOT. EOF()
    DISP OFF NEXT 15
    WAIT 'Q to abort, any other key to continue ' TO mcont
    IF UPPER(mcont)='Q'
        EXIT
    ENDIF
    SKIP
ENDDO &&while not eof
```

This program displays 15 records on the screen and then pauses, giving the user an opportunity to continue or to abort.

Selecting Specified Fields and Records

Remember that the SET FIELDS TO and SET FILTER TO can be used in conjunction with a LIST to select specified fields and records.

Practical Examples

With the accounts payable example that is used throughout this book, it might be necessary to perform these functions:

1. Generate a listing of all checks written between certain dates.
2. Generate a listing of all checks written to a given vendor.

The DISPLAY command can be quite useful for implementing both of these functions.

Generating a List of All Checks Written between Two Dates

To generate an on-screen list of all checks written between two dates, the following code can be used:

```
* datelist.prg
* program to list all checks written between two specified dates
* vendor codes are listed for each check

SET STATUS OFF
SET TALK OFF

* get dates
    mdate1 = CTOD('01/01/88')
    mdate2 = DATE()
    CLEAR
    @ 1,1 SAY 'List checks between two dates'
    @ 3,1 SAY 'Enter beginning date ' GET mdate1
    @ 3,40 SAY 'Enter ending date     ' GET mdate2
    READ
    USE apmaster
    SET FILTER TO date >= mdate1 .AND. date <= mdate2
    GO TOP
    SET FIELDS TO date,ckno,pvendno,amt

        DO WHILE .NOT. EOF()
            @ 4,0 CLEAR
            DISP OFF NEXT 15
            mcont = SPACE(1)
            @ 22,1 SAY 'Q to abort, any other key to continue ' GET mcont

            READ
            IF UPPER(mcont) = 'Q'
                EXIT
            ENDIF
            SKIP
        ENDDO &&while not eof
```

First, this code gets the two dates between which the checks are to be listed. When the dates are initialized, mdate1 is set equal to an earlier date, and mdate2 is set equal to the system date. These dates can be changed by the user at input time. The checks are then listed on the screen, 15 at a time. Note that vendor codes rather than the full vendor names are shown. See chapter 10 about including the full vendor name.

Generate a Listing of All Checks Written to a Given Vendor

The previous program can be modified slightly to show all the checks written to a given vendor by replacing all of the lines prior to the SET FIELDS statement with

```
* vendlist.prg
* program to list all checks for a given vendor

SET STATUS OFF
SET TALK OFF

* get vendor
    @ 1,1 SAY 'Display all checks for a given vendor'
    mvendor=SPACE(5)
    @ 3,1 SAY 'Enter vendor     ' GET mvendor PICTURE '@!'
    READ
    USE apmaster
    SET FILTER TO pvendno=mvendor
    GO TOP
```

The program will then display all checks to a given vendor.

Using IIF() with LIST

The IIF() function can be used in conjunction with a LIST command. In an example that has a due date field indicating when a bill is to be paid, the following command will output each account and flag those that are overdue

```
LIST OFF ACCTNAME,IIF(duedate <date(),'OVERDUE',DTOC(duedate))
```

The IIF() function is like a spreadsheet IF function. There are three arguments: the condition to be checked, the value to be returned if the condition is true, and the value to be returned if the condition is false.

For each record the due date will be checked. If it is less than the system date, the word OVERDUE will be output. Otherwise, the actual due date must be shown. The due date field must be converted to a character since OVERDUE is a character.

Longer messages can be stored in a memory variable and used with IIF(), as shown in this example:

```
    m1 = 'this account is overdue'
LIST OFF ACCTNAME,IIF(duedate <date(),m1,DTOC(duedate))
```

Using PICTURE Statements with LIST

PICTURE functions and templates can be used with a LIST command in conjunction with the TRANSFORM function. To format numeric values with commas as part of a LIST command, the following syntax can be used:

```
LIST    lname,TRANSFORM(contribamt,'999,999.99')
```

Sending LISTs to the Printer

The output of the LIST command can be directed to the printer by using SET PRINT ON. SET PRINT ON also directs the output of ?, REPORT, and DISPLAY to the printer. Another way to send the output of LIST to the printer is to add the TO PRINT switch to the command, as in

```
LIST TO PRINT
```

Problem of Losing the Last Line

The way that dBASE sends data to the printer, the last line sometimes gets lost in the printer buffer with some printers. This problem can be eliminated by sending an extra blank line or by executing an EJECT. Use either of the following forms of syntax:

```
LIST TO PRINT
EJECT
```

or

```
SET PRINT ON
LIST
EJECT
SET PRINT OFF
```

The EJECT command causes a page eject to be executed at the printer.

SENDING PRINTER CONTROL CODES

Printer control codes can be sent directly to the printer, using the following syntax. If the printer control code to turn on compressed print is Escape C, this code will turn on compressed print:

```
SET PRINT ON
? CHR(27)+'C'
```

CHR(27) sends an Escape to the printer, followed by an upper case *C*.

Each type of printer uses different control codes, so the printer manual must be checked to see which control codes to send.

USING @...SAY STATEMENTS

@...SAY statements provide programmers with the maximum control over both screen and printed output. @...SAY statements must be used when simple row and column output, such as that generated by LIST, is not sufficient.

The syntax for an @...SAY statement is

@ *r,c* SAY '<*string*>' + *variable*

r is the row coordinate with the ranges

0–24	for screen output
0–255	for printer output

c is the column coordinate and has ranges

0–79	for screen output
0–255	for printer output

Directing Output to the Printer

The output of @...SAY statements can be directed to the printer by using SET DEVICE TO PRINT. To redirect output to the screen, the command is SET DEVICE TO SCREEN.

Cautions:

1. Variable types cannot be combined with a single @...SAY. For example, this statement will generate a syntax error if mnum is a numeric value.

@ 2,1 SAY 'The answer is '+ *mnum*

This statement attempts to output a number and a character string with the same @...SAY statement. The correct syntax is

```
@ 2,1 SAY 'The answer is '+STR(mnum)
```

This syntax is correct because both values are now string values.

2. When @...SAY statements are used to output to the screen, the order of the coordinates does not matter. Row 5 could be output before row 3, for instance. However, if output is directed to the printer, the ordering becomes much more critical. Outputting row 5 and then row 3 will result in a page eject at the printer. This occurs because, after row 5 is printed, a page eject must be performed to print row three on the next page.

3. PICTURE clauses apply to the entire @...SAY statement. Thus the command

```
@ 2,1 SAY 'The answer is '+STR(contribamt);
    PICTURE '$999,999.99'
```

would result in problems. The output would be

```
$he ,ans.er
```

This occurs because the PICTURE clause is applied to the entire @...SAY statement starting with *The answer is*.

The correct syntax is

```
@ 2,1 SAY 'The answer is '
@ 2,16 SAY contribamt PICTURE '$999,999.99'
```

4. If a program that sends @...SAYs to the printer aborts abnormally while SET DEVICE TO PRINT is in effect, all subsequent @...SAYs and GETs will be directed to the printer. This means that if a menu is the next option to be generated and it is generated using @...SAYs, it will be printed on the printer or, if the printer is not ready, the computer may appear to freeze up. One workaround is to include a SET DEVICE TO SCREEN in a menu loop as described in chapter 11.

A PICTURE Statement Is Worth a Thousand Words: Formatting @...SAY Output with PICTURE Clauses

@...SAY output can be formatted using two types of PICTURE statements.

PICTURE Template Clauses

A PICTURE template clause requires one PICTURE template character for each character to be output. For example,

```
@ 2,1 SAY mchar PICTURE '!!!!!!!!!!!!'
```

will convert any alphabetic output contained in the memory variable or field to all upper case for output purposes. It will not change the underlying values of the data in the field or memory variable.

This example assumes that the variable *mchar* is 12 characters long. One exclamation point is required for each of the 12 characters.

The advantage of using PICTURE templates is that various characters in the string can be formatted differently. For example, the following template will convert the first character to upper case and leave the others as they are entered.

```
@ 2,1 SAY mchar PICTURE '!XXXXXXXXXXX'
```

PICTURE Functions

PICTURE functions allow applying a single template character to all characters in the variable to be output.

```
@ 2,1 SAY mchar PICTURE '@!'
```

This expression converts all alphabetic output to upper case by using the *at sign* (@) to indicate a PICTURE function and following it with an exclamation point (!) to indicate converting the whole string to upper case. In some cases, PICTURE templates and functions can be combined in a single output statement.

The expression above converts all alphabetic characters contained in the memory variable mchar to capitals. By using @ to indicate a PICTURE function and following it with the *!* template character, you apply the single template character to the entire string.

Examples of Using PICTURE Statements to Format Output

Inserting Formatting Characters into Output

Some values, such as social security numbers and telephone numbers, are routinely displayed with hyphens and/or parentheses in appropriate locations.

For example, a social security number is commonly displayed in the format

```
123-45-6789
```

It is a waste of disk space to store two hyphens within each field. If a social security number field is created as nine characters long, it can be formatted for output with

```
@ 2,1 SAY ssn PICTURE '@R 999-99-999'
```

or

```
@ 2,1 SAY ssn FUNCTION 'R' PICTURE '999-99-9999'
```

Blank spaces are important in the syntax of this command. A blank space must follow the word *PICTURE*. The @R PICTURE function tells dBASE to insert extraneous characters into the field for outputting. The three 9's tell dBASE to take the first three characters from the field and insert a hyphen; take the next two characters and insert a hyphen; and then take the last three characters from the field.

A similar approach can be used for formatting telephone numbers. A standard telephone number is 10 characters long, but it is displayed in the format

```
(123) 456-7890
```

This statement can be formatted using the following command, assuming that mphone is a 10-character character variable.

```
@ 2,1 SAY mphone PICTURE '@R (999) 999-9999'
```

Formatting Currency Output

One common need is to format numeric output to include commas (,), decimal points (.), and dollar signs ($).

If *mnum* is a numeric memory variable initialized in the following manner

```
mnum =1234567.89
```

then the @...SAY command

```
@ 2,1 SAY mnum
```

will result in

```
1234567.89
```

To insert commas,

```
@ 2,1 say mnum picture '999,999,999.99'
```

can be used, which will result in

```
1,234,567.89
```

Floating $ Sign

In generating printouts of currency output for applications such as check writing, it is important to have a *$* with no spaces between the *$* and the first digit of the number it precedes.

Ashton-Tate's solution to the *$* problem is

```
@ 2,1 SAY mnum PICTURE '$$$,999,999.99'
```

which results in

```
$$1,234,567.89
```

This approach pads the number with leading *$*'s. However, for appearances, it may be preferable to have a single *$* with no space before the first number.

The following statement will format a number with commas and a single leading *$*:

```
@ 2,1 SAY '$'-LTRIM(TRANSFORM(mnum,'999,999,999.99'))
```

Enclosing Negative Numbers in Parentheses

In accounting applications, it is often useful to enclose negative numbers in parentheses. This can be accomplished using the @(function.

```
@ 2,1 SAY mnum PICTURE '@( $$$,999,999.99'
```

will enclose negative numbers in parentheses, pad with leading *$*'s and insert commas. Using TRANSFORM, the syntax is

```
@ 2,1 say '$'-LTRIM(TRANSFORM(mnum,'@( 999,999,999.99'))
```

in which case, the *$* would be *outside* the parentheses.

AN ACCOUNTS PAYABLE EXAMPLE

An accounts payable check writing example is used throughout this book to demonstrate important concepts.

This example shows how to use dBASE output tools to generate checks from a temporary file. In chapter 6, an example of inputting check information to a temporary file called aptemp is given. The following example shows how to print out the checks from that file. The address of each vendor is stored in a vendor file, called vendor. For each check the address is looked up in the vendor file.

The check number is assigned to each check sequentially as it is printed. Thus the *ckno* field in aptemp is also used as a flag to see whether or not the check was printed. If a check number is filled in, the check has been printed. The assumption is made that the checks will be printed on prenumbered check forms. Since checks can be *eaten* by the printer as they are being generated, an option is provided that enables the user to reprint checks:

WRITECHE.PRG 12/05/88

```
* writeche.prg
* program to print checks
* check numbers are assigned after the check is printed
* users are given the opportunity to reprint checks in case
* checks were damaged in printing
* aptemp open in A, vendor open in B

```

```
CLEAR
? 'Setting up—Please wait'
SET DEVICE TO SCREEN
* find highest check number in master file
SELE A
USE apmaster
GO BOTTOM
maxcheck=ckno
* find maximum check number in aptemp
USE aptemp
LOCATE FOR VAL(ckno) > VAL(maxcheck)
DO WHILE .NOT. EOF()
    STORE ckno TO maxcheck
    CONTINUE
ENDDO
maxcheck =STR(VAL(maxcheck)+1,5)
SELE B
USE vendor INDEX vendor
SELECT A
* ask if ready to print
mprint=' '
CLEAR
@ 10,1 SAY 'Is Printer Ready and Check Stub lined up at top of form ? Y OR N'
@ 11,1 GET mprint PICTURE '!'
READ
IF mprint <> 'Y'
    CLOSE DATA
    RETURN
ENDIF
* allow to reprint checks that may have been damaged
```

```
mreprint=' '
@ 13,1 SAY 'Do you want to reprint checks? Y or N' GET mreprint
READ
IF UPPER(mreprint)='Y'
    * reprint bad checks
    STORE SPACE(5) TO mstart,mend
    @ 20,1
    @ 20,1 SAY 'Starting Check Number to Reprint' GET mstart
    @ 21,1 SAY 'Ending Check Number to Reprint   ' GET mend
    @ 22,1 SAY 'Blank Ending Number to Reprint all above starting number'
    READ
    IF VAL(MSTART)>0
        LOCATE FOR TRIM(LTRIM(ckno))=TRIM(LTRIM(mstart))
        IF EOF()
            @ 20,1
            @ 20,1 SAY 'CHECK NUMBER '+mstart+' NOT FOUND'
            WAIT
        ELSE
            IF VAL(mend) <> 0
                REPL ckno WITH ' ' FOR VAL(ckno) >= VAL(mstart) .AND. VAL(ckno)<=VAL(MEND)
            ELSE
                REPL ckno WITH ' ' FOR VAL(ckno) >= VAL(mstart)
            ENDIF &&MEND NOT 0
        ENDIF &&EOF
    ENDIF &&VAL(mstart)>0
  @ 20,1
  @ 21,1
  @ 22,1
ENDIF &&reprint
* get starting check number for current run
mckno = maxcheck
@ 15,1 SAY 'Enter Starting Check Number (all zeroes to abort)' GET mckno
```

```
READ
IF VAL(mckno)=0
    SET DEVICE TO SCREEN
    CLOSE DATA
    RETURN
ENDIF

* validate check number
DO WHILE VAL(mckno) < VAL(maxcheck)
    @ 20,1 SAY 'Enter check number as greater than '+maxcheck
    @ 3,60 GET mckno
    READ
ENDDO

* find first blank checknumber
SET FILTER TO ckno =' '
GO TOP
IF EOF()
    CLEAR
    ? 'All checks have been printed'
    WAIT
ELSE
       SET DEVICE TO PRINT
          * SET top of form ON PRINTER
          * MODIFY PRINTER CONTROL CODES AS NEEDED
          ** reset printer
          @ 0,3 say CHR(27)+'@'
          * set page length to 42 lines
          @ 0,5 SAY CHR(27)+CHR(67)+CHR(42)
          ** turn letter quality on
          @ 0,8 SAY CHR(27)+'x'+'1'

* print checks that have not been printed
DO WHILE .NOT. EOF()
  n=1
  ? 'Position check to top of form. Q to quit'
  WAIT TO mprint
  IF UPPER(mprint)='Q'
    SET DEVICE TO SCREEN
    CLOSE DATA
```

```
    RETURN
ENDIF



DO WHILE .NOT. EOF() .AND. N < 10
    * do look up in payee file to find address
        mvendno=pvendno
        SELE B
        SEEK TRIM(mvendno)
        IF EOF()
          ? 'Vendor '+mvendno+ ' not found'
          WAIT
          @ 20,0
          SELE A
          SKIP
          LOOP
        ENDIF
        SELE A

      * print check stub
        @ 2,1 SAY 'CHECK STUB'
        @ 3,20 SAY B->vendname
        @ 4,20 SAY DATE()
        @ 5,20 SAY comment1
        @ 6,20 SAY 'AMOUNT    '+'$'-LTRIM
        (TRANSFORM(amt,'999,999.99'))

    * print check

        @ 30,53 SAY DATE()
        @ 30,68 SAY '$******'-LTRIM(TRANSFORM(amt,'999,999.99'))
        @ 31,10 SAY B->vendname
        @ 32,10 SAY B->straddr
     IF B->CITY <> ' '
        @ 33,10 SAY TRIM(B->city)+', '+B->state+' '+B->zip
     ENDIF
```

```
        * assign check number
        REPL ckno WITH mckno
        STORE STR(VAL(mckno)+1,5) TO mckno
        SKIP
        STORE N+1 TO N


ENDDO   &&N< 10
ENDDO &&NOT EOF

ENDIF &&EOF
    ** reset printer
    @ 0,3 SAY CHR(27)+'@'
SET DEVICE TO SCREEN

WAIT 'Ok to post to master file? (Y/N)' TO mch
IF UPPER(mch)='Y'
    * check if all checks have been printed
    GO TOP
    IF .NOT. EOF()
        ? 'Some checks have not been printed'
        ? 'Please print all checks before posting to master'
        WAIT


        CLOSE DATA

        RETURN
    ENDIF

    DO POST
ENDIF
CLOSE DATA


SET DEVICE TO SCREEN
RETURN
```

NOTE: For documentation purposes, the convention of using the end of an ENDDO or an ENDIF as a comment is used. In dBASE III PLUS, double ampersands (&&) are not required if a space is left after the ENDDO or ENDIF. In dBASE IV, if the && is not used, the compiler will generate an *extra character's ignored* message, but the program will run.

NOTE: Longer program listings in this book are printed with line numbers for ease of reference. *When entering the program, do not type the line numbers.*

The structure of the aptemp file is

```
Structure for database: C:aptemp.dbf
Number of data records:        5
Date of last update    : 11/01/88
Field   Field Name      Type        Width    Dec
    1   DATE            Date            8
    2   CKNO            Character       5
    3   PVENDNO         Character       5
    4   PACCTNO         Character       5
    5   AMT             Numeric        10      2
    6   COMMENT1        Character      20
    7   COMMENT2        Character      20
    8   PACCTNO2        Character       5
    9   PAMT2           Numeric        10      2
** Total **                            89
```

The first part of the program determines the highest check number, based on the checks already written. First the file, *apmaster*, is opened. Next, GO BOTTOM positions the record pointer at the last physical record in the file, which, since checks are appended to the master file in sequential order, also contains the highest check number.

Then the maximum check number in the temporary file is determined. Since the assumption is made that the temporary file will stay relatively small, it is not indexed. To determine whether or not check numbers exist that are higher than the check numbers in the master file, the command LOCATE FOR VAL(*ckno*) > VAL(*maxcheck*) is used on line 21.

The DO WHILE loop in lines 23–26 uses the CONTINUE statement to find the highest check number in the temporary file. Each successively higher check number is stored to the memory variable maxcheck. maxcheck is set then to the value of *maxcheck* plus 1 to equal the number of the next check to be written.

Next, the vendor.dbf file is opened in work area B. The user is asked if the printer is ready and if the check stub is lined up at the top of the form. The user is then given a chance to abort by entering any letter other than *Y* for *yes*.

The user is asked next if checks need to be reprinted. This option covers the eventuality of prenumbered checks being *eaten* by the printer so that they must be reprinted. If this option is selected, the starting check number and ending check number to be reprinted are prompted for. If no ending check number is entered, all check numbers above the starting number are replaced. The actual REPLACE statements are on lines 68 and 70. If the ending check number is not specified, all checks with values above the starting number are replaced with blanks.

On line 83, the default starting check number is displayed. The user can override this number by entering a higher number or by entering all zeroes to abort.

Lines 85–89 contain an IF...ENDIF statement for determining if all zeroes have been entered, to allow aborting. Lines 92–96 contain a DO WHILE loop to make sure that a check number that is too low has not been entered.

Lines 99–101 find the first check number that has not been printed by using the command SET FILTER TO *ckno*=' ' and GO TOP. A GO TOP when a SET FILTER is in effect will position the record pointer at the first record matching the filter. If no such record is present, EOF() is True. The *ckno* field is used both to store the check number and as a flag to determine whether the check has been printed. If all checks have been printed, a message is shown.

If there are still more checks to print, the device is set to print and printer control codes are sent. The printer control codes shown are for an EPSON LQ printer and may vary for other printers. These functions are performed.

1. The page length is set to 42—the length of the check plus check stub.
2. The printer is reset.
3. Letter quality is turned on.

Next, a SET FILTER TO *ckno*=' ' is used to filter out checks that have been printed already. Note that a GO TOP occurs immediately after the SET FILTER command to position the record pointer at the first record that meets the condition.

Two DO WHILE loops are used to print the checks. The outer DO WHILE loop from lines 117–172 is DO WHILE .NOT. EOF(). An inner DO WHILE loop from lines 129–171 is based on a counter. This counter causes printing to stop after every nine checks so that they can be realigned if necessary.

For each check that is printed, a look-up is done in the vendor file to extract the address for the given vendor so that it can be printed in the address portion of the check.

The check stub is printed in lines 145–149. The check itself is printed in lines 153–159. After the check is printed, the *ckno* field is replaced with the value of the check number in *mckno* and *mckno* is incremented. A SKIP is done to move to the next record.

After printing has been completed and the DO WHILE loops exited, the printer is reset in line 176.

Next, the user is prompted to select whether or not the checks should be posted to the master file. If so, then a test is made to see if any checks remain that have not been printed. All checks in the temporary file must be printed before any checks can be posted to the master file. The test to see if any checks remain to be printed is based on the GO TOP in line 182. Since a SET FILTER TO *ckno*=' ' is in effect, if all checks have been printed, then the GO TOP will position the record pointer at EOF(). If this is the case, then the post routine is executed as described in chapter 9.

dBASE IV

dBASE IV provides several enhancements that are useful for output.

PRINTSTATUS()

One of the most useful enhancements is the inclusion of a PRINTSTATUS() function that allows checking the printer status. This function returns a logical False if the printer is not ready and a logical True if it is ready. All print routines should include a routine such as the following prior to sending any output to the printer:

```
DO WHILE .NOT. PRINTSTATUS()
   @ 20,0 SAY CHR(7)+'Printer is not ready'
   WAIT 'Press Q to abort printing, any other key to continue';
      TO mprint
   IF UPPER(mprint)='Q'
      RETURN
   ENDIF
ENDDO
```

Printer Drivers

dBASE IV now includes printer drivers that may be installed for specific printers. This installation consists of setting up memory variables that control various printer attributes and that are automatically sent to the printer when the command PRINTJOB is issued.

During the installation program, the user is asked to identify the printer or printers to be used. The appropriate printer drivers (a file with a .pr2 extension) is copied from the installation disk to the user's hard drive. The name of the default printer is stored in the config.db file in the form

```
PDRIVER              = GENERIC.PR2
```

This feature adds no new capabilities to the language, but it makes it potentially easier to control printer output. The parameters that control printing are set in system memory variables whose names begin with an *underline* character (_). The printer control settings also apply to MODIFY COMMAND.

The name of the installed printer driver is stored to a system memory variable called *_pdriver*. To check the value of this memory variable, the command

```
? _pdriver
```

can be used. To change the name of the installed driver, the value in *_pdriver* can be changed, as in

```
_pdriver='generic.pr2'
```

dBASE IV includes a new program control structure, PRINTJOB... ENDPRINTJOB. PRINTJOB must be issued after the command is issued to direct output to the printer: SET PRINT ON or SET DEVICE TO PRINT. PRINTJOB works in conjunction with system memory variables. The names of these system memory variables begin with an underline(_) and their contents determine which actions will be taken when printing takes place. PRINTJOB, in conjunction with the system memory variables, is most useful for directing the output of ? commands or the REPORT FORM to the printer. When PRINTJOB is issued after output is directed to the printer, the following events occur:

1. The starting printer codes defined by *_pscode* are sent to the printer.
2. If *_peject* is set to 'BEFORE' or 'BOTH' a page eject is issued.
3. *_pcolno* is set to 0.

These actions are taken when ENDPRINTJOB is issued:

1. Send the ending printer codes from the system variables (*_pecode*).
2. Send a page eject if *_peject* is set to 'AFTER' or 'BOTH'.
3. Loop back to PRINTJOB the number of times defined by the memory variable *_pcopies*.

dBASE IV includes an ON PAGE [AT LINE *<expN>* *<command>*] that causes dBASE to execute specified commands during the printing process at a specified line number.

CAUTION: If any of the beginning system variables are changed after the PRINTJOB command is issued, they will not be directed to the printer. For example, it is not possible to change the value of *_alignment* in the middle of the print job in order to have some of the text justified and the rest of it not justified.

Print System Memory Variables

All printer system memory variables begin with an underline(_). Some of these variables only apply to output generated with the ? command.

_alignment pub C "LEFT"

Specifies whether text is left justified ("LEFT"), centered ("CENTER"), or right justified ("RIGHT") when output is produced with the *?* command and *_wrap* is set to True.

_box pub L .T.

Controls whether defined boxes are printed.

_indent pub N 0 (0.000000000000000000)

Specifies the indentation of the first line of each new paragraph printed with the *?* command.

_lmargin pub N 0 (0.000000000000000000)

Defines the left margin for both displayed and printed text produced by the *?* command when *_wrap* is set to True.

_padvance pub C "FORMFEED"

Determines how the printer advances the paper. The default is 'FORMFEED'

_pageno pub N 3 (3.000000000000000000)

Used to determine the current page number or to set the page number to a specific value. The value of *_pageno* is increased by 1 each time a page eject is issued. The value of *_pageno* must be less than or equal to the value of *_pepage* to print any page.

_pbpage pub N 1 (1.000000000000000000)

Contains the beginning page for the print job. The default is 1.

_pcolno pub N 21 (21.00000000000000000)

Contains the column position of the printhead.

_pcopies pub N 1 (1.000000000000000000)

Contains the number of copies to be printed by a print job. It determines the number of times a PRINTJOB...ENDPRINTJOB loop is executed.

_pdriver pub C "LX80.PR2"

Contains the name of the current printer driver.

_pecode pub C ""

Contains the ending control codes for a print job. The default is a null string. This variable could be used to turn off any special attributes that have been used to set up the printer for the print job just ended.

_peject pub C "BEFORE"

Determines whether a page eject is issued before or after a print job or not at all. The options are "BEFORE"—eject before print job; "AFTER"—eject after print job; "BOTH"—eject both before and after; "NONE"—eject neither before nor after.

_pepage pub N 32767 (32767.00000000000000)

Contains the page number on which to end the print job. The default is 32767.

_pform pub C ""

Contains the name of a print form file that has the desired print settings.

_plength pub N 66 (66.0000000000000000)

Contains the number of lines on the printed page.

_plineno pub N 44 (44.0000000000000000)

Contains the number of the current line. It can be used prior to a print job to position the printer paper. During a print job, dBASE increments *_plineno* as each line is printed.

_ploffset pub N 0 (0.000000000000000000)

Contains the offset on the left side of the page for printed output only.

_ppitch pub C "DEFAULT"

Used to set the printer pitch. The available pitch options depend on the printer being used.

_pquality pub L .F.

Used to set near-letter quality On or Off on dot matrix printers. The variable is set to a logical True for near-letter quality On and a logical False for Off.

_pscode pub C ""

Contains the starting control codes for a print job. This code can be used for turning on printer attributes such as compressed print that will be used for the current print job. If, for a given printer, the code to turn on compressed print is Escape-C, *_pscode* could be set thusly to cause compressed print to be turned on. *_pscode*="{27}{67}" Note that the decimal ASCII values are enclosed in curly braces and the entire string is enclosed in quotes.

_pspacing pub N 1 (1.000000000000000000)

Specifies the line spacing.

_pwait pub L .F.

Specifies whether the printer pauses after each page.

_rmargin pub N 80 (80.00000000000000000)

Contains the right margin for output generated with ? commands if *_wrap* is set to True.

_tabs pub C ""

Used to set one or more tabs.

_wrap pub L .F.

Sets word wrap On or Off

Of the memory variables above, these apply to formatting the printed page.

_plength. The page length in lines, including the top and bottom margins.
_ploffset. The page offset at the left side of the page.
_lmargin. The left margin. The total space on the left side of the page is _ploffset+_lmargin.
_rmargin. The right margin.

Setting System Memory Variables

It may be desirable to allow the user to set the system memory variables that will control how a report generated with the CREATE REPORT command will look when printed. This program displays the current values of the system memory variables and allows the user to change them.

```
* printsel.prg
medit='Y'
DO WHILE UPPER(medit)='Y'
    CLEAR
    @ 0,0 TO 23 ,79
    @ 1,3 SAY 'Printer driver          ' GET _pdriver
    @ 2,3 SAY 'Letter Quality          ' GET _pquality
    @ 3,3 SAY 'Lines/page              ' GET _plength
    @ 4,3 SAY 'Page offset             ' GET _ploffset
    @ 5,3 SAY 'Left Margin             ' GET _lmargin
    @ 6,3 SAY 'Right Margin            ' GET _rmargin
    @ 7,3 SAY 'Alignment               ' GET _alignment
    @ 8,3 SAY 'Starting codes          ' GET _pscode
    @ 9,3 SAY 'Page Eject              ' GET _peject
    @ 10,3 SAY 'Ending Code            ' GET _pecode
    @ 11,3 SAY 'Number of Copies       ' GET _pcopies
    @ 12,3 SAY 'Beginning Page         ' GET _pbpage
    @ 13,3 SAY 'Ending Page            ' GET _pepage
    @ 14,3 SAY 'Printer Pitch          ' GET _ppitch
    @ 15,3 SAY 'How advances           ' GET _padvance
    @ 16,3 SAY 'Print form             ' GET _pform
    @ 17,3 SAY 'Line spacing           ' GET _pspacing
    @ 18,3 SAY 'Wait at end of page    ' GET _pwait
    @ 19,3 SAY 'Indent                 ' GET _indent
    @ 20,3 SAY 'Wrap                   ' GET _wrap
    READ
    @ 24,0 SAY 'Do you want to edit? Y or N' GET medit
    READ
ENDDO
```

If some variables, such as *_pdriver*, should not be changed by the user, then the variables should be removed from the program. Note that *_pscode*, *_pecode*, and *_pform* default to a null so that the GET will not be activated.

To allow the user to change these values, some value such as a blank must be stored to each variable prior to executing the program.

Formatting Long Expressions

dBASE IV provides options for formatting long expressions that are basically memo fields or long character fields.

These new options are in the form of new PICTURE functions that can be used with the *?* command. These functions include

H	Horizontal stretch
V<*n*>	Vertical stretch
I	Center a field within a column
B	Left align
J	Right align

NOTE: There must be a space between the word *FUNCTION* and the function letter in quotes.

The H function wraps a memo field within the margins established by *_rmargin* and *_lmargin* only if *_wrap* is set to True. If *_wrap* is set to False, the memowidth established with SET MEMOWIDTH TO is used. The following example demonstrates how to use this PICTURE function.

```
. _rmargin=60
     60
. _wrap=.T.
.T.
. ? m1 FUNCTION 'H'
This is the time for all good men to come to the aid of
their party.
```

The V<*n*> function wraps the field within the width established by <*n*>.

```
. ? m1 FUNCTION 'V25'
This is the time for all
good men to come to the
aid of their party.
```

The I function can be used in conjunction with the V function to center text within a column as follows:

```
. ? m1 FUNCTION 'IV25'
  This is the time for all
good men to come to the
    aid of their party.
```

If the I function is used by itself, text is centered within the column established by the SET MEMOWIDTH TO <*n*>. The following example is based on the default memowidth of 50.

```
. ? m1 FUNCTION 'I'
This is the time for all good men to come to the
                aid of their party.
```

The B function allows the left aligning of text and can be used in conjunction with the V function.

```
. ? m1 FUNCTION 'BV25'
This is the time for all
good men to come to the
aid of their party.
```

The J function forces right aligning of text, as in the example:

```
. ? m1 FUNCTION 'JV25'
   This is the time for all
good men to come to the
        aid of their party.
```

New Output Options

dBASE IV adds the capability to use windows. In dBASE III PLUS, windows can be simulated with boxes, using such commands as

```
@ 1,0 TO 12,40
```

to create boxes on the screen. However, boxes are simply lines on the screen. If text is later output over parts of the box, the box is overprinted.

By contrast, dBASE IV offers the option to use windows—rectangular areas of the screen where output occurs. If the output is too wide for the window, it wraps to the next line. Windows are useful for editing memo fields and for directing output such as LIST or DISPLAY.

When a window is invoked, attempting to execute an @...SAY with coordinates outside the window will generate an error message. @...SAY coordinates must be relative to the window. For example, if a window is defined from 17,1 to 23,79, row 18 becomes row 0 for that window. Row 19 becomes row 1, etc. This means that the following command would generate an error message because the coordinates are outside the window

@ 18,5 SAY 'Title'

The correct command to print on row 18 is

@ 0,5 SAY 'Title'.

NOTE: SET STATUS OFF must be executed to define a window that covers the status line.

Thus if a window is defined from *r1*,*c1*, to *r2*,*c2* with the command

DEFINE WINDOW test FROM *r1*,*c1* TO *r2*,*c2*

the valid row coordinates are from 0 to $r2-r1-2$, and the valid column coordinates are from 1 to $c2-c1-2$. In both cases, 2 must be subtracted to allow for the borders.

dBASE IV also adds features to support pop-up and pull-down menus, which are discussed in chapter 11.

Windows

Windows provide a way to direct the output of certain operations to a specified area of the screen.

The steps for setting up and using a window are as follows:

1. Define the Window

The full syntax of the DEFINE WINDOW command is

DEFINE WINDOW <*window name*> FROM <*row1*>,<*col1*>
TO <*row2*>,<*col2*> [DOUBLE/PANEL/NONE/<*border*

```
definition string>] [COLOR [<standard>]
[,<enhanced>] [,<frame>]]
```

Basically, the DEFINE WINDOW command is used to specify the name, screen location, and display attribute of the window and its border. The default border is a single-line. A double-line box, a highlighted panel, or none can be specified for the border, using the SET BORDER TO command.

For instance, to define a window to display vendor codes, we can use

```
DEFINE WINDOW vendor FROM 2,40 TO 15,79
```

Make sure in defining the window that it is large enough to contain the information that is to be displayed.

2. Activate the Window

When the window is ready to be used, it must be activated by using the syntax

```
ACTIVATE WINDOW vendor
```

Once a window is activated, the output of all subsequent commands, including MODIFY COMMAND, will be directed to the window until it is DEACTIVATEd.

3. Enter Commands That Will Cause Output to Be Displayed in the Window

The output of all subsequent commands will appear in the window until it is DEACTIVATEd. For our vendor example, the following code will display the vendor code and vendor names in the window:

```
USE vendor
DISPLAY ALL vendno,vendname
```

The output of the DISPLAY command will be directed to the window defined above. The DISPLAY command automatically adjusts the number of records displayed to fit into the window.

4. Deactivate the Window

After a window's purpose has been served, it is necessary to DEACTIVATE it so that subsequent output will not be directed to the window. The command is

DEACTIVATE WINDOW vendor

After this command is issued, the window definition is still saved in memory so that it can be ACTIVATEd again.

5. Release the Window from Memory

After the window's usefulness has been exhausted, it can be released from memory in order to free up memory space. The command is

RELEASE WINDOW vendor

When working with multiple windows that occupy the same area of the screen, each subsequent window that is ACTIVATED overwrites the previous window. When a window is DEACTIVATEd, it disappears from the screen, and text from any previous window that it overwrote is restored.

Other Window Commands

The following additional functions can be performed with windows:

1. ACTIVATE SCREEN. Redirects output to the full screen while leaving the window in the foreground.

2. CLEAR WINDOWS. DEACTIVATEs all windows and releases them from memory.

3. SAVE WINDOW. Saves window definitions to a disk file. The syntax is

SAVE WINDOW <*name list*>/ALL TO <*file name*>

This command creates a file with a .win extension. To save the vendor window, the syntax is

SAVE WINDOW vendor TO vendor

4. RESTORE WINDOW. The inverse of SAVE WINDOW. The syntax to restore the window saved above would be

RESTORE WINDOW vendor FROM vendor

When the RESTORE WINDOW command is issued, the window is loaded into memory and must be ACTIVATEd.

5. MOVE WINDOW. After a window is defined, it can be moved. The syntax of the command is

MOVE WINDOW <*name*> TO <*r*>,<*c*>/BY <*n1*>,<*n2*>

The window can be moved to a new set of absolute coordinates, or it can be moved by a certain number in each direction.

The following rather silly program demonstrates how to move a window.

```
* movwind.prg
*1.     define the window:
        DEFINE WINDOW test FROM 2,5 TO 10,10
*2.     activate the window
        ACTIVATE WINDOW test
*3.     move the window
        r=1
        c=1
        DO WHILE r < 10
            DO WHILE c < 10
                MOVE WINDOW test BY r,c
                c=c+1
            ENDDO
            r=r+1
        ENDDO
```

6. SET WINDOW OF MEMO TO <*window name*>

Defines a special window for editing memo fields. If a memo field is being edited, by pressing Ctrl-Home in the Edit or Append mode, or in response to an @...GET, the editing will take place in the specified window. The window specified for editing memo fields can be overridden or changed using the window clause of the @...SAY/GET.

Chapter 6

INPUT

Communication is expectation. We perceive, as a rule, what we expect to perceive . . .

Before we can communicate, we must, therefore, know what the recipient expects to see and hear.

—*Peter Drucker,* Management: Tasks, Responsibilities, Practices

Input validation is the antidote to *Garbage In, Garbage Out* (GIGO). For the results of a data base query to be accurate, the data entered into the data base must be valid. It is the job of the programmer to communicate to the user what is expected in the way of input. Various tools are available to the programmer.

Making an input screen look like a paper form
Providing help screens
Checking for valid input and prompting the user if the input is not valid.

THE INPUT PROCESS

In previous chapters we showed dBASE's built-in interactive commands for adding new records and editing existing records. While such commands may be acceptable for use with files in which data integrity is not critical, when data integrity *is* important, more sophisticated programming techniques must be used. When data integrity is critical, it is the job of the programmer to restrict the user's access to the data. For example, it would not be desirable to allow users to BROWSE through a file containing accounting data and to allow them to change numbers randomly.

To support data integrity and to facilitate data entry, the following three-step process will be used for examples in the remainder of this book.

1. Input to memory variables first. Instead of inputting directly to a file, input is done first to memory variables. The input is validated as it is entered into the memory variables.

2. After the user has reviewed the data entered into memory variables and confirmed its accuracy, post the data from memory variables to a temporary file.

3. The data is posted from the transaction or temporary file to the master file.

This chapter will cover steps 1 and 2 while chapter 9 will cover step 3. This approach may seem to require a lot of programming, but it will have benefits in the long run. Some of the principles that underlie this method of input are

1. Never post directly to the master file. There are several reasons for this.

   a. When data is posted directly to the master file, indexes must be updated. This index update process may require several minutes. It would waste the inputter's time to wait several minutes after entering each record while the index files are updated. The above approach—inputting to memory variables and then to a temporary file—causes virtually no delay. The temporary file is generally not indexed, so no update time is required. After input is completed, a posting routine can be executed to post the temporary file to the master file automatically. Since no one has to be at the computer for posting, the slow process of updating the index files is separated from the relatively faster process of inputting data.

   b. It is a good idea not to have the master file open any longer than necessary. The longer the file is open, the more likely is the possibility that it will be corrupted.

2. Allowing users to change their minds. It is always a good idea in programming to allow users to change their minds at many points throughout the program. This approach makes changes of mind easy. If the data were to be input directly to the master file, the first step would have to be appending a

blank record. Thus, if the users changed their minds, that blank record would have to be deleted and the file packed in order to remove the blank record. No such problems occur when the approach above is used.

3. Appending records in groups and updating the indexes all at once, rather than appending single records and updating indexes, reduces file fragmentation on the hard disk.

MODIFICATIONS

Sometimes it makes sense to use a modification of the above approach in which steps 1 and 2 are combined. In this modified approach, a temporary file is created with the same structure as the master file, and input is done directly to the temporary file. However, only in extremely few cases would it make sense to input directly to the master file.

INPUT VALIDATION

One of the most important jobs of the programmer is to validate user input. The programmer knows what type of input the program requires. It is the programmer's job to communicate this knowledge to the user through documentation, on-line help, and input validation that forces the user to input valid information. Unless this approach is followed, the old adage "garbage in, garbage out" may well apply.

dBASE supplies various tools for validating input. With these tools, virtually any kind of input validation can be accomplished. In this chapter we will review the various tools dBASE provides.

Input Validation through Initializing Memory Variables

There is much confusion about the various input validation tools provided by dBASE. In many cases, initializing a variable properly will take care of all of the input validation that is required.

The memory variable type is determined by how it is initialized. If a variable is set equal to a character string, it is a character type variable. If it is set equal to a number, then it is a numeric type. If it is set equal to a date, then it is a date type. If it is set equal to a logical value, then it is a logical memory variable.

```
mchar='This is a test'  &&initializing a character variable
mnum=0.00               &&initializing a numeric variable
```

```
mdate = DATE()          &&initializing a date variable
mlogic = .T.            &&initializing a logical variable
```

The initialization process not only determines the variable type, but, with a character variable, the initialization also determines the length of the variable. In the above example, *mchar* is 14 characters long because the string to which it is initialized is 14 characters long. If an attempt is made to input more than 14 characters to *mchar*, everything over 14 characters will be truncated.

When a numeric memory variable is initialized, the number of places to the right of the decimal point is determined. In the above example, *mnum* will have two places to the right of the point. When initializing numeric memory variables, it is important to think through the amount of precision that will be required in the numbers to be tracked. If three places to the right of the point are needed, then *mnum* must be initialized in the following way:

```
mnum = 0.000
```

If no places to the right of the point are required, then *mnum* can be initialized with

```
mnum = 0
```

While the initialization statement controls the number of places to the right of the decimal point, dBASE defaults to numeric memory variables containing 10 places to the left of the point. To increase that to the full 16 digits of precision allowed, a larger number can be stored to the memory variable.

In defining memory variables for input, it is important to define the memory variable as having the same precision as the numeric field to which it will eventually be stored. As stated in chapter 3, when a numeric field is created, the total length (including the decimal point) must be specified, and the number of places to the right of the point must be specified.

An initialization statement is only good until another initialization statement is issued for the same variable name. Consider these two statements

```
memvar = 'This is a test'
memvar = DATE()
```

The second statement completely overrides the first, making *memvar* a date type memory variable containing the system date. The most recent initialization statement for a memory variable name determines its type and content.

By defining a memory variable as a certain type, dBASE does some input validation. For example, dBASE will only allow users to enter numeric data into a numeric memory variable. If an attempt is made to enter a letter into a numeric memory variable, the computer will beep, and nothing will be entered into the memory variable. This feature of dBASE is useful as a first defense against erroneous information being entered into a memory variable.

By defining a memory variable as a date type memory variable, dBASE will only allow valid dates to be entered into a date memory variable. dBASE knows how many days each month has and will only allow valid dates to be entered. If an attempt is made to enter 02/31/88 into a date type memory variable, a prompt will appear saying *Invalid date (press Space)*. The user must press the Space Bar and try again.

The automatic type checking by dBASE saves programmers from having to write their own input validation routines to perform these functions.

NOTE: PICTURE statements can be used to define precision. For example, a memory variable can be initialized to be 0 and PICTURE '99.99' added to the GET to force two decimal places of precision. SET FIXED ON in conjunction with SET DECIMALS TO 2 will not accomplish the same result and will cause misleading results to be displayed.

Picture Statements

Picture statements provide the next level of input checking provided by dBASE. dBASE provides PICTURE symbols for formatting both input and output. The use of PICTURE statements for output is discussed in chapter 5.

Since dBASE automatically restricts numeric variables to numbers and date variables to dates, PICTURE statements are most useful in conjunction with character type fields.

Some of the most useful PICTURE statements for formatting input include

! converts alphabetic characters to upper case.
9 restricts input of character fields to numbers. The 9 PICTURE is most often used with fields such as zip code and telephone number, which are character fields containing numbers.
A restricts input into character fields to alphabetic characters.

As described in chapter 5, PICTURE statements can include either PICTURE template characters, which provide one PICTURE template character for each character in the variable, or PICTURE functions in which one PICTURE character is applied to the whole variable.

Some examples of using PICTURE templates for input include the following:

```
mzip=SPACE(5)
@ 5,10 GET mzip PICTURE '99999'
READ
```

This PICTURE template would restrict input into mzip to 5 characters, all of which must be numbers. It does not require that all 5 spaces be filled in, however. It only requires that if a character is entered, it must be a number.

Surprisingly, in dBASE III PLUS the expected function version of this command will *not* work in restricting input to numbers.

```
mzip=SPACE(5)
@ 5,10 GET mzip PICTURE '@9'
READ
```

It may be desirable to restrict input into a last name field to all upper case. This can be accomplished with either of these methods:

```
mlname=SPACE(20)
@ 5,10 GET mlname PICTURE '!!!!!!!!!!!!!!!!!!!!'
READ
```

or

```
mlname=SPACE(20)
@ 5,10 GET mlname PICTURE '@!'
READ
```

The first method uses the template approach in which there is one PICTURE character for each character in the variable. In the second method a PICTURE function is used so that a single character can apply to the whole variable. It could be rewritten using the less common, but sometimes useful, syntax.

```
mlname=SPACE(20)
@ 5,10 GET mlname FUNCTION '!'
READ
```

Note that the *!* character does not restrict input to alphabetic characters, and numbers can still be entered. When a lower case character is entered, it is converted to upper case.

Using @R

Sometimes it is necessary to insert extraneous characters into a string for formatting purposes. One example is a social security number where a hyphen is inserted between the third and fourth characters and between the fifth and sixth characters. While it is possible to physically store the hyphens in the field in the file, it would waste 2 bytes per record. dBASE provides a PICTURE statement to format values for input and output without requiring extraneous characters to be stored in the field.

```
mssn = SPACE(9)
@ 5,1 SAY 'Enter social security number ' GET mssn ;
    PICTURE '@R 999-99-9999'
READ
```

When this command is executed, the following display will appear on the screen if the digits 1–9 are entered.

```
Enter social security number 123-45-6789
```

The entry field will appear to be 11 characters long, even though the memory variable is only 9 characters long. The @R PICTURE function used in conjunction with a PICTURE template tells dBASE that in the PICTURE template, extraneous characters—in this case, hyphens—are to be inserted at the places shown in the field. The @R function is used to format the variable for output.

A phone number can be formatted similarly:

```
mphone = SPACE(10)
@ 5,1 SAY 'Enter phone number ' GET mphone ;
    PICTURE '@R (999) 999-9999'
READ
```

The display would appear on the screen as

```
Enter Phone Number (123) 456-7890
```

Even though the field is only 10 characters long, the @R function formats the input field to include 2 parentheses, a space, and a hyphen.

Range Statements

The next level of input validation provided by dBASE is the RANGE statement that allows specifying the range for numeric or date type memory variables.

Following is an example that uses the RANGE statement to restrict a test score to 0–100:

```
mscore=0
@ 5,1 SAY 'Enter score ' GET mscore RANGE 0,100
READ
```

No PICTURE statement is needed for the variable *mscore*. Since it is initialized as numeric, only valid numbers can be entered.

If a number entered is outside the range 0–100, the following prompt will appear:

```
RANGE is 0 to 100 (press SPACE)
```

The user must press the Space Bar and then re-enter the number.

Range checking is only done when data is input from the keyboard. If the program initializes the variable to a value outside the range and the user presses Enter to confirm it, the *Range Error* message will not be triggered.

The RANGE function can also be used to check for valid dates. For example, to limit a date to a value between July 1, 1987 and June 30, 1988, this format can be used:

```
mdate=CTOD('07/01/87')
@ 5,1 GET mdate RANGE CTOD('07/01/87'),CTOD('06/30/88')
READ
```

The above discussion shows how to use dBASE's built-in error checking functions. However, some things cannot be checked that way. Virtually any condition can be checked using the following approaches.

DO WHILE Loops for Input Validation

Any input validation that cannot be accomplished with the previous commands can be done with DO WHILE loops. PICTURE '99999' can insure that all digits in a 5-digit zip code are numbers, but it cannot insure that all digits are entered. In using a DO WHILE loop for input validation, the DO WHILE condition is the error condition, so the loop is only executed if there is an error condition, and then the user is "trapped" in the DO WHILE loop until a valid value is entered.

For example, to see whether all digits in a zip code have been entered to a memory variable mzip, the following DO WHILE loop can be used

```
DO WHILE AT(' ',mzip) > 0
    @ 19,0 SAY 'Please enter all 5 digits for the zipcode'
    @ 10,35 GET mzip PICTURE '99999'
    READ
ENDDO
```

The user will be trapped in this loop until a valid zip code is entered. The AT function will only be greater than zero if the mzip memory variable contains a space.

Another example is inputting values to a 1-character character variable, mgrade, that has valid values of 'K123456'. Since one of the valid values is a letter, a simple RANGE statement cannot be used, but the following DO WHILE loop will work.

```
mgrade=SPACE(1)
@ 2,1 SAY 'Enter grade ' GET mgrade PICTURE '!'
    READ
DO WHILE .NOT. mgrade $ 'K123456'
    @ 20,0 SAY 'Enter grade as K123456'
    @ 2,1 SAY 'Enter grade ' GET mgrade PICTURE '!'
    READ
ENDDO
```

This program makes use of the $ function to see whether or not one string is contained within another. If the string in the memory variable mgrade is not contained in the string 'K123456', an error condition exists, and the user is locked into the DO WHILE loop until the required value is entered.

A SIMPLE INPUT PROGRAM

This program is useful for inputting name and address information first to memory variables and then to a temporary file.

```
* getaddr.prg

^ program to input contributor data

* initialize environment
SET TALK OFF
SET ECHO OFF
SET STATUS OFF
SET DEVICE TO SCREEN

* initialize memory variables
mlname=SPACE(20)
mfname=SPACE(15)
mtitle=SPACE(15)
mcompany=SPACE(20)
mstraddr=SPACE(20)
mcity=SPACE(15)
mstate=SPACE(2)
mzip=SPACE(5)
mphone=space(10)
mcontrib=0

* get input
mflag=.T.
CLEAR
DO WHILE mflag
     @ 1,0 to 14,79
     @ 5,5 SAY 'First name 'GET mfname
     @ 5,45 SAY 'Last name ' GET mlname PICTURE '@!'
     @ 6,5 SAY 'Title          ' GET mtitle
     @ 7,5 SAY 'Company name ' GET mcompany
     @ 8,5 SAY 'Street address ' GET mstraddr
     @ 9,5 SAY 'City ' GET mcity
     @ 9,35 SAY 'State ' GET mstate PICTURE '@!'
     @ 9,47 SAY 'Zip ' GET mzip PICTURE '99999'
@ 10,5 SAY 'Phone number ' GET mphone PICTURE '@R (999) 999-9999'
     @ 11,5 SAY 'Contribution Amount ' GET mcontrib
     READ
@ 20,1 SAY 'Do you want to edit? (Y/N)' GET mflag PICTURE 'Y'
     READ
 ENDDO
```

```
    @ 20,0
    * check if valid name entered
    IF mfname=' ' .OR. mlname= ' '
        RETURN
    ENDIF

    DO WHILE ' ' $ mzip
        @ 20,0 SAY 'Please enter full five-digit zip code'
        @ 9,47 SAY 'Zip ' GET mzip
        READ
    ENDDO

    * get names in proper format
    mfname=LTRIM(mfname)
    mfname=UPPER(SUBSTR(mfname,1,1));
-LOWER(SUBSTR(mfname,2,14))

    * show user what has been entered
    CLEAR
    @ 1,0 to 14,79
    @ 5,5 SAY 'First Name 'GET mfname
    @ 5,45 SAY 'Last Name ' GET mlname
    @ 6,5 SAY 'Title          ' GET mtitle
    @ 7,5 SAY 'Company Name ' GET mcompany
    @ 8,5 SAY 'Street Address ' GET mstraddr
    @ 9,5 SAY 'City ' GET mcity
    @ 9,35 SAY 'State ' GET mstate
    @ 9,47 SAY 'Zip ' GET mzip
    @ 10,5 SAY 'Phone number ' GET mphone PICTURE '@R (999) 999-;
    9999'
    @ 11,5 SAY 'Contribution Amount ' GET mcontrib
    CLEAR GETS
    mpost=SPACE(1)
@ 20,1 SAY 'Do you want to save this address? (Y/N)' GET mpost PICTURE;
'Y'
        READ
    IF UPPER(mpost)='Y'
        USE tempaddr
        APPEND BLANK
        REPL fname WITH mfname
        REPL lname WITH mlname
```

```
        REPL title WITH mtitle
        REPL company WITH mcompany
        REPL straddr WITH mstraddr
        REPL city WITH mcity
        REPL state WITH mstate
        REPL zip WITH mzip
        REPL phone WITH mphone
        REPL contrib WITH mcontrib
    ENDIF post
```

Inputting to Memory Variables First

The first section of this program initializes the environment. When a program is executed, it is useful to initialize the environment first in order to reset any conditions that may have been set by other programs.

SET TALK OFF suppresses dBASE's default of displaying the results of certain commands on the screen.
SET ECHO OFF turns off the feature of dBASE that displays each line of code on the screen as it is executed.
SET STATUS OFF turns off the status display at the bottom of the screen.
SET DEVICE TO SCREEN redirects @...SAY output to the screen. This SET command is included in case a previous program had aborted abnormally while SET DEVICE TO PRINT was in effect. If this was the case, output would be directed to the printer until the SET DEVICE TO SCREEN command was issued.

The *initialize variables* section of the program sets up the memory variables into which data will be input. It is important that the memory variables be initialized to the same type and length as the fields in the file to which the data will be input.

The next section of the program sets up a DO WHILE loop that enables the user to edit the information that has been entered. The memory variable *mflag* is initialized to *Y*. The user can reset the value of that memory variable in response to the @...SAY...GET which asks 'Do you want to edit?'

The remainder of the loop consists of @...SAY...GET statements that allow the user to input each item of data. PICTURE '@!' is used with the memory variable *mlname* to force the last name field into upper case. This is done for retrieval purposes so that the last name will always be all upper case. Note that a space is required between the key word PICTURE and the PICTURE clause.

A PICTURE clause is also used for the *state* and *zip* memory variables. PICTURE '@!' insures that the 2-character *state* field will be input as upper case. Even though the *zip* field contains numbers, the numbers are not manipulated numerically. For that reason, the *zip* field is defined as a character field rather than as a numeric field, and PICTURE '99999' is used to insure that only numbers can be input to this character field. If it were defined as a numeric field, leading zeroes would be suppressed.

The *phone number* field is another character field containing numbers. The PICTURE clause used with the *phone number* field not only insures that input will be numeric, but also causes the phone number to be formatted properly. A phone number with an area code consists of 10 characters. It is a waste of disk space to include formatting characters such as parentheses around the area code. Formatting characters can be added for input and output purposes using the @R PICTURE function in conjunction with the PICTURE template shown. The @R tells dBASE that extraneous characters will be included in the screen display for formatting purposes, but that these extraneous characters will not be saved to the memory variable or field. In this case, the extraneous characters are the parentheses around the area code and the hyphen between the phone number exchange and the last four digits.

Since *mcontrib* is a numeric field, no PICTURE statements are needed. The fact that it is a numeric field restricts the input to numeric data. PICTURE 'Y' is used with the *mflag* field to restrict input to *Yes* or *No*.

After a READ to get input has been executed, the user is then asked whether or not to edit the data input. If the answer is *Yes*, the loop is executed again to allow a change of mind. Only when the user says *No* is the loop exited.

Next, an IF statement is used to see whether first or last name is blank. If this is the case, the program is exited with a RETURN statement.

A DO WHILE loop checks whether the full zip code has been entered, using the condition ' ' $ *mzip*. If a blank is contained in the *mzip* memory variable, then an error condition exists and the loop is executed in order to force the user to enter the full zip code.

The first name is formatted then to remove all leading blanks and to force the first letter to be in upper case and the remaining letters to be in lower case.

Posting the Information to a Temporary File

After the data is entered to memory variables, the contents of the memory variables are transferred to a temporary file. This task is accomplished by displaying the entered data on the screen and asking the user for confirmation that the address is to be saved. Note that a CLEAR GETS is substituted for a READ.

This approach is used so that the data entered will be displayed in inverse video, and the user will not be permitted to change it.

Only if the user confirmed saving the address by entering a *Y* will a blank record be appended to the temporary file and the data from the memory variables transferred to the record in the temporary file.

Converting This Program to Add Multiple Records

As written, the program only provides for adding a single record. However, the program can be modified to add multiple records by putting a DO WHILE loop around the whole program. At the beginning of the program, add these lines:

```
madd='Y'
DO WHILE madd='Y'
```

At the end of the program add

```
   @ 20,0 SAY 'Do you want to add another address? Y or N' ;
      GET madd PICTURE '!'
   READ
ENDDO &&WHILE madd='Y'
```

Changing to an Edit Routine

The program can be changed from an add routine to an edit routine by taking these steps:

1. At the beginning of the program, ask the user to identify the key field for the record to be edited.

2. See whether or not that record exists. If it does, position the record pointer to that record; if not, inform the user and allow the key field to be re-entered.

3. If the record exists, set the memory variables equal to the current values in the fields.

4. In the routine to REPLACE the field values, take out the USE tempaddr and the APPEND BLANK since the record pointer is already pointing to the proper record.

PROGRAM TO ENTER A CHECK

This program is used to enter a check. Account distributions may be up to two accounts. The check is posted to a temporary file named aptemp. When a vendor code is entered, it is validated in a vendor file. Accounts codes are validated in an account file. The structures of files accessed by the program are shown below.

```
Structure for database: C:aptemp.dbf
Number of data records:        5
Date of last update     : 11/01/88
Field       Field Name      Type        Width     Dec
   1        DATE            Date            8
   2        CKNO            Character       5
   3        PVENDNO         Character       5
   4        PACCTNO         Character       5
   5        AMT             Numeric        10       2
   6        COMMENT1        Character      20
   7        COMMENT2        Character      20
   8        PACCTNO2        Character       5
   9        PAMT2           Numeric        10       2
** Total **                                89

Structure for database: C:vendor.dbf
Number of data records:        131
Date of last update     : 10/19/88
Field       Field Name      Type        Width     Dec
   1        VENDNO          Character       5
   2        VENDNAME        Character      26
   3        DEFAUAMT        Numeric        10       2
   4        DEFAUACCT       Character       5
   5        STRADDR         Character      25
   6        CITY            Character      15
   7        STATE           Character       2
   8        ZIP             Character       5
** Total **                                94

Structure for database: C:ACCOUNT.dbf
Number of data records:        20
Date of last update     : 09/06/88
```

Field	Field Name	Type	Width	Dec
1	ACCTNO	Character	2	
2	ACCTNAME	Character	15	
** Total **			18	

CHECK ENTRY PROGRAM

```
* enter.prg
* Program to enter checks and post to temporary file—aptemp
* Allow to post to up to two accounts per check
SET TALK OFF
SET STATUS OFF
* open files
SELECT A
USE aptemp
GO BOTT
mrecno=RECNO()+1
SELE B
USE vendor INDEX vendor
SELECT C
USE account INDEX account
* initialize variables
mchoice='Y'
mtotal=0.00
mdate=DATE()
mline=REPLICATE('-',80)
CLEAR
DO WHILE UPPER(mchoice)='Y'
     mfound=SPACE(1)
     mpayee=SPACE(5)
     mamt=0.00
     macct=SPACE(5)
     macctno=SPACE(5)
```

```
   STORE SPACE(20) TO mcomment1, mcomment2

   CLEAR
   @ 2,0 SAY mline
   @ 20,0 SAY 'Press Return in Payto field to exit'
   @ 5,5 GET mdate
   @ 5,53 SAY mrecno
   @ 8,5 SAY 'Pay to ' GET mpayee PICTURE '!!!!!'
   READ
   @ 20,0

   ** allow to exit by entering blank for payee
   IF mpayee=" "
     CLOSE DATA
     CLEAR
     RETURN
   ENDIF

* input validate vendor
   SELE B
   mpayee = TRIM(mpayee)
   SEEK mpayee

   * trap if invalid payee
   DO WHILE EOF()
     @ 22,1 SAY 'Vendor not found in file—Please re-enter'
@ 23,1 SAY 'Press Enter to abort, A to add new vendor, R to review; vendors'

     mpayee=SPACE(5)
     @ 8,5 SAY 'PAY TO ' GET mpayee PICTURE '!!!!!'
     READ
     DO CASE

       * exit error routine
       CASE MPAYEE= " "
         GOTO 1
         mfound='N'

       * review vendor codes
```

```
      CASE UPPER(mpayee) = "R" .AND. SUBSTR(mpayee,2,1) = ' '
        GO TOP
        DO WHILE .NOT. EOF()
          @ 8,0 CLEAR
          DISPLAY NEXT 12 vendno,vendname
          WAIT 'Press Q to quit, any other key to continue' TO mquit
          IF UPPER(mquit) = 'Q'
            EXIT
          ENDIF
        ENDDO
        CLEAR
        mfound = 'N'
        EXIT
      * add new vendor
      CASE UPPER(MPAYEE) = 'A' .AND. SUBSTR(MPAYEE,2,1)  =  ' '
        DO VENDADD
        mfound = 'N'
      OTHERWISE
        SEEK TRIM(mpayee)
    ENDCASE
  ENDDO && end of vendor error trapping loop
  @ 22,1
  @ 23,1
  * if vendor not found, re-enter
  IF mfound = 'N'
    LOOP
  ENDIF
  * extract payee information from vendor file and display
  * vendor name
  mvendname = vendname
  mamt = defauamt
  macct  = defauacct
```

```
@ 8,5
@ 8,12 SAY mvendname
@ 8,57 SAY “AMT” GET mamt
READ
**CHECK FOR 0 AMT
IF mamt=0
     LOOP
ENDIF
r=10
@ 10,5 SAY “ACCT # ” GET macct
mamt1=mamt
@ 10,20 say '$' GET   mamt1 RANGE 1,mamt
READ
IF macct= ' '
     LOOP
ENDIF
macctno=macct
DO checkacc
macct=macctno
* check if macct blank
IF mpayee=“ ” .OR. macct= “ ”
   LOOP
ENDIF
@ 10,38 SAY acctname
IF mamt1 <> mamt
     r=11
     macct1=SPACE(5)
     @ 11,5 SAY 'ACCT # ' GET macct1
     @ 11,20 SAY '$'+STR(mamt-mamt1)
     READ
     IF macct1= ' '
          LOOP
     ENDIF
     macctno=macct1
```

```
        DO checkacc
        macct1=macctno
        IF macct1=' '
            LOOP
        ENDIF
          @ 11,38 SAY acctname
        ENDIF &&second distribution
      @ 12,0 SAY mline
      @ 14,2 SAY 'COMMENT 1 ' GET mcomment1
      @ 15,2 SAY 'COMMENT 2 ' GET mcomment2
      @ 17,0 SAY mline
      READ
    ** if ok to post, store to temp file
      mpost=SPACE(1)
      @ 20,1 SAY 'Ok to post? Y or N' GET mpost
      READ
      IF UPPER(mpost)='Y'
        SELE A
        APPEND BLANK
        REPL date WITH mdate
        REPL amt WITH mamt, comment1 WITH mcomment1
        REPL comment2 WITH mcomment2
        REPL pvendno WITH mpayee, pacctno WITH macct
        IF mamt1 <> mamt
          REPLACE pacctno2 WITH macct1
          REPLACE pamt2 WITH mamt1
        ENDIF
        mtotal=mtotal+mamt
        mrecno=mrecno+1
    ENDIF && post
    @ 20,1 SAY 'Total disbursed this session =:'+STR(mtotal,10,2)
```

```
    @ 22,1 SAY 'Enter another? Y OR N' GET mchoice
    READ



ENDDO &&WHILE mchoice Y

```

```
** vendadd.prg
** program to add a new vendor

mcont   =   'Y'

DO WHILE UPPER(mcont)='Y'
    flag = 'Y'
    store SPACE(5) TO mvendno,mdefauacct
    mvendname = SPACE(26)
    mvamt     = 0.00
    mstraddr  = SPACE(25)
    mcity     = SPACE(15)
    mstate    = SPACE(2)
    mzip      = SPACE(5)


    DO WHILE UPPER(flag)='Y'
        CLEAR
        @ 2,1 SAY 'Enter vendor information'

        @ 4,2 SAY 'Vendor code      ' GET mvendno PICTURE '!!!!!'
        @ 5,2 SAY 'Vendor name      ' GET mvendname
        @ 6,2 SAY 'Street address   ' GET mstraddr
        @ 7,2 SAY 'City             ' GET mcity
        @ 7,35 SAY 'State '             GET mstate
        @ 7,45 SAY 'Zip '               GET mzip PICTURE '99999'
        @ 8,2 SAY 'Default amount   ' GET mvamt
        @ 9,2 SAY 'Default account  ' GET mdefauacct PICT '!!!!!'
```

```
        READ

        @ 10,1 SAY 'Enter Y to Edit, Q to Quit, any other key to;
        continue'
        @ 11,1 GET flag
        READ
    ENDDO &&WHILE flag=y

** check for blank account code
    IF UPPER(flag)='Q' .OR. mvendno=' ' .OR. mvendname= ' '
        GOTO 1
        RETURN
    ENDIF


    ** input validate default account
      r=18
      macctno=mdefauacct
      DO checkacc
      mdefauacct=macctno

    IF mdefauacct= " "
        @ 20,1 say 'Enter another vendor? Y or N' get mcont
        READ
        LOOP
    ENDIF

    SELECT B
    mvendno=TRIM(mvendno)
    SEEK mvendno
    IF EOF()
      APPEND BLANK
      REPLACE vendno WITH mvendno
      REPLACE vendname WITH mvendname
      REPLACE defauamt WITH mvamt
      REPL defauacct WITH mdefauacct
      REPL straddr WITH mstraddr
      REPL city WITH mcity
      REPL state WITH mstate
```

```
      REPL zip WITH mzip
    ELSE
      @ 12,1 SAY 'Vendor number '+mvendno +' is already in file'
    ENDIF



  @ 20,1 say 'Enter another vendor? Y or N' get mcont
  READ
ENDDO &&WHILE mcont=Y
```

```
* checkacc.prg
* program to input validate account number
SELE C
macctno=trim(macctno)
SEEK macctno
DO WHILE EOF()
        @ 22,1 SAY 'Account number not found in file—Please re-enter'
        @ 23,1 SAY 'Press Enter to abort this entry'
        macctno=SPACE(5)
        @ r,5 SAY "Acct # " GET macctno
        READ
        IF macctno= " "
          RETURN
        ENDIF
        macctno =TRIM(macctno)
        SEEK macctno
ENDDO &&WHILE EOF()
@ 22,1
@ 23,1
```

NOTE: Longer program listings in this book are printed with line numbers for ease of reference. *When entering the program, do not type the line numbers.*

WHAT THESE PROGRAMS DO

There are three separate programs: enter.prg, vendadd.prg, and checkacc.prg

enter.prg

Lines 5 and 6 set up the environment with

```
SET TALK OFF
SET STATUS OFF
```

Lines 8–16 open three separate files in three separate work areas. In area A the aptemp file is opened with no index. This is the temporary file in which checks will be stored as they are entered. Each check is assigned a temporary number based on its record number in the temporary file. The actual check number will be assigned when the check is printed. The memory variable *mrecno* contains the temporary number of the check.

The vendor file, with its index based on vendor number, is opened in area B and the account file with its index on account number is opened in area C.

Lines 21–24 initialize memory variables that are used throughout the program and that are best initialized prior to the DO WHILE loop. The memory variable *mchoice* is the one that determines whether a user wants to enter additional checks. *mtotal* will store the cumulative total of check amounts entered. *mdate* is the date that will be recorded for the check. *mline* contains 80 hyphens that will be used for graphic separation on the screen.

The CLEAR on line 26 clears the screen. The DO WHILE loop is executed once each time a check is entered. When the user no longer wants to enter checks, the DO WHILE loop is exited.

The DO WHILE loop, which starts on line 28, is executed each time a check is entered. Lines 30–35 reinitialize memory variables which must be re-entered for each check. *mfound* is a flag that is set to *N* when an attempt is made to find a nonexistent vendor. *mpayee* is used to store the vendor code. *mamt* is the amount of the check. *macct* is the account number for the first account distribution. *macctno* is the account number of the second account distribution. *mcomment1* and *mcomment2* are two separate comments that can be entered for each check.

Lines 37–44 display the top part of the screen, which allows entering the vendor code and confirming the date. The memory variable *mdate* is initialized to the system date of the computer, but it can be changed at this time with the GET on line 40. *mrecno* holds the temporary number that is assigned to the check until print time. *mrecno* is based on the record number of the check in the temporary file. A prompt is displayed on line 20 that tells the user to press Return in the *payto* field to exit the program. The PICTURE statement on line 42 forces any letters that are entered in the *payto* field to be converted to capitals. The READ activates the GETs to permit the user to enter the information. The @ 20,0 on line 44 blanks out the prompt on line 20 to press Return to exit the program.

Lines 46–51 permit the user to exit the program if a blank vendor code was entered. If the memory variable *mpayee* contains a blank, the data base (.dbf) files are closed, the screen is cleared, and the program is exited.

Lines 54–56 check whether the vendor for which the code has been entered exists in the vendor file. SELECT B is executed to access the vendor file that is open in work area B.

Lines 59–99 contain a DO WHILE loop that is executed only if the specified vendor is not found in the vendor file. If the vendor is found, EOF() is not true and program control goes to line 100. If the vendor is not found, EOF() is true and control goes to line 60, which displays an error message that the vendor was not found.

The code on lines 64–65 gives users another opportunity to enter the vendor code. The DO CASE statement in lines 66–96 takes actions based on what the user entered in response to the code on lines 64–65. The first case traps whether a blank was entered, in which case the memory variable *mfound* is set to n. The GO TO 1 in line 70 makes sure that EOF() is not true so that the DO WHILE loop will be exited. Control then goes to line 100, where the value of *mfound* is tested, and LOOP is used to return control to the DO WHILE on line 28.

The second CASE from lines 74–87 is executed if the user entered an R to review existing vendors. The GO TOP in line 76 positions the record pointer at the beginning of the vendor file. The DO WHILE loop from lines 77–84 displays the vendor codes and names on the screen 12 lines at a time. At the end of each screen the user is given an option to quit or continue.

The third CASE from lines 90–92 is executed if the user wants to add a new vendor code. If this is the case, the vendadd routine is executed.

The OTHERWISE CASE is executed if none of the previous CASEs are true, it is assumed that a vendor code was entered, and it is checked for validity by SEEKing it. When the ENDCASE is encountered, control is returned to the DO WHILE in line 59. If EOF() is true, meaning that the vendor was not found, the DO WHILE loop is re-executed. If EOF() is not true, control passes to the instruction after the ENDDO in line 100.

When line 111 is executed, it is assumed that the vendor search has been successful and that the record pointer is pointing to the proper record in the vendor file. Three values are extracted from the vendor file into memory variables: *mvendname* is set equal to *vendname*, *mamt* to the default amount of payment for that vendor, and *macct* to the value of the default account. Next the vendor name is displayed on the screen.

Lines 119–120 get the amount of the check, while lines 123–125 check for a zero amount. If the amount is zero, control is returned to the DO WHILE in line 28 so that another check can be entered.

Lines 127–130 get the account number and the amount to be allocated to that account. Lines 131–133 see whether a blank account was entered, in which case control is returned to the DO WHILE in line 28.

Lines 134–136 check whether a valid account number was entered. The account number entered in *macct* is stored to the memory variable *macctno* which is then checked in the program checkacc. After that program is exited, *macct* is set equal to *macctno* in case an invalid account number was entered and *macctno* was changed in the program checkacc.

Lines 140–142 check whether the account number is blank because the user decided to abort the entry. If it is, control is returned to the DO WHILE in line 28. If a valid account number was entered, the name of the account is displayed according to the code in line 143.

The IF...ENDIF from lines 144–160 is only executed if a second account distribution is to be made for this check as evidenced by making the amount allocated to the first account less than the amount of the check. The code in line 148 displays the amount remaining to be allocated, and the code in line 147 gets the account to which it is to be allocated. The IF...ENDIF in lines 150–152 test whether a blank account was entered.

If a nonblank account was entered, the code in lines 153–155 calls checkacc to see if the account was valid. If an invalid account was entered and the user chose to abort, the IF...ENDIF in lines 156–158 will return control to the DO WHILE in line 28. If a valid account was entered, the code in line 159 displays the second account name on the screen.

The code in lines 163–167 allows entering two separate comments.

The remainder of the code asks the user if it is all right to post. If a *Y* is entered, a new record is created in the aptemp file, and REPLACE is used to transfer the contents of the memory variables to the fields in that file. After the posting is completed, the total distribution for this session is shown, and the user is asked whether another check is to be entered. If an affirmative answer is given, control is returned to the DO WHILE in line 28 and another check can be entered.

vendadd.prg

vendadd is a program that adds a record to a file based on the principles discussed earlier in this chapter. Memory variables are set up, and the user is prompted to enter the desired information on which input validation will be performed. In this example the default account is validated against the account file. If all input validation tests are passed, including verification that the vendor is not already in the file, and if the user wants to add the record to the file, a record is added to the vendor file.

checkacc.prg

The checkacc program checks for a valid account number by doing a SEEK in the account file. If the account number is not found, the user is given a choice of entering a new account number to be verified or a blank to abort.

dBASE IV INPUT ENHANCEMENTS

dBASE IV adds features to support input validation while simplifying programming.

Enhancing the @...SAY

dBASE IV adds various enhancements that could change the way the input program above is written.

The @...SAY statement has various new switches designed to simplify programming.

The VALID clause allows specifying any error condition such as would have been used as the DO WHILE condition in the previous examples. The ERROR clause is used in conjunction with the VALID clause to specify the error message to be displayed if the condition of the VALID clause is not met. If the ERROR clause is not included, a generic error message will be displayed when the VALID condition is not met. The generic error message says *Editing condition not satisfied (press SPACE)*. Thus, if a VALID clause is used, an ERROR clause should also be used to tell the user what type of error has occurred.

One example is

```
@ 2,1 GET mstate PICTURE '!!' VALID mstate='CA' ;
   .OR. mstate='NY' ERROR 'State must be CA or NY'
```

Here the PICTURE clause forces any alphabetic values that are entered to be converted to upper case. The VALID clause requires that *CA* or *NY* must be entered. If *CA* or *NY* is not entered, an error message saying *State must be CA or NY (press SPACE)* is displayed. The VALID clause eliminates the necessity of having a READ and a DO WHILE loop after each GET in order to trap an error condition.

The following code could be used to validate the state as being any of the 50 states.

```
* states.prg
mstate =SPACE(2)
states = "AK,AL,AR,AZ,CA,CO,CT,DC,DE,FL,GA,HI,IA,ID,IL,IN,KS,KY,LA," ;
+"MA,MD,ME,MI,MN,MO,MS,MT,NC,ND,NE,NH,NJ,NM,NV,NY,OH,OK,OR," ;
+"PA,PR,RI,SC,SD,TN,TX,UT,VA,VT,WA,WI,WV,WY"
CLEAR
@ 5,5 SAY 'State ' GET mstate PICTURE '!!' VALID mstate $ states ;
   ERROR 'Invalid state'
READ
```

An additional switch on the @...SAY...GET is the MESSAGE switch. It can be used to display a message at the bottom of the screen when a variable that is being gotten is highlighted.

In addition, a COLOR switch on the @...SAY...GET enables the attribute for each variable to be set.

These PICTURE function symbols have been added.

1. The L function displays leading zeroes. Using

```
mnum=123
@ 4,1 SAY mnum FUNCTION 'L'
READ
```

will result in

```
0000000123
```

2. The *$* function works correctly to show the $ right before the numbers.

```
. mnum=123.45
. @ 4,1 SAY mnum FUNCTION '$'
    $123.45
```

3. The *M* function is for enumerated types. It enables specifying the desired contents of a field. The following code will permit only the state abbreviations *CA* or *NJ* to be entered into the state variable.

```
mstate=SPACE(2)
@ 2,1 GET mstate PICTURE '@M CA,NJ'
READ
```

Other Modifiers to the @...SAY...GET

WINDOW

The WINDOW modifier allows specifying a predefined window in which a memo field will be edited. If m1 is a memo field in a file and if memoedit is a predefined window, the following syntax can be used:

```
@ 2,1 GET m1 WINDOW memoedit
READ
```

The user will see the word *MEMO* in inverse video, and will need to press Ctrl-Home in order to activate the window for editing.

WHEN

Using the WHEN modifier is like putting the whole @...SAY...GET within an IF statement. A logical condition can be specified using the WHEN modifier. A READ will activate the GET only if the logical condition specified by the WHEN clause is true.

This modifier is most useful when one piece of input is dependent on another. In our input example, for instance, we only ask for a second account allocation if the first account allocation is not equal to the total amount of the check.

```
mamt=0.00
@ 8,57 SAY "AMT" GET mamt
READ
```

```
mamt1 = mamt
@ 10,20 SAY '$' GET mamt1
READ
    macct1 = SPACE(5)
    @ 11,5 SAY 'ACCT # ' GET macct1 WHEN mamt <> mamt1
    READ
```

Unfortunately, two limitations of the WHEN modifier make it virtually unusable for this purpose:

1. The WHEN modifier must be used with a GET: it won't work with just a SAY.

2. If the WHEN condition is not true, the GET is displayed, but the READ is not activated. Generally, in this kind of situation, we would not want the GET to be displayed at all.

DEFAULT

The default modifier enables specifying a default value for the variable that is being input with the GET. Of course, the default value can be specified when the memory variable is initialized as discussed above. The DEFAULT clause just gives another way of specifying the default.

RANGE

The RANGE modifier has been expanded in two ways:

1. A character range can now be expressed. Thus, to limit input to a range of character values, such as a range of zip codes in a character field, the following expression can be used.

```
mzip = SPACE(5)
@ 2,1 SAY 'zip' GET mzip RANGE '94700','94706'
READ
```

2. Only a lower limit needs to be expressed. Thus in the example above, to require the zip code to be greater than or equal to '94700' this formulation can be used.

```
mzip=SPACE(5)
@ 2,1 SAY 'zip' GET mzip RANGE '94700'
READ
```

Doing Input Validation from Other Files

The syntax for verifying referential integrity by seeing whether a record exists in another file has been simplified.

Two new functions, LOOKUP() and SEEK(), have been added. The SEEK() function works on files that are indexed, while the LOOKUP() function does not require an index.

The SEEK() function is similar to the SEEK command in that it checks an index to see whether a value exists. The SEEK() function, like the SEEK command, must be used in conjunction with an index. The SEEK() function returns a logical True if the key exists in the index and a False if it does not.

The syntax of the SEEK() function is

```
SEEK(key value[,alias])
```

The key value is the value to be compared against the index keys. The optional alias is the alias of the work area where the file is open.

Compare the following examples with line 54 to the end of the above enter.prg program example.

This function is probably most useful in cases such as input validation, when an attempt is made to do a SEEK in a nonselected area as in the following example.

```
USE vendor ORDER vendor IN A
SELECT B
USE aptemp
mvendor=SPACE(5)
@ 10,1 SAY 'Enter Vendor Code ' GET mvendor
READ
DO WHILE .NOT. SEEK(TRIM(mvendor),'Vendor')
    @ 20,0 SAY 'Vendor '+ mvendor +' not found in file'
    @ 10,1 SAY 'Enter Vendor Code ' GET mvendor
    READ
ENDDO
```

The code could be simplified further by combining the SEEK function with the VALID clause of the @...SAY:

```
USE vendor ORDER vendor IN A
SELECT B
USE aptemp

mvendor=SPACE(5)
@ 10,1 SAY 'Enter vendor code ' GET mvendor   ;
    VALID SEEK(TRIM(mvendor),'Vendor')        ;
    ERROR 'Vendor '+ mvendor +' not found in file'
READ
```

The problem with using the SEEK() function in conjunction with a VALID clause is that it does not give the user options such as reviewing existing vendors or aborting, as is done in the enter.prg program.

Another similar function is LOOKUP(). The LOOKUP() function can be used with either indexed or nonindexed files. The syntax is

```
LOOKUP(<return field>,<key value>,<field to check>)
```

For example,

```
. ? LOOKUP(vendor->vendname,'BELL',vendor->vendno)
```

This expression will check for a record with a vendor code of 'BELL' and will return the vendor name. If no such vendor is found, the record pointer will be positioned at EOF() so that all fields will be blank, and a blank will be returned for vendor name.

NOTE: The field to be returned must be a field. A constant there will produce an error message.

Using the Report Generator and the Quick Screen Generator

In dBASE IV, the Report Generator and the Quick Screen Generator produce program code. The code produced is stored in a file with an .frg or .fmt extension and can then be modified by using the principles discussed in this chapter and in the chapter on output.

While the Quick Screen generator may occasionally be useful for quickly generating the @...SAY...GETS for input or output screens, it has several drawbacks:

1. The program code generated assumes that input is done directly to fields rather than to memory variables. So, to use the principles discussed in this chapter, the code would have to be modified to do the input to memory variables. This modification can be accomplished by putting an *m* in front of all field names and having a section at the beginning to initialize the memory variables.

2. Once the code in the .fmt or .frg file is modified, it is not possible to go back into the Quick Forms Generator or Report Generator to modify it further.

Chapter 7

ACCESSING RECORDS BY USING INDEXES

Good order is the foundation of all good things.
—Edmund Burke

The commands discussed in this chapter are

INDEX ON
USE file INDEX file name
SEEK
INDEX ON
SET ORDER TO
REINDEX
LOCATE

dBASE provides two basic methods of accessing data: sequential search and indexed access. Indexing is one of the most powerful features of dBASE and is used for several purposes:

1. To order records for generating reports and other output.
2. To locate a record in a file quickly. If an index is in effect, any record in the file can be located almost instantaneously based on its key value.
3. To find a group of records based on their key fields.

TYPES OF SEARCHES

To locate a record or group of records in a file quickly, various types of searches may be desirable:

1. Searching for a unique record when there is an exact match on the entire value of the key field.

2. Searching for all of the records that match a certain part of the key field; for example: finding all of the people with the last name Smith.

3. Searching for a string being contained in a key field. An example of this type of search is a key word search. It is implemented by having a field for key words and listing all of the key words for a record in that that field. Unfortunately, this type of searching is not accomplished with indexes but by sequential access and is thus quite slow.

```
LOCATE FOR 'CARDIAC' $ UPPER(keyword)
```

HOW INDEXES ARE CREATED

An index is conceptually a table consisting of a listing of all the key fields in the file with a record pointer positioned to the appropriate record.

An index is created by using the following syntax

```
USE <file name>
INDEX ON <expression> TO <file>
```

The key expression can be any valid dBASE expression up to 100 characters long. The longer and more complex the expression is, the more time it will take to reindex or to update the index when records are added. Building an index from scratch takes a significant amount of time and should be done as infrequently as possible. It is usually possible to open indexes for updating when records are added.

After the INDEX command is executed or the .dbf file is USEd with an index, the file appears to be in logical or indexed order as discussed in chapter 3.

dBASE III PLUS saves each index in a separate file. The default extension for an index file is .ndx. After the above commands are executed, both the .dbf file and the .ndx file are open.

INVOKING INDEXES

Indexes that have been created previously, may be invoked or opened using the syntax

```
USE file INDEX ind1,ind2,ind3,ind4,ind5,ind6,ind7
```

Up to seven indexes can be opened at one time, but only the first index is the master or controlling index that is used for ordering the records. The other indexes are only opened so that, if records are added, they will be updated.

When indexes are open, blank records can be added and the fields changed with a series of REPLACEs. This process causes all the open indexes to be updated.

CAUTION: When appending a number of records to a file with an open index, it is useful to maintain a counter so that the file can be opened and closed periodically in order to update the indexes. dBASE stores information in memory buffers in RAM until a file is closed. If too many records are added without opening and closing the file, records can become corrupted.

The following sample program fragment shows a method for maintaining a counter of the number of records added and for closing and reopening the file after each 10 records is added.

```
USE file INDEX ind1,ind2,ind3,ind4,ind5,ind6,ind7
------
---------
    ctr=ctr+1
    IF ctr > 10
        USE
        USE file INDEX ind1,ind2,ind3,ind4,ind5,ind6,ind7
        ctr=1
    ENDIF
    APPEND BLANK
    REPL....
```

This fragment counts how many records have been added. After 10 records have been appended, the file is closed to flush the changes from memory buffers onto disk. The file and all of its indexes are then reopened.

If records are added to a file while an index is not in use, the entire index must be rebuilt.

Another caution, discussed in chapter 9, involves appending a whole file to another file with indexes open. In this case, because of the time required to update the index or indexes and because of the risk of the index becoming unbalanced, it may be better to append the file with the indexes closed and then to rebuild the indexes. This approach is only practical when appending a large number of records at once.

CHANGING THE MASTER OR CONTROLLING INDEX

It is often necessary to change master indexes. One of the powers of a computerized data base system is that it is easy to switch between different ways of ordering a file. For example, an address file needs to be viewed in both last name and zip code order with frequent changes between the two views. There are several forms of syntax for switching between indexes.

Prior to dBASE III PLUS, if ind3 (from the program fragment above) was to become the master index, the following syntax would have been used.

```
SET INDEX TO ind3,ind1,ind2,ind4,ind5,ind6,ind7
```

This command closes all of the indexes and reopens them in the stated order; ind3 would then become the controlling index. The order in which the indexes are listed after the first one is not important. The problem with this approach was that each index file had to be physically closed and then reopened, which required a substantial amount of time.

In dBASE III PLUS, the SET ORDER TO command was introduced, which enables changing the master index without physically opening and closing files. The same result shown above can be accomplished by the command

```
SET ORDER TO 3
```

without any physical opening and closing of files. When the index files are opened, they are numbered implicitly:

```
                 (1)  (2)  (3)  (4)  (5)  (6)  (7)
USE file INDEX  ind1,ind2,ind3,ind4,ind5,ind6,ind7
```

To turn off all indexes, the command is

```
SET ORDER TO 0
```

FINDING RECORDS

Records can be found almost instantaneously, based on their complete key value or on the leftmost part of the key value. The syntax is

```
SEEK <expression>
```

If a file is indexed on zip code, the following can be used:

```
SEEK "94704"
    OR
mkey='94704'
SEEK mkey
```

TESTING FOR NO FIND

After a SEEK it is imperative to test whether or not the record was found. The test is performed in the following manner.

```
IF EOF()
    ? 'Record not found for '+mkey
ENDIF
```

It is not good programming practice to execute a SEEK without testing whether or not it was successful. A test, such as the one listed above, should follow each SEEK.

FIND VS. SEEK

The SEEK command was added in dBASE III. dBASE II users may remember the FIND command. In contrast to the SEEK command, FIND expects a literal value as an argument. The following is a comparison of FIND and SEEK:

```
FIND SMITH          SEEK "SMITH"
     or                  or
mkey='SMITH'        mkey='SMITH'
FIND &mkey          SEEK mkey
```

Since FIND expects a literal value, when the value is in a memory variable, macro substitution must be used to put the actual value of that variable into the command line. By contrast, SEEK expects an expression or memory variable as an argument, so that if a literal value is used, it must be enclosed in quotes (“ ”).

SEEKING PART OF A KEY

Under certain circumstances, the leftmost part of the key expression can be the basis for a SEEK. If the command

```
SET EXACT OFF
```

is executed and if the argument of the SEEK contains the leftmost characters in a key field, as soon as a match is found on the leftmost characters, the matching record will be found.

Conversely, the command

```
SET EXACT ON
```

can be issued so that a full character-by-character match would be required for a SEEK to be successful.

CONSIDERATIONS IN FINDING RECORDS

It is important to remember that the expression to be found must match exactly the way in which the index was created. The command

```
* Case 1:
INDEX ON lname+fname TO name
```

will create an index table such as

Anderson	Mary
Jones	Frank
Smith	John

The full contents of the last name field (including all trailing blanks) plus the full contents of the First Name field (including all trailing blanks) are included in the index.

By way of contrast, the index command

```
* Case 2:
INDEX ON TRIM(lname)+fname
```

will create a table such as the following

AndersonMary
JonesFrank
SmithJohn

It is important to know the exact index expression when you do a SEEK or FIND based on the whole index key. For a search to be successful on both first and last name in case 1, the SEEK expression must be

```
SEEK "Smith          John"
```

In case 2, it must be

```
SEEK "SmithJohn"
```

The index key that is sought must match exactly the index as it was created.

FINDING ON LAST NAME ONLY

Finding on last name only, after SET EXACT OFF has been executed, will be exactly the same:

1. To find the first occurrence of a last name beginning with *J*.

```
FIND J
   or
SEEK "J"
```

2. To find the first occurrence of last names beginning with *Jon*, assuming that last names are stored in all upper case.

```
FIND JON
   or
SEEK "JON"
```

3. For finding based on the contents of a memory variable.

```
mlname=SPACE(20)
@ 2,1 SAY 'Enter last name ' GET mlname;
    PICTURE '@!'
READ
```

When finding based on part of the last name in a memory variable, several cautions must be observed. If the user types *J* and presses Enter, for example, the memory variable will contain *J* followed by 19 blanks or "J   ".

Even if EXACT is set off, the command

```
SEEK mlname
```

will not find a match because there is no entry in the index consisting of a *J* followed by 19 blanks. Thus, to use the contents of the memory variable to find on part of the last name,

```
SEEK TRIM(mlname)
```

must be used regardless of the indexing method employed.

FINDING ON THE FULL KEY

When finding is based on the full key, it is important to understand which indexing method has been used. If method 1 was used for indexing, the SEEK condition must be

```
SEEK 'Smith          John'
```

If case 2 was used, the following syntax must be used:

```
SEEK 'SmithJohn'
```

Thus, when getting the contents into memory variables, the following must be used:

```
mlname=SPACE(15)
mfname=SPACE(15)
@ 2,1 SAY 'Enter last name ' GET mlname
```

```
@ 3,1 SAY 'Enter first name ' GET mfname
READ
```

The memory variables should be initialized with the same length as the fields. If the index was created by using method 1, the following SEEK must be used, assuming that the case is correct:

```
SEEK mlname+mfname
```

Any trailing blanks must explicitly be left in the SEEK condition. If method 2 was used, the SEEK condition would be

```
SEEK TRIM(mlname)+mfname
```

WHICH METHOD TO USE

Case 2 is slower than case 1 because of the additional time required to call the TRIM function for each record when it is indexed, but the index would be smaller.

USING INDEX KEYS TO DO SORTS WITHIN SORTS

Index keys can be used to do sorts-within-sorts. For instance, to arrange names alphabetically within each zip code, the syntax would be

```
INDEX ON zip+lname+fname
```

When this INDEX command is executed, records are arranged first by zip code, and then names are sorted alphabetically within each zip code.

Retrievals by Zip Code

As long as SET EXACT OFF has been executed, retrievals can be done on the leftmost part of the key, such as:

```
SEEK "94704"
```

Retrievals by the Zip Code Plus Part of the Last Name

```
SEEK "94704J"
```

This syntax would result in retrieving the record of the first person in the 94704 zip code whose last name starts with *J*.

CASE SENSITIVITY

For a retrieval to be successful, the case of the key sought must be exactly the same as the case of the contents of the key field. For this reason, it is important to have a fixed method of storing the last name, such as 1) all letters in upper case using

```
REPLACE lname WITH UPPER(mlname)
```

or 2) first letter in upper case and all remaining letters in lower case.

```
REPLACE lname WITH UPPER(SUBSTR(mlname,1,1)) + ;
    LOWER(SUBSTR(mlname,2))
```

Whichever format is desired, *all* last names must be stored in the same format.

WATCH OUT FOR LEADING AND TRAILING BLANKS

When you enter the key to be sought into a single memory variable, it is important to watch out for leading and trailing blanks. For this reason a lot of trouble can be avoided by using

```
mkey = LTRIM(TRIM(mkey))
SEEK mkey
```

THE OVERHEAD OF INDEXES

While indexes provide a quick method of accessing data, using them can have drawbacks. Indexes have overhead:

1. Indexes take up disk space.

2. Indexes must be maintained. When records are added or key fields are changed, indexes must be updated, which can take a significant amount of time.

3. Indexes can become corrupted, which can cause unpredictable results in programs.

4. Indexes count against the total number of files open. In dBASE III PLUS, the total number of files of all kinds that can be open is 15.

Unfortunately, dBASE does not have a good built-in way to verify the validity of indexes. Thus, programmers must devise various means for checking indexes to avoid index corruption. One such method is discussed below.

SEQUENTIAL ACCESS VS. INDEX ACCESS

While indexed access is quick, it does have drawbacks. By contrast, sequential access is slow, but it has no overhead. The following command can be used when no index is present:

```
LOCATE FOR lname='SMITH' .AND. zip='94704'
```

Sequential access is used for searches that are not performed frequently and when it is not worth the overhead of having an index. The LOCATE command works by searching each record in the file until it finds the first match. Then DISPLAY or a similar command must be used to display the record. The record pointer can be moved to the next record that matches the criteria by entering CONTINUE. Figure 7-1 compares the virtues of sequential vs. indexed access.

Following a LOCATE statement should be a test for whether or not the LOCATE was successful.

```
IF EOF()
    ? 'Record not found'
ENDIF
```

Multiple records that meet the LOCATE condition can be found by using the CONTINUE command. The following short program uses the LOCATE command to find all occurrences of a condition.

```
USE address
LOCATE FOR lname='SMITH' .AND. zip='94704'
DO WHILE lname='SMITH' .AND. zip='94704'
    DISPLAY
    CONTINUE
ENDDO
```

INDEXED ACCESS

Advantages	*Disadvantages*
Immediate access to records	Overhead of indexes disk space time to update risk of corruption

SCANNED ACCESS (Virtually any command with a FOR clause)

Advantages	*Disadvantages*
No overhead Flexible query conditions	Slow access time

Figure 7-1. Comparison of advantages and disadvantages of sequential vs. indexed access.

What This Program Does

This program uses the LOCATE command to move the record pointer to the first record where the last name is SMITH and the zip code is 94704. It searches every record in the file, starting with the first record, until a match is found, then the DO WHILE loop is executed, and the record is displayed. The CONTINUE causes LOCATE to look for the next matching record. If it is found, the record is displayed. If the CONTINUE command does not result in finding a matching record, the loop is not executed, and the next command after the ENDDO is executed instead.

CAUTION: *Be careful about mixing indexed and sequential access.* If a LOCATE command is used on a file when an index is open, it will execute much more slowly than if the index were not open. The reason is that the LOCATE command starts with the first record in the file and checks each record, looking for a match. When no index is open, it can check the file in the physical order of the records. If an index is open, it must go to the index to find the first logical record before it can check that record against its FOR condition. The extra step of checking the index each time slows down the LOCATE operation significantly.

TESTING FOR CORRUPTED INDEXES

Indexes can be corrupted in several ways:

1. adding records to a .dbf file without having indexes open
2. shutting off the computer without properly closing files
3. random reasons such as power surges

Remarkably, dBASE provides no simple and reliable way to test for index validity. One solution to the problem of corrupted indexes is to rebuild indexes every day or each time the program is started up. This approach is inefficient. The following approach will work in most cases to check for corrupted indexes.

```
USE file
GO BOTT
mkey=keyfield
mfieldn1=FIELD(1)
mfield1=&mfieldn1
mfieldn2=FIELD(2)
mfield2=&mfieldn2
SET FILTER TO &mfieldn1=mfield1 .and. &mfieldn2=mfield2
SET INDEX TO ind1
SEEK mkey
IF EOF()
    ? 'Reindexing—Please wait'
    REINDEX
ENDIF
```

What This Program Does

First this program uses the file without an index. The GO BOTT command moves the record pointer to the last physical record in the file. The key field for the index to be tested is stored to the memory variable mkey. Then, to account for possible records with duplicate index keys, the contents of FIELD(1) are stored to a memory variable named mfield1 and the contents of FIELD(2) are stored to a memory variable named mfield2. The SET FILTER TO command insures that only records that match on the contents of the first two fields for the last record are looked at. Next, the index to be checked is opened by SET INDEX TO ind1. Then, a SEEK mkey is performed. For this SEEK to be successful, a record must be found where the key field is equal to mkey, the contents of

FIELD(1) are equal to mfield1, and FIELD(2) is equal to mfield(2). Hopefully, the only matching record will be the last physical record. If the SEEK is not successful, the index is rebuilt.

This approach is not foolproof but is relatively effective for checking the validity of indexes, particularly if the index has been corrupted by adding records when the index file is not open.

SET FILTER TO WITH INDEX

The underlying principle in the example above is how a SET FILTER TO works with an index. Basically dBASE "ANDs" the filter with the index. Thus for a SEEK to be successful when a filter is in effect, the record must match both the SEEK condition and the filter condition.

SPEED COMPARISONS

If we have an address file with a zip code field, the following methods can be used to list the names of all people living in zip code 94704.

Method 1:

```
USE <file name>
LIST fname+lname FOR zip='94704'
```

Method 2:

```
SET INDEX TO zip
SEEK '94704'
DO WHILE zip='94704'
    DISPL fname+lname
    SKIP
ENDDO
```

Method 3:

```
SEEK '94704'
LIST fname+lname WHILE zip='94704'
```

In each of these methods, all names for residents of the '94704' zip code would be displayed. However, there are tremendous speed differences that become apparent when these methods are used with larger files. Each successive method takes about half the time of the previous method depending on the type of machine used and the size of the file. Much of the slowness associated with accessing data comes from programmers' not understanding the differences between these methods.

Even though Method 1 is the slowest, there are times when it must be used. Methods 2 and 3 require an index. Method 1 uses sequential access and can be used when an index is not present based on the key value. Method 1 is slow because it requires dBASE to check every record in the file to see if the FOR condition is true for that record.

Method 2 is slower than Method 3 because of the overhead of the DO WHILE loop. However, Method 2 is the one that must be used when some processing of records is required, such as accumulating subtotals. Method 2 is faster than Method 1 because the SEEK command moves the record pointer to the first record where zip ='94704'. Since in an indexed file all records with the same key values appear to be grouped together, the DO WHILE loop results in displaying all appropriate records, and it stops as soon as a record with a different zip code is found.

Method 3 is the fastest method to use and is appropriate for generating simple lists from indexed files. Method 3 utilizes the WHILE clause of the LIST command. Method 3 works in a manner similar to Method 2 but is faster because it does not incur the overhead of a DO WHILE loop.

The WHILE clause works in this manner:

1. It checks the WHILE condition against the fields in the record to which the record pointer is pointing. If the WHILE condition is not true for that record, the command is not executed.

2. If the WHILE condition was true for the record to which the record pointer was pointing, it displays that record, skips to the next record, and then checks the condition again. As soon as it finds a record where the condition is not true, it stops executing.

The key thing to be aware of with the WHILE condition is that the command prior to using a WHILE modifier must make the WHILE condition true. In this case the SEEK makes the WHILE condition true. As soon as a record is found that does not meet the WHILE condition, execution stops.

COMPARING FOR AND WHILE CLAUSES

The following table shows a comparison of FOR and WHILE clauses.

FOR	*WHILE*
1. starts with first record	starts with current record
2. checks each record for the FOR condition	as soon as it finds a record where the WHILE condition is not true, execution stops

The principles presented in this section represent the crux of how to speed up accessing records.

USING WHILE WITH OTHER COMMANDS

The WHILE clause can also be used with such commands as LIST, DISPLAY, AVERAGE, SUM, REPORT, and COUNT. Unlike using these commands with a FOR clause, the record pointer is not positioned to the beginning of the file when using WHILE. Rather, the WHILE clause is evaluated against the current record. If the WHILE clause is true, it executes; otherwise, it does not. As soon as a record is encountered for which the WHILE clause is not true, the command stops executing. The WHILE clause is best used in conjunction with an indexed file after a SEEK to make the WHILE clause true: for example,

```
SEEK 'Smith'
SUM WHILE lname='Smith'
```

USING FOR AND WHILE CLAUSES TOGETHER

A WHILE clause can be used in conjunction with a FOR clause to look selectively at records meeting the WHILE condition:

```
SEEK 'Smith'
LIST WHILE lname='Smith' FOR state='CA'
```

This approach, based on using an index on last name only, would immediately go to the first Smith record and then selectively list all Smith records where the state='CA'. This example is one of the few cases in dBASE where indexed and sequential access can be combined for effective results.

Additional examples of combining FOR and WHILE clauses are covered in chapter 8.

PAGING MULTIPLE RECORDS

Often, when finding on a key field that is not unique, it is useful to allow users to enter the key field, and then, if multiple records with that key field exist, to display all of them on the screen and allow the user to access the desired record by number.

To keep track of people, it is best to use the social security number as a primary key if it is available. However, users often don't want to type in social security numbers, or the social security number is not available. In that case, it is possible to allow users to access by last name using a program like the following, which would be useful in a mailing list or in any example where users are accessed by name.

access.prg 12/30/88

```
** access.prg
** program to access by last name

PARAMETERS CALLPRG
SET HEADING OFF
SELECT a
USE address INDEX name

DO WHILE .T.

    mlname=SPACE(15)
    CLEAR
    @ 2,10 say 'Enter last name to search for '
    @ 3,10 SAY 'Press Return to exit'
    @ 4,10 GET mlname PICTURE '@!'
    READ
    IF mlname=' '
        RETURN
    ENDIF
    SEEK TRIM(mlname)
    IF EOF()
        ? 'No records found for last name ' +mlname
```

```
            WAIT
            LOOP
    ENDIF
    CLEA
    N=1
    DO WHILE lname=mlname .AND. .NOT. EOF()
        @ N+2,10 SAY STR(N,2)+' '+lname+fname
        N=N+1
        SKIP
    ENDDO
* if more than one record found, give choice
    IF n >2
        STORE 0 TO mnum
        @ 20,1 SAY 'Enter desired number. Press Return to abort' GET;
        mnum
        READ
        DO WHILE mnum<0 .OR. mnum>n-1
            mnum=0
            @ 20,1 SAY 'Enter number between 1 and '+STR(n-1) GET;
            mnum
            READ
        ENDDO
        IF mnum=0
            LOOP
        ENDIF
* find desired record
    SEEK TRIM(mlname)
    IF EOF()
        LOOP
    ENDIF
    SKIP mnum-1
  ELSE && if one record found
    SKIP-1
  ENDIF N>2
```

```
60
61      * DO desired program
62      DO &callprg
63      SELECT a
64
65 ENDDO WHILE T
```

What This Program Does

This program has a single parameter called callprg. This feature allows this program to be called from anywhere in the system in order to position the record pointer to the desired record so that a specific function can be performed. The function that will be performed is done in the program whose name is passed as the parameter. After the record pointer is positioned, DO &callprg executes the desired program.

In line 7, the file address is used with the name index which is based on last name. The rest of the program is enclosed in a DO WHILE loop, which allows entering the name until a match is found. If a carriage return is pressed in response to the READ so that mlname contains blanks, the program is exited.

Next, a SEEK is performed on TRIM(mlname). If a match is not found, program control loops back to the top of the loop so that the user can re-enter a name.

If a match is found, a variable named, *n*, is initialized to 1 and each record with a corresponding last name is displayed on the screen with an associated number. As written, this program assumes that all records found will fit on a single screen. It could be modified to allow paging through multiple screens.

The IF...ENDIF construct from lines 34–59 positions the record pointer. If a single record is found that matches the last name, the record pointer is positioned to that single record. Otherwise, the user is prompted to select the number of the desired record. If a 0 is entered, control loops back to entering the name. Once a valid number has been entered, the record pointer is positioned to that record by doing a SEEK to find the first matching record again and then SKIPping the number of the record selected minus 1 to position the record pointer to the desired record.

Finally, the indicated program is executed with the command DO &callprg. The function of access.prg is to position the record pointer in the address file before DOing the next program.

INDEXING ON COMPOUND KEYS INVOLVING VARIOUS FIELD TYPES

Indexing on compound keys, involving various field types, provokes special problems. All fields in the key must be converted to the same field type that, in effect, means a character field type.

Indexing on Character Plus Date

Indexing on just a date field is simple. However, when a date type is mixed with a character type, certain problems result. The default date type is SET DATE AMERICAN in which the date is displayed in the form mm/dd/yy. If an index is created solely on a date field, the records will be arranged in proper order, arranged by day within month within year. However, in the syntax

```
INDEX ON crsenum + DTOC(cdate)
```

the contents of the date field are converted to a character. If SET DATE AMERICAN is in effect, dates will be converted to the mm/dd/yy format, meaning that dates will be arranged in year order within day within month, which is not the proper order for indexing. This problem can be overcome by taking advantage of SET DATE ANSI, which makes the date format yy/mm/dd, the proper format for indexing. Thus, to index records properly when a date field is converted to character, the following syntax must be used:

```
SET DATE ANSI
INDEX ON crsenum + DTOC(cdate)
SET DATE AMERICAN
```

The date is set ANSI for indexing purposes and then back to AMERICAN for output purposes.

When you add a record to a file with this index open, this syntax must be used to properly update the indexes:

```
SET DATE ANSI
APPEND BLANK
REPLACE...

SET DATE AMERICAN
```

If this syntax is not used, the indexes will not be updated properly.

Indexing on a Character Plus a Number

Sometimes it is desirable to print out an address file with street number arranged sequentially for each street with streets listed alphabetically, such as

```
342 FRONT ST.
444 FRONT ST.
12 MAIN
14 MAIN
16 MAIN
```

If a space always appears between the street number and the street name, the following syntax could be used

```
INDEX ON UPPERTRIM(SUBSTR(straddr,AT(' ',straddr), ;
  LEN(straddr)-AT(' ',straddr)))) +STR(VAL(straddr),6)
```

This approach assumes that the name of the street falls after the first space.

INDEXING ON UNUSUAL COMBINATIONS

Indexing on Reverse Alphabetical Order

Occasionally it may be necessary to index in reverse alphabetical order. Perhaps the easiest solution to this problem is to index in alphabetical order and then look at the file in reverse order:

```
INDEX ON lname+fname TO name
GO BOTT
DO WHILE .NOT. BOF()
    DISP
    SKIP-1
ENDDO
```

Indexing on Negative Date

To index on date in descending order, simply subtract the date field from a later date.

```
INDEX ON CTOD('12/31/99') -date
```

TROUBLESHOOTING

If a key that is known to be there is being sought, but it is not found, TRIM the memory variable.

```
mkey=TRIM(mkey)
SEEK mkey
```

COMMANDS NOT TO USE

There are several dBASE commands that are best not to be used by programmers. SORT physically reorders a file by creating another file in sorted order. For programming purposes it is generally more efficient to use indexes rather than SORTs.

SET UNIQUE ON creates an index that only allows one value of each key field and hides records with duplicate key values. It is better to check for duplicates at input time rather than use SET UNIQUE ON.

HOW INDEXES ARE HANDLED IN dBASE IV

As discussed in chapter 3, dBASE IV gives users a choice of either using stand-alone .ndx files with the syntaxes discussed so far in this chapter, or using an .mdx (multiple index file) which allows storing up to 47 logical indexes in a single file. Each logical index in an .mdx file is referred to as a TAG. For each .dbf file, a production .mdx file with the same name as the .dbf file is automatically created when the first TAG is created. Whenever the .dbf file is opened, the production .mdx file is also automatically opened, although no TAG is invoked until a SET ORDER TO TAG command is used. To invoke a tag from an .mdx file, the following syntax is used.

```
SET ORDER TO TAG <tag name>
```

The advantages of having multiple index tags in a single .mdx file as opposed to having each index in a separate .ndx file are

1. Up to 47 index tags can be accessed while only incurring the overhead of opening a single DOS file.

2. From an end-user standpoint, indexes are updated automatically—the .mdx file is automatically opened with the .dbf file. However, this means that in a very large file, as each record is added, there could be a significant time delay when the indexes are updated. This may be a disadvantage for programmers who want to control when indexes are updated.

Comparison of INDEX and TAG Syntax

In the following comparison, the syntax for using a separate .ndx file (dBASE III PLUS or dBASE IV) is shown on the left, and the syntax for using .mdx files (dBASE IV) is shown on the right.

1. Opening a file with an index

USE file INDEX ind1,ind2	USE file ORDER tag1

2. Changing indexes once a file is open

SET ORDER TO 2	SET ORDER TO TAG <*tag name*>

3. Create a new tag or index

INDEX ON <*key*> TO <*file name*>	INDEX ON <*key*> TAG <*tag name*>

4. Rebuild indexes

REINDEX	REINDEX

5. Turn off all indexes (with SET ORDER TO the indexes will still be updated if records are added)

SET INDEX TO	SET ORDER TO

Index tags can now be created in descending order by using the syntax

INDEX ON duedate DESCENDING TAG <tag name>

Note that the DESCENDING switch only works when creating TAGs, not when creating stand-alone .ndx files.

Remember to Delete Tags

Keeping unused index tags will unnecessarily increase the index update time whenever a record is added to the file. For this reason it is important to delete unneeded tags using the command:

DELETE TAG <*tag name*>

Index Functions

The following functions that pertain to indexes have been added in dBASE IV.

KEY(*n*) returns the key field of the *n*th tag in the current .mdx file.

MDX(*n*) returns file name of .mdx file containing the tag at the *n*th position in the index list. If no .mdx files are open, it returns a blank.

NDX(*n*) returns name of the *n*th .ndx file in the index list

ORDER([*n*]) if no argument specified, returns master index tag for current work area. If number specified, returns master index for that work area.

SEEK(<*key value*>,[alias]) returns logical True if key value is in specified index. See chapter 6 for further discussion.

TAG(*n*) returns the *n*th tag from the currently open .mdx file

Here is an example of using these index-related functions.

```
.USE account ORDER acctno
Master index: ACCTNO
. ? NDX(1)
. ? MDX(1)
C:ACCOUNT.MDX
. ? KEY(1)
acctno
. ? TAG(1)
ACCTNO
. ? ORDER()
ACCTNO
. ? SEEK('XY')
.T.
. ? SEEK('ZX')
.F.
```

The USE command uses the file account and selects the acctno tag from the production .mdx file. If the ORDER switch is not specified, the file will be USEd without the acctno tag being the master index and will be in the order in which the records were physically put in the file.

? NDX(1) returns a blank because no index file has been specified. ? MDX(1) returns the name of the open .mdx file, Account.mdx. ? KEY(1) returns the key value of the first tag in the .mdx file. ? TAG(1) returns the name of the first tag in the .mdx file. ? ORDER() returns the key value of the tag that is in effect, and thus the currently selected order of the .dbf file.

? SEEK('XY') returns a logical True because an account named *XY* exists in the file. SEEK('ZX') returns a False because there is no such account in the file.

SET NEAR ON

dBASE III PLUS defaults to moving the record pointer to end of file if a SEEK was not successful. dBASE IV allows the option of a *soft seek* or an attempt to find the closest match. With SET NEAR ON, the record pointer will move to the next record after the value being searched for in the index when a SEEK is unsuccessful. If this feature is used, the FOUND() function must be used to test whether or not an exact match was found. The following code fragment will work if the file is open with an index and the key value corresponding to the index is stored in the memory variable keyvalue. This code fragment warns the user if an exact match has not been found.

```
SET NEAR ON
SEEK TRIM(keyvalue)
IF .NOT. FOUND()
    ? 'No exact match was found—The closest record is'
ENDIF
DISP
```

NOTE: If SET NEAR ON has been executed, the FOUND() function rather than .NOT. EOF() must be used as a test as to whether or not the SEEK was successful. Since with SET NEAR ON, the record pointer will stop at the nearest match if an exact match is not found, the record pointer will not be at EOF() if the SEEK fails. In dBASE IV a SET NEAR OFF should be executed if EOF() is used for a test of not finding a record.

Concatenating Date Fields with Character Fields

The problem discussed above—of indexing on a date field plus a character field—can be resolved in dBASE IV by using the DTOS() function. The DTOS() function takes a date value and puts it in index format when concatenating with a character field.

If code is a character field and date is a date field, the following index expression will arrange records in ascending date order within each code.

```
INDEX ON code+DTOS(date) TAG codedate
```

SOUNDEX()

dBASE IV includes a SOUNDEX() function that converts a character string to a phonetic code and thus allows looking up a name or other word by its sound. This feature is useful when records are accessed by last name and it isn't known how all of the last names are spelled.

This feature can be utilized in the following manner to create an index based on the SOUNDEX() code of the last name.

```
USE address
INDEX ON SOUNDEX(lname) TO soundname
```

To access a name by its sound, the following code can be used.

```
mname = SPACE(20)
@ 2, 0 SAY 'Enter last name to match ' GET mname
READ
SEEK SOUNDEX(mname)
IF FOUND()
    LIST WHILE SOUNDEX(lname) = SOUNDEX(mname)
ENDIF
```

The access.prg program presented above to show multiple instances of a last name can be modified to show multiple instances of last names that sound alike by making the following changes.

1. Invoke an index created on SOUNDEX(lname)
2. Change both SEEKs to: SEEK SOUNDEX(mlname)
3. Change the DO WHILE condition to

```
DO WHILE SOUNDEX(mlname) = SOUNDEX(LNAME);
    .AND. .NOT. EOF()
```

An example of using SOUNDEX() is presented in chapter 16.

Chapter 8

EXTRACTING SUMMARY STATISTICS FROM A FILE

Everything should be made as simple as possible, but not simpler.
—Albert Einstein

This chapter discusses extracting summary data from a single file. The chapter on SET RELATION TO discusses extracting data from multiple files. The principles needed to understand this chapter are discussed in chapter 7.

dBASE III PLUS provides various built-in commands for extracting simple summary statistics from a file:

SUM
COUNT
TOTAL
AVERAGE

More complex summary data can be generated by programming.

EXTRACTING NUMBERS FROM THE FILE

Perhaps the simplest example involves summing the contents of a single numeric field. If a .dbf file contains a numeric field called *amt*, the following command will sum the value of that field for all records:

```
SUM amt TO totamt
```

This command makes a single pass through the file. Each record is looked at and summed. The same result can be accomplished using the following DO WHILE loop, however, the SUM command executes more quickly.

```
totamt=0
DO WHILE .NOT. EOF()
    totamt=totamt+amt
    SKIP
ENDDO
```

Certain records can be summed selectively using the syntax

```
SUM amt TO totamt FOR zip='94704'
```

Multiple fields can be summed. For instance, if we have numeric fields named *amt1*, *amt2*, and *amt3*, and we want the sum for each field, the following syntax can be used

```
SUM amt1 TO totamt1
SUM amt2 TO totamt2
SUM amt3 TO totamt3
```

However, there is a problem. The above command requires three passes through the file. Each time the SUM verb is executed, dBASE starts at the first record in the file and sequentially searches through all records. The same result can be accomplished much faster with only one pass through the file, using the syntax

```
SUM amt1,amt2,amt2 TO totamt1,totamt2,totamt3
```

The values of numeric fields in records meeting a given condition can be quickly SUMmed using the WHILE clause as shown in the following syntax.

```
SEEK '94704'
SUM amt1 TO totamt WHILE zip ='94704'
```

In this example the amt1 field is SUMmed only for records in which the zip code is equal to 94704. SEEK '94704' positions the record pointer at the first record that meets the condition, and the WHILE clause assures that only records whose zip = 94704 are SUMmed.

THE COUNT COMMAND

The COUNT command performs in a similar manner as the SUM command but counts records instead of SUMming numeric fields. For instance, we can make a count based on a condition:

```
COUNT TO totzip FOR zip='94704'
```

This command will return a count of all records whose zip code is 94704. We can do a count for multiple conditions in the same manner, but it would require multiple passes through the file.

```
COUNT TO totzip FOR zip='94704'
COUNT TO totzip1 FOR zip='94706'
```

As shown, this approach will work, but it would require two separate passes through the file.

SUMMING AND COUNTING AT THE SAME TIME

The objective when extracting data from a file is to minimize the number of passes through the file. For instance, it might be desirable to sum certain numeric fields and to count at the same time. This result can be accomplished through an innovative use of the SUM command. Assume a contribution data base in which we want to count the number of contributors in a certain zip code as well as to sum their contributions. This command would accomplish that result.

```
SUM contribamt,1 TO totcontrib,totnum FOR zip='94704'
```

This command, with a single pass through the file, would sum the contribamt field to a memory variable named *totcontrib*. Also, for each record that meets the FOR condition, the memory variable *totnum* would be increased by 1. SUM 1 TO totnum means that each time a record is encountered that meets the FOR condition, the memory variable totnum is increased by 1.

THE AVERAGE COMMAND

The AVERAGE command will return a number that is the average of a numeric field.

```
AVERAGE amt TO avamt
```

will look at each amt field in the file and return the average value. The AVERAGE command does a SUM and a COUNT and divides the SUM by the COUNT.

SUMMING ON MULTIPLE CONDITIONS

The problem gets more complex if we try to sum for various conditions. For example we could get sums by zip code in the following manner:

```
SUM amt1 TO totamt FOR zip='94704'
SUM amt1 TO totamt1 FOR zip='94706'
```

This approach will work but will require two passes through the files.

THE TOTAL COMMAND

Some of the problems of summing or counting based on multiple conditions can be solved by using the TOTAL command. In contrast to the SUM, COUNT, and AVERAGE commands that return a number, the TOTAL command returns a file. The file that is created contains a summary record for each unique key and subtotals numeric fields based on the key field. For example,

```
USE file1 INDEX zip
TOTAL ON zip TO totzip
```

This command creates a file named totzip which will contain one record for each unique zip code in file1. Each numeric field in the summary record will contain a subtotal of the values of that numeric field by zip code.

Cautions

1. The file to be TOTALed must be indexed on or physically in the order of the field that is used as the key field for the TOTAL command. In other words, the field that is TOTALed on should be the same as the index key.

2. It is best to TOTAL to a file that does not exist already. Let the TOTAL command create the file.

3. The TOTAL command can only total on a single field. To total on the concatenation of two or more fields, another field must be added to the structure of the file and replaced with the concatenation of the multiple fields to be TOTALed on. Then INDEX on the new field and TOTAL on the new field.

While the TOTAL command defaults to subtotaling all numeric fields, the process can be sped up by specifying only certain numeric fields to be subtotaled:

```
TOTAL ON zip TO totzip FIELDS amt,amt1
```

Examples

The examples below demonstrate extracting data from a file with the following structure and indexed on region. While only five records are shown for the sample file, the approaches used will work equally well with 5,000 or 50,000 records. In fact, the efficiency of these approaches become more evident when used with larger files.

```
Structure for database: C:region.dbf
Number of data records:        5
Date of last update    : 12/06/87
Field   Field Name      Type        Width   Dec
    1   REGION          Character       2
    2   OFFICENAME      Character      15
    3   SALES           Numeric        10
    4   NUM_EMPL        Numeric         6
** Total **                            34
```

With sample records such as

```
Record#  REGION  OFFICENAME     SALES     NUM_EMPL
      1  AT      Atlanta Main   1100000         98
      2  AT      West Side      1800000        105
      3  BO      Boston Main    3400000        210
      4  CH      Downtown       3900000        280
      5  CH      Evanston       1500000        110
```

what is the most efficient way to extract the following information?

1. Show the total sales for each region.

```
USE region INDEX region
TOTAL ON region TO regtot
USE regtot
LIST region,sales
```

The TOTAL command is used to generate a file called regtot that contains one record for each region and in which all the numeric fields, including the sales field, are summed. Thus, using regtot and doing LIST region, sales will list each region and the total sales for that region.

2. Show the number of employees for each region.

```
USE region INDEX region
TOTAL ON region TO regtot
USE regtot
LIST region,num_empl
```

As in case 1, the TOTAL command is used to generate a record for each region. The only difference is that the final listing details region and the total number of employees for each region.

3. Show the sales per employee for each office.

```
USE region
LIST officename,sales/num_empl
```

This example is solved by a simple LIST, using a calculated value of sales/num_empl. Note that when the TOTAL command is used, as in examples 1 and 2, the detail about each office is lost.

4. Show the average sales per employee for each region.

```
USE region INDEX region
TOTAL ON region TO regtot
USE regtot
LIST region,sales/num_empl
```

This example uses the TOTAL command in conjunction with the LIST command listing calculated fields.

5. Show the average sales per office for each region.

```
USE region INDEX region
DO WHILE .NOT. EOF()
    key=region
    AVERAGE sales WHILE region=key TO mav
    ? 'The average sales per office in the '+key+' region is';
    '+STR(mav)
ENDDO
```

In this example, the region index is invoked so that the file will appear to be in region order. The name of the first region is saved to a memory variable called key, then the AVERAGE verb is used to average the sales for that region to a memory variable mav. Note that when the AVERAGE command stops executing, the record pointer will be pointing to the first record for the next region. Thus, each time the DO WHILE loop is executed, the name of the next region will be stored to the memory variable key. The AVERAGE WHILE then averages the sales for that region and positions the record pointer to the first record for the next region.

6. Show the offices in the Chicago region with sales greater than $1 million.

```
USE region INDEX region
SEEK "CH"
LIST WHILE region='CH' FOR sales > 1000000
```

This approach combines indexed and sequential access. The key field of region is used to find the first occurrence of the Chicago region. The WHILE clause of the LIST command assures that all records in which region ='CH'' are looked at, but the FOR clause then selects from those records the ones where sales>1000000.

7. Show the office in the Chicago region with the highest sales per employee.

```
USE region
INDEX ON region+STR(sales/num_empl,10) TO hsales
SEEK "CH"
* record found will be record with lowest sales per employee
* find last Chicago record
SET CONSOLE OFF
LIST WHILE REGION='CH'
SET CONSOLE ON
SKIP-1
DISPLAY
```

This example illustrates a problem with ASCII sorts of numeric data. A straight ASCII sort of left justified numeric data results in the ordering

```
100
11
20
```

This can be avoided by using the dBASE STR function that inserts leading blanks and makes the numeric data right justified, resulting in a proper ordering.

The solution shown above results in indexing on region plus sales/ num_empl. In this case, the first record in the Chicago region would be the one with the lowest sales per employee because indexes are built in ascending order. To find the record after the last Chicago record, the console is turned off and a LIST WHILE region='CH' is performed. This command effectively positions the record pointer at the record after the last Chicago record. SKIP–1 moves the record pointer to the last Chicago record or the Chicago record with the highest sales per employee. The DISPLAY then displays that record.

8. Show the office in the Chicago region with the lowest sales per employee.

```
USE region
INDEX ON region+STR(sales/num_empl,10) To hsales
SEEK "CH"
DISPLAY
```

This example constructs an index based on region+STR(sales/ num_empl) so that the record with the lowest sales in the region will be the first record for that region.

9. Show the offices in the Chicago region with above-average sales for the region.

```
USE region INDEX region
FIND CH
AVERAGE sales TO av WHILE region='CH'
FIND CH
LIST WHILE region='CH' FOR sales >av
```

This approach uses a FIND first to position the record pointer to the first Chicago record. The average command is used to average sales for the region using a WHILE clause. At the conclusion of the AVERAGE command, the record pointer is positioned at the first record after the last Chicago record. Next, another FIND CH is used to again position the record pointer at the first Chicago record. The LIST WHILE is then used to look at all of the Chicago records again. This time, however, the FOR sales > av clause is used to extract the records where sales are greater than average.

10. Show the offices in the Chicago region with below average sales.

```
USE region INDEX region
FIND CH
AVERAGE sales to av WHILE region='CH'
FIND CH
LIST WHILE region='CH' FOR sales <av
```

This approach is exactly the same as the one in the previous example except that in the last instruction FOR sales <av is used instead of sales > av.

11. Show the offices by region in order of ascending sales.

```
USE region
INDEX ON region+STR(sales,10) TO regionsales
LIST
```

This case indexes on region plus sales within each region in ascending order. The simple LIST command then displays the records in that order.

12. Show the offices by region in order of ascending sales per employee

```
USE region
INDEX ON region+STR(sales/num_empl,10) TO regionsales
LIST
```

This approach uses the index to arrange the data base in order of ascending sales per employee within each region. The LIST command then lists them in that order.

13. Generate a list of offices alphabetically by region.

```
USE region
INDEX ON region+officename TO regoffice
LIST
```

This example uses an index on region + officename to alphabetize by office name within each region. A LIST then displays the records in that order.

The SQL solutions to these problems are shown in chapter 13. However, the approaches shown here will execute significantly faster than the SQL approaches.

THE dBASE IV CALCULATE COMMAND

dBASE IV adds a CALCULATE command to allow extracting data based on a single pass through the file. The basic syntax of the command is

```
CALCULATE [<scope>] <option list>
    [FOR <condition>] [WHILE <condition>]
    [TO <memvar list>/TO ARRAY <array name>]
```

It can be used in conjunction with one or more of the following functions:

AVG(<*expN*>) calculates the average of the specified field or field expression such as

```
CALCULATE AVG(amt)
```

CNT() has no argument, but calculates the number of records based on the FOR or WHILE clause with the CALCULATE statement. CALCULATE CNT() counts all records. CALCULATE CNT() FOR zip='94704' counts all records with the zip code of 94704. Two or more functions can be combined, as in

```
CALCULATE CNT(),AVG(amt) FOR zip='94704'
```

MAX(<*expression*>) calculates the maximum value for a field expression as in

```
CALCULATE MAX(amt)
```

MIN(<*expression*>) calculates the minimum value of a field or expression such as

```
CALCULATE MIN(amt)
```

NPV(<*rate*>,<*flows*>,<*initial*>) calculates the net present value based on an interest rate, various cash flows, and an initial sum of money, where each expression can be a field or a field expression.

STD(<*expN*>) calculates the standard deviation based on a numeric field or field expression. This function makes the most sense when combined with AVG().

```
CALCULATE AVG(amt),STD(amt)
```

SUM(<*expN*>) sums the numeric fields or field expression

```
CALCULATE SUM(amt)
CALCULATE SUM(amt) FOR zip='94704'
```

VAR(<*expN*>) variance is another statistical function best used with AVG() and STD().

```
CALCULATE AVG(amt),STD(amt),VAR(amt)
```

The CALCULATE command can be used with the WHILE clause for maximum effectiveness by first using a SEEK to position the record pointer at the proper record.

For instance, the dBASE IV CALCULATE command can be used to implement example 7 above, using the approach

```
. FIND 'CH'
. CALCULATE MAX(sales/num_empl) WHILE region='CH'
```

Chapter 9

TRANSACTION PROCESSING

Simplify, simplify.
—Henry David Thoreau, Walden

The last step of the input process is posting the transaction file to the master file. As discussed in chapter 6, it is most effective generally to input first to memory variables and then to a transaction file. This section will discuss the posting of the transaction file to the master file.

In general, there are two major types of transaction postings:

1. Posting historical data from one file to another with the same structure. This type of posting can be accomplished with

APPEND FROM <*file*>

An example is posting a temporary file containing journal entries to the master journal file.

2. Updating. Another common type of posting involves updating account balances from another file. For instance in the accounts payable example, the balances in each general ledger account in the general ledger file would need to be updated based on the checks written.

In this section, the following examples will be used from the accounts payable example above.

1. Posting each account distribution for each check in the temporary file and posting it to an account distribution file

2. Posting the temporary file created when a check is written to the check journal

3. Posting the impact of all account distributions on all accounts in the general ledger file

REASONS FOR USING TRANSACTION PROCESSING

The following are some of the reasons for using transaction processing, rather than posting records directly to the master file.

1. To separate the slow index updating process from the fast input process. If an inputter has to pause several minutes between entering records while indexes are being updated, it wastes the inputter's time.

2. To allow transaction rollback. The transactions are not finalized until they are posted to the master file.

3. To reduce accesses to the master file in order to minimize the possibility of corruption.

4. To insure that all input validation is done at the transaction file level before it gets to the master file.

APPENDING FROM

When appending a file of significant size to a large indexed file, it is best to rebuild the master file index.

Do not do this:

```
USE master INDEX ssn
APPEND FROM temp
```

Do this

```
USE master
APPEND FROM temp
INDEX ON ssn TO ssn
```

When a large number of records is appended to a file that is indexed and an attempt is made to update the index, the index may become unbalanced from the attempt to insert all the new key values into the index. For that reason, it is best to use the approach above.

POSTING THE CHECK FILE

In our input example we entered data for checks to a temporary file called aptemp. Now the account distributions for each check need to be recorded in a file called acctdist. In addition, aptemp is appended onto the end of apmaster, which is essentially a check register. Both aptemp and apmaster have the following structure:

```
Structure for database: C:aptemp.dbf
Number of data records:        5
Date of last update    : 11/01/88
Field    Field Name     Type        Width    Dec
    1    DATE           Date            8
    2    CKNO           Character       5
    3    PVENDNO        Character       5
    4    PACCTNO        Character       5
    5    AMT            Numeric        10      2
    6    COMMENT1       Character      20
    7    COMMENT2       Character      20
    8    PACCTNO2       Character       5
    9    PAMT2          Numeric        10      2
** Total **                            89
```

Two types of records must be maintained:

1. A chronological check journal file that contains a listing of all checks written

2. A distribution file that maintains information about which checks are associated with which accounts

The first function is accomplished by the apmaster file. Since both aptemp and apmaster have the same structure, the posting is done through a simple APPEND FROM. The apmaster file can be used to look up checks by check number and to determine the amount and vendor and check distributions. However, it will be necessary also to generate reports by account: to see which vendors were paid out of a given account and how much they were paid.

Remember, in this simplified example we are allowing only two distributions per check.

In this example we show how to generate the file from which questions about check distributions can be answered. In chapter 10 we will look at how to generate the report. At this point, it might be desirable to look at the file structures outlined in chapter 2.

The structure of the distribution file will be

```
Structure for database: C:acctdist.dbf
Number of data records:          86
Date of last update     : 11/01/88
Field      Field Name      Type          Width      Dec
    1      DDATE           Date              8
    2      DCKNO           Character         5
    3      DACCT           Character         5
    4      DAMT            Numeric          10        2
** Total **                                 29
```

Note that there are only four fields. The primary key that will uniquely identify a record is the check number(dckno) plus the account number (dacct). Now we must write a program to post the apmaster file to acctdist. Note that we cannot do a simple APPEND FROM because the files have different structures, and each record in apmaster will have one or two records in acctdist.

The following program will perform the posting.

```
* post.prg

CLOSE DATA
SELECT A
USE aptemp
LOCATE FOR CKNO= ' '
IF .NOT. EOF()
    @ 20,0 SAY 'Some checks have not been printed '
    WAIT
    USE
    RETURN
ENDIF
```

```
GO TOP
SELECT B
USE acctdist
@ 20,0 SAY 'Posting—Please wait'
COPY STRU TO acctdtemp
USE acctdtemp

SELECT A
DO WHILE .NOT. EOF()

          SELECT B
          APPEND BLANK
          REPLACE ddate WITH A->date
          REPLACE dckno WITH A->ckno
          REPLACE dacct WITH A->pacctno
          REPLACE damt WITH A->amt-A->pamt2

          * check if second distribution
          IF A->pamt2 >0
               APPEND BLANK
               REPLACE ddate WITH A->date
               REPLACE dckno WITH A->ckno
               REPLACE dacct WITH A->pacctno2
               REPLACE damt WITH A->pamt2
          ENDIF &&second distribution

          SELECT A
          SKIP
ENDDO  &&while not eof

* post acctdtemp to acctdist
CLOSE DATA
USE acctdist
APPEND FROM acctdtemp
SET INDEX TO acctcheck
REINDEX

* post aptemp to apmaster
USE apmaster
APPEND FROM aptemp
USE aptemp
ZAP
```

What This Program Does

This program posts the data from the apmaster file to the acctdist file.

This is accomplished by first opening the aptemp file in work area A. A LOCATE FOR ckno= ' ' is performed as a final test to see if any checks remain unprinted. If this is the case, a message is displayed and the program is aborted.

Next, the acctdist file is opened in work area B. A copy STRU TO acctdtemp is performed to create a temporary file to which the new records will be appended. Then the temporary file is opened.

The DO WHILE loop goes through every record in the aptemp file and creates at least one record in acctdtemp. If only one account distribution is performed per check, only one record is appended to acctdtemp. If a second account distribution is associated with the check, a second record is appended.

After all of the records have been added to acctdtemp, it is appended to acctdist and index acctcheck is invoked and rebuilt.

Last, the aptemp file is appended to apmaster and the records in aptemp are deleted, using ZAP.

POSTING TO GL FILE

In another type of posting, the check distribution file is posted to a general ledger file. A general ledger file maintains the current balance in each account. It has the following structure:

```
Structure for database: C:gl.dbf
Number of data records:          5
Date of last update     : 12/12/88
Field    Field Name    Type         Width    Dec
    1    DATE          Date             8
    2    DACCT         Character        5
    3    AMT           Numeric         10      2
** Total **                            24
```

This posting could be done to update the gl file.

```
* update.prg
CLOSE DATA
USE acctdtemp
INDEX ON dacct TO tempacct
TOTAL ON dacct TO accttot
USE accttot
```

```
SELECT B
USE gl
UPDATE ON dacct FROM accttot ;
    REPLACE amt WITH amt +a->damt
```

What This Program Does

This program makes use of the dBASE UPDATE command to update the balances of each record in the gl file.

First the acctdtemp file created in the program above is opened. This file contains one record for each account distribution. The file is then indexed on account number and TOTALed on account number. This process has the effect of creating a single record in the accttot file for each account number. The amt field in this record contains the sum of the amounts effecting that account.

Next the gl file is opened in work area B. The UPDATE command is used to tell dBASE to go through each record in the gl file and look for a record with the corresponding account number in the accttot file. If one exists, the value of the amt field in gl is replaced with its current value plus the value of the damt field from accttot.

Note that accttot is physically in account number order. gl is assumed to be in account number order also.

USING UPDATE

When using the UPDATE command these cautions must be observed.

1. The key field on which the UPDATE is to be performed, in this case dacct, must be present in both files.

2. Both files must be either indexed on that key field or physically be in order of the key field. In this case they were physically in the order of that field.

3. If values of the key field exist in the file being updated from, in this case dacct, which are not present in the file being updated, in this case gl, no warning is given that data is being lost.

RECAPPING

In this chapter we showed how to take a file with the structure

```
Structure for database: C:aptemp.dbf
Number of data records:         9
Date of last update    : 12/11/88
```

Field	Field Name	Type	Width	Dec
1	DATE	Date	8	
2	CKNO	Character	5	
3	PVENDNO	Character	5	
4	PACCTNO	Character	5	
5	AMT	Numeric	10	2
6	COMMENT1	Character	20	
7	COMMENT2	Character	20	
8	PACCTNO2	Character	5	
9	PAMT2	Numeric	10	2
** Total **			89	

and do the following with it.

1. Post it to a file with the same structure, apmaster, by using APPEND FROM.

2. Create another file to record account distributions with the following structure.

Structure for database: C:acctdist.dbf
Number of data records: 161
Date of last update : 12/11/88

Field	Field Name	Type	Width	Dec
1	DDATE	Date	8	
2	DCKNO	Character	5	
3	DACCT	Character	5	
4	DAMT	Numeric	10	2
** Total **			29	

3. From the temporary account distribution file, post the changes in account balances to the gl file, which has the structure

Structure for database: C:gl.dbf
Number of data records: 5
Date of last update : 12/12/88

Field	Field Name	Type	Width	Dec
1	DATE	Date	8	
2	DACCT	Character	5	

3	AMT	Numeric	10	2
** Total **			24	

These examples illustrate one of the things at which dBASE is very good—manipulating data in whole files.

dBASE IV TRANSACTION PROCESSING

dBASE IV adds a new program structure designed for transaction processing. That program structure is BEGIN TRANSACTION...END TRANSACTION. The purpose of this program structure is to handle the case when a system crash or other problem occurs in midtransaction and to allow rolling back the transactions. This can be accomplished in other ways in dBASE III PLUS, such as by making a backup copy of each file to be modified prior to beginning the transaction.

dBASE IV offers the following built-in tools:

BEGIN TRANSACTION All postings to files after this statement are logged until an END TRANSACTION statement is encountered. When changes are made to a .dbf file as part of a transaction, an integrity check flag is set in the header of the .dbf file.

END TRANSACTION terminates a transaction.

ROLLBACK [<*database file name*>] restores a file that was part of a transaction to its condition prior to the start of the transaction.

RESET resets the integrity check flag. This needs to be done when a transaction terminates abnormally and a ROLLBACK is not executed.

If a CANCEL command is executed within a BEGIN TRANSACTION...END TRANSACTION construct, the transaction is automatically rolled back. If the program is SUSPENDed, the transaction remains active and all commands that are issued while the program is SUSPENDed become part of the transaction. If a ROLLBACK is issued while the program is SUSPENDed, RESUME will cause the next line of code after the END TRANSACTION to be executed.

Within a BEGIN TRANSACTION...END TRANSACTION construct, commands that delete files or overwrite whole files cannot be used because of the impossibility of executing a ROLLBACK once the file is overwritten.

These functions are offered to test the status of a transaction.

COMPLETED() returns True if transaction completed.

ISMARKED() returns True if transactions are being added to file, meaning that a transaction has not been completed.

ROLLBACK() determines whether the last ROLLBACK command was successful.

Why use all of this? In a way, all of this could be avoided by simply making a backup copy of all files to be impacted prior to the beginning of a transaction. In general the programming practices advocated in this book minimize the need for this new feature.

Chapter 10

RELATING FILES WITH SET RELATION TO

The basic relational model is simpler than are other data-modeling techniques, as it views data as if they were formatted into tables.
—*Mary Loomis,* The Database Book

The commands discussed in this chapter are

SET RELATION TO
SET SKIP TO (dBASE IV)

THE CONCEPT

When you work in a relational data base management situation, it is often necessary to relate files based on a common key field. dBASE provides several alternatives for implementing relations between files.

TYPES OF RELATIONS

Before you implement the relations among files, it is helpful to understand logically the types of relations involved. The two most common types of relations that are encountered are the following.

Many-to-One Relations

If a course has a single instructor, looking up information about an instructor from an instructor file, based on an instructor ID in the course file, is an example of a many-to-one relation. There are many courses taught by a single instructor. For each course in the course file there is one and only one record in the instructor file.

One-to-Many Relations

In some cases a one-to-many relation exists. In an invoice example, the invoice file contains one record for each invoice. A line item file contains one record for each line item on the invoice. A one-to-many relation exists between the invoice and line item files. For each invoice record, there are many line item records.

The relationship of the instructor file to the course file is also a one-to-many relation. For each instructor in the instructor file, there are many course records in the course file. *Many* means zero to *n*.

THE IMPLEMENTATION OF MANY-TO-ONE RELATIONS

The SET RELATION TO command is perhaps the most misunderstood command in the dBASE language.

The SET RELATION TO command is best suited to many-to-one relations. However, it can also be used for one-to-many relations. The SET RELATION TO command is really a shorthand for several lines of dBASE code; it allows linking two files based on a common key field. Based on understanding what the SET RELATION TO command actually does it can be used in a more powerful way.

Linking the course and instructor files could be done in the following manner, using SET RELATION TO.

The structures for the files used are as shown:

```
Structure for database: C:FACULTY.dbf
Number of data records:        2
Date of last update     : 12/06/85
Field       Field Name      Type          Width      Dec
    1       FACSSN          Character         9
    2       NAME            Character        15
    3       ADDRESS         Character        20
** Total **                                  45
```

```
Structure for database: C:COURSE.dbf
Number of data records:        3
Date of last update    : 12/18/88
Field       Field Name     Type         Width     Dec
    1       CRSENUM        Character        5
    2       CRSENAME       Character       12
    3       FACSSN         Character        9
    4       DEPT           Character        3
    5       ROOM           Character        5
** Total **                                35
```

The facssn index must have been created previously by indexing faculty on facssn to facssn.

```
* facourse.prg
SELE A
USE course
SELE B
USE faculty INDEX facssn
SELE A
SET RELATION TO facssn INTO faculty
LIST crsename,faculty->name
```

Things to Know about SET RELATION TO

In this program we open the course file in area A. The course file may be in any order. For each record in the course file, whenever a facssn is encountered, the name of the faculty member will be looked up in the faculty file.

In area B we open the faculty file. The faculty file must be indexed on the key field based on which the relation will be set.

Then we SELECT A and SET RELATION TO facssn INTO faculty. This command essentially links the two files based on the facssn field. When the record pointer in the course file is moved, the record pointer in the faculty file will be moved to the faculty member with the corresponding faculty ID.

The LIST command makes use of this linkage. It lists the name of the course from the course file and the name of the faculty member from the faculty file. The appropriate record is pulled from the faculty file because a relation has been set between the two files based on faculty ssn.

One anomaly of SET RELATION TO is that, if the records looked up in the second file are flagged for deletion, the deletion flag is ignored and the records are displayed.

When a match is not found for a key value in the file into which the relation is set, a blank is displayed for the field or fields pulled from that file.

THE LONGHAND WAY FOR MANY-TO-ONE RELATIONS

To understand what is going on, the program above can be rewritten in the following longhand manner.

```
* faclook.prg
SET TALK OFF
SELE B
USE faculty INDEX facssn
SELE A
USE COURSE
DO WHILE .NOT. EOF()
    mssn=facssn
    SELECT faculty
    SEEK TRIM(mssn)
    IF EOF()
        SELECT course
        ? '        '+crsename
    ELSE
        SELECT course
        ? '        '+crsename+' '+faculty->name
    ENDIF
    SKIP
ENDDO
```

This program produces the same results as the previous program, but it does it without SET RELATION TO. This approach could be implemented in dBASE II which does not have a SET RELATION TO command.

In this example the DO WHILE loop goes through each record in the course file. It stores the faculty social security number to a memory variable called mssn. Then a SEEK is done in the faculty file to find the corresponding record. If a matching record is found, the faculty member's name is displayed after the course name. If it is not found, blanks are displayed in place of the faculty name. Note that the alias faculty->name must be used to identify the name field as being from the nonselected work area. Note also that SELECT course must be included within each option of the IF statement because a test for EOF in the faculty file is done as the condition of the IF statement.

THE ACCOUNTS PAYABLE EXAMPLE

There are a number of cases in the accounts payable example in which it may be necessary to relate files. Following are two examples.

1. For a given account, look up all the checks written and who they were written to during a specified time period.

2. Show all checks written between two dates with the vendor name spelled out.

LOOKING UP BY ACCOUNT: ONE-TO-MANY

The first problem is to look up all the checks for a given account. It can be implemented using this program:

```
* acctlook.prg
* for a given account, look up all checks written
* and who they were written to
CLEAR
? 'Setting up—Please wait'
* set up the following relation
* acctdist->checks->vendor
CLOSE DATA
SET EXACT OFF
SET TALK OFF
SELECT A
USE account INDEX account
SELECT B
* index acctdis on acctno+check

USE acctdist INDEX acctcheck
SELECT C
USE apmaster INDEX checkno
SELECT B
SET RELATION TO TRIM(dckno) INTO apmaster
SELECT D
USE vendor INDEX vendor
```

```
SELECT C
SET RELATION TO TRIM(pvendno) INTO vendor
DO WHILE .T.

    CLEAR
    macct=SPACE(5)

    @ 2,0 SAY 'Enter account to look up ' GET macct
    READ
    IF macct=' '
        CLOSE DATA
        RETURN
    ENDIF
    * input validate account number
    SELECT A
    SEEK TRIM(macct)
    IF EOF()
        @ 20,0 SAY 'Account '+macct+' does not exist'
        WAIT
        @ 20,0
        LOOP
    ENDIF
    SELECT B
    SEEK TRIM(macct)
    IF EOF()
        @ 20,0 SAY 'No checks found for account '+macct
        WAIT
        @ 20,0
        LOOP
    ENDIF
    * display checks found
    CLEAR
    ? 'Checks written for account '+a->acctno+' '+a->acctname

    SET HEADING OFF
    DISPLAY OFF ddate,dckno,vendor->vendname,damt;
      WHILE dacct=trim(macct)
    WAIT

ENDDO WHILE T
```

What This Program Does

SET RELATION TO allows linking files based on a common key field so that the record pointer in the files can be moved in tandem.

This program opens four files: account, account distribution, apmaster (which contains the checks), and vendor. We essentially establish a daisy-chain relationship. First, when an account number is entered, the account file is used to verify that it is a valid account.

If the account is valid, a SEEK is used to position the record pointer in the account distribution file at the first record showing a distribution to that account if one exists.

Next the SET RELATION TO TRIM(dckno) INTO apmaster automatically positions the record pointer in the apmaster file at the check associated with the distribution record in the distribution file. The purpose of this relation is to extract the vendor code so that a lookup can be done in the vendor file to find the vendor name. The SET RELATION TO (pvendno) INTO vendor takes care of this last lookup.

```
ACCTDIS            APMASTER              VENDOR

ddate              date
dckno -----------  ckno
dacct              pvendno -------------- vendno
damt               amt                   vendname
                   comment1              defauamt
                   comment2              defauacct
                                         straddr
                                         city
                                         state
                                         zip
```

The first record with the desired account number is found in the acctdis file using SEEK(TRIM(macct)). The first SET RELATION automatically positions the record pointer in APMASTER at the corresponding check. Then the second SET RELATION automatically positions the record pointer in the vendor file to the appropriate vendor. When a SKIP is done in the acctdis file, the record pointers are automatically repositioned in the other two files.

SAYING IT WITH dBASE IV SQL

The same query could be done using the single SQL command

```
SELECT ddate,dckno,vendname,damt
FROM vendor,apmaster,acctdist
WHERE acctdist.dckno=apmaster.ckno
  AND apmaster.pvendno=vendor.vendno
```

Using SQL allows the program above to be expressed in one SQL statement. However, because of the way SQL is implemented in dBASE IV, it will tend to execute more slowly.

dBASE IV SET SKIP

The program above can be modified to make use of the dBASE IV SET SKIP command, which can be used for implementing one-to-many relations.

SET SKIP TO substitutes for a WHILE clause with commands that support WHILE clauses, such as DISPLAY or LIST. For instance, in the previous program, after the files are opened and the relations are set, a SET SKIP TO command could be added. Note that the .ndx index syntax is used.

```
* testskip.prg
SELECT A
USE account INDEX account
SELECT B
* index acctdis on acctno+check
*
USE acctdist INDEX acctcheck
SELECT C
USE apmaster INDEX checkno
SELECT B
SET RELATION TO TRIM(dckno) INTO apmaster
SELECT D
USE vendor INDEX vendor
SELECT C
SET RELATION TO TRIM(pvendno) INTO vendor
SET SKIP TO acctdist,apmaster,vendor
```

The above code sets relations in the form

```
acctdist->apmaster->vendor
```

Note that a many-to-one relation exists between acctdist and apmaster: more than one distribution may correspond to one check found in apmaster. A many-to-one relation exists between apmaster and vendor. Each check in apmaster has only one vendor, but each vendor can have many checks. Once a record positioning command is executed to move the record pointer in acctdist, the fact that a relation is set causes the record pointers to be positioned at the first corresponding record in apmaster and vendor. If there are many records that match, the SET SKIP command insures that all of these records will be displayed if a LIST or DISPLAY is executed.

For instance, if SEEK '1000' is executed to move the record to the first record where dacctno='1000' in the acctdis file, the fact that SET relation is used will cause the record pointer in the apmaster file to be moved to the first record where ckno is equal to the check number in the current record in acctdist. Then, since a relation is set between apmaster based on vendno, the record pointer in vendor would be moved to the first record in vendor where vendno=pvendno from the apmaster file.

SET SKIP TO is useful only if many records exist in the files into which the relation is set. In this case SET SKIP TO acctdist,apmaster,vendor would insure that if a LIST were executed, all corresponding records would be shown.

SET SKIP TO has limited utility. In the example above, using SET SKIP TO would save only part of a program line. It would allow elimination of the WHILE clause used to modify the DISPLAY in the third line from the end of the program.

For SET SKIP TO to show any results, either a SET FIELDS statement must be used or a fields list with DISPLAY or LIST to reference fields in more than one file.

Note that when SET RELATION TO is set, a SKIP or SEEK takes more time because the record pointer must be positioned in all related files.

To make use of the relations set above, a SET FIELDS command could be used to determine the fields to be displayed, such as

```
SELECT acctdist
SET FIELDS TO dckno,damt,vendor->vendname
DISPLAY
```

In this case a display would display dckno and damt from the acctdist file. Dckno would be used to find the corresponding record in apmaster from which pvendno would be looked at to find the corresponding vendor record in the vendor file. Thus to display the vendor name correctly above a lookup has to be done in both apmaster and vendor.

REPORTS

The following program is a modification of the program shown in chapter 5 to show relating two files in a report. In the version in chapter 5, only the vendor number is shown. In this case a SET RELATION TO is used to show the actual vendor name.

```
* datelist.prg
* program to list all checks written between two specified dates
* vendor names are listed for each check

SET STATUS OFF
SET TALK OFF

* get dates
  mdate1=CTOD('01/01/88')
  mdate2=DATE()
  CLEAR
  @ 1,1 SAY 'List checks between two dates'

  @ 3,1 SAY 'Enter beginning date ' get mdate1
  @ 3,40 SAY 'Enter ending date    ' get mdate2
  READ
  SELECT A
  USE apmaster
  SET FILTER TO date >=mdate1 .AND. date <=mdate2
  SET FIELDS TO date,ckno,pvendno,amt
  SELECT B
  USE vendor INDEX vendor
  SELECT A
  SET RELATION TO TRIM(pvendno) INTO vendor
    DO WHILE .NOT. EOF()
        @ 4,0 CLEAR
        DISP OFF NEXT 15 date,ckno,vendor->vendname,amt
        mcont=space(1)
        @ 22,1 SAY 'Q to abort, any other key to continue ' GET mcont
```

```
        READ
        IF UPPER(mcont)='Q'
            EXIT
        ENDIF
    ENDDO while not eof
```

What This Program Does

Note that the following changes have been made to the program presented in chapter 5.

1. apmaster is opened in area A.
2. vendor is opened in area B with its index.
3. A relation is set from area A to area B based on vendor number.
4. The DISPLAY statement has been changed to show the vendor name from the vendor file.

SETTING MULTIPLE RELATIONS OUT OF AN AREA

One of the criticisms of dBASE III PLUS is that it is impossible to use the SET RELATION TO command to set multiple relations out of an area. For instance, it might be desirable to go through the apmaster file and print out the vendor name and the account name for each check. This approach involves setting a relation from the apmaster file to the account file and to the vendor file. This can be done directly in dBASE IV using the SET RELATION TO commands. In dBASE III PLUS it would require slightly more programming.

The dBASE III PLUS Approach

The following program shows the dBASE III PLUS approach for setting two relations out of an area without explicitly using the SET RELATION TO command.

```
* 2relat3.prg
* program to set two relations out of an area
CLEAR
CLOSE DATA
SET TALK OFF
SELECT A
USE apmaster
SELECT B
```

```
USE vendor INDEX vendor
SELECT C
USE account INDEX account
SELECT A
r=5
DO WHILE .NOT. EOF()
     SELECT B
     SEEK TRIM(A->pvendno)
     IF EOF()
          mvendor=SPACE(26)
     ELSE
          mvendor=vendname
     ENDIF
     SELECT C
     SEEK TRIM(A->pacctno)
     IF EOF()
          macct=SPACE(15)
     ELSE
          macct=acctname
     ENDIF
     SELECT A
     @ r,5 SAY ckno+' '+mvendor+' '+macct+' '+STR(amt-pamt2)
     r=r+1
     IF PAMT2>0
          SELECT C
          SEEK TRIM(A->pacctno2)
          IF EOF()
               macct=SPACE(15)
          ELSE
               macct=acctname
          ENDIF
          SELECT A
          @ r,5 SAY ckno+' '+mvendor+' '+macct+' '+STR(pamt2)
          r=r+1
     ENDIF

     IF R>20
            WAIT
            CLEAR
            r=5
```

```
    ENDIF
    SKIP
ENDDO
```

This program first opens the three files to be related: apmaster, vendor, and account. A row counter, r, is set equal to five. The DO WHILE loop then goes through each record in the apmaster file. For each record, the vendor number is looked up in the vendor file. If a match is found, the vendor name is stored to the memory variable vendname, otherwise mvendor contains blanks. Then the account file is selected. A SEEK is done in the account file. If a match is found, the account name is stored to the memory variable, macct. If no match is found, macct is set equal to blanks. Finally, one line is displayed for each check showing check number, vendor name, account name, and the amount. Next a check is done to see if there was a second account distribution for this check. If there was, the second account is looked up and the information displayed on the screen. Then the row counter is incremented and a SKIP is executed to move to the next record in the apmaster file.

The dBASE IV Approach

dBASE IV allows setting multiple relations out of an area. The above program could be rewritten as follows in dBASE IV. Note that the SET RELATION TO command now supports multiple relations out of an area.

```
*2relat4.prg
* program to set two relations out of an area
CLEAR
CLOSE DATA
SET TALK OFF
SELECT A
USE APMASTER
SELECT B
USE vendor ORDER vendor
SELECT C
USE account ORDER acctno
SELECT A
SET RELATION TO TRIM(pvendno) INTO vendor, TRIM(pacctno) INTO
account
GO TOP
r=5
```

```
DO WHILE .NOT. EOF()
     SELECT A
     @ r,5 SAY ckno+' '+b->vendname+' '+c->acctname+' '+STR(amt)
     r=r+1
     IF PAMT2>0
          mvendor=b->vendname
          SELECT C
          SEEK TRIM(A->pacctno2)
          IF EOF()
               macct=SPACE(15)
          ELSE
               macct=acctname
          ENDIF
          SELECT A
          @ r,5 SAY ckno+' '+mvendor+' '+macct+' '+STR(pamt2)
          r=r+1
     ENDIF
     IF R>20
            WAIT
            CLEAR
            r=5
     ENDIF
     SKIP
ENDDO
```

Chapter 11

PROGRAM STRUCTURE AND MENUS

The right answer is whatever structure enables people to perform and to contribute. For liberation and mobilization of human energies—rather than symmetry or harmony—is the purpose of organization.
—*Peter Drucker,* Management: Tasks, Responsibilities, Practices

The commands discussed in this chapter are

IF...ELSE...ENDIF
DO WHILE...ENDDO
DO CASE...ENDCASE
DO
ADDED IN dBASE IV
SCAN WHILE...ENDSCAN

STRUCTURING CODE WITHIN A PROGRAM

dBASE provides various program control statements for branching to program instructions based on a condition.

Two-Valued Logic

The IF...ENDIF statement is most useful for testing conditions of true and not true. The syntax is

IF *<condition>*
    <program instructions>

```
ELSE
    <program instructions>
ENDIF
```

as in the following example

```
IF ISCOLOR()
    ? 'This is a color monitor'
ELSE
    ? 'This is not a color monitor'
ENDIF
```

The ELSE branch is optional. Multiple statements can be included in each branch of the statement.

Multiple Choice—The DO CASE

When there are more than two possible conditions, the DO CASE is the program control statement of choice.

```
DO CASE
    CASE <condition1>
        <program instructions>

    CASE <condition2>
        <program instructions>
    CASE <condition3>
        <program instructions>
  OTHERWISE
        <program instructions>
ENDCASE
```

Multiple statements may be contained between each CASE clause. The OTHERWISE is optional and is executed only if none of the other case statements are true. The first true condition is executed. The instructions after that CASE are executed until the next CASE is encountered, and then program control is transferred to the statement after the ENDCASE.

If multiple cases are true, then the first one that is true will be used. This means that when using restrictive conditions, the most restrictive should be listed first.

```
DO CASE
    CASE score > 90
        grade='A'
    CASE score > 80
        grade='B'
    CASE score > 70
        grade='C'
    CASE score > 60
        grade='D'
    OTHERWISE
        grade='F'
ENDCASE
```

Performing Instructions Repetitively—The DO WHILE

The DO WHILE statement is useful when instructions are to be executed more than once. The syntax is

```
DO WHILE <condition>
    <program instructions>

ENDDO
```

If the DO WHILE condition is true, then the statement after the DO WHILE is executed, otherwise the instruction after the ENDDO is executed. If the condition is true, each instruction within the loop is executed until the ENDDO is encountered. Program control then reverts to the DO WHILE where the condition is again checked. If it is true, the loop is again executed, otherwise control goes to the statement after the ENDDO.

Ways of Exiting a DO WHILE Loop

A DO WHILE loop can be exited in any of these ways.

1. When the ENDDO is encountered, control returns to the DO WHILE. If the condition is no longer true, control reverts to the instruction after the DO WHILE.

2. When an EXIT command is encountered in a DO WHILE, program control goes to the statement after the ENDDO.

3. When a LOOP command is encountered in a DO WHILE, control goes to the DO WHILE statement. If the condition is true, control goes to the statement after the DO WHILE, otherwise control goes to the statement after the ENDDO.

```
DO WHILE <condition>
        <instruction1>
        <instruction2>
    LOOP
    EXIT
ENDDO
```

Nested DO WHILEs

One DO WHILE can be used within another DO WHILE. A simple example would involve generating a multiplication table on the screen.

```
col=1
row=1
CLEAR
SET TALK OFF
DO WHILE row <=9
    DO WHILE col<=9
        @ row+3,col*5 SAY row*col PICTURE '999'
        col=col+1
    ENDDO WHILE col<=9
    row=row+1
    col=1
ENDDO WHILE row <=9
```

What This Program Does

This program initializes two counters, row and column, each equal to 1. CLEAR clears the screen. SET TALK OFF suppresses output of the results of calculations to the screen. Then two DO WHILE loops are executed. Each time the outer DO WHILE is executed, a row of numbers is printed. Each time the inner DO WHILE is executed, one item is printed in each row. The value of the counters is used to calculate the row and column positions. After a single row is printed, the value of the row pointer is increased and the column pointer is reset to 1.

Finding Duplicates—A Common DO WHILE Example

A common use of a DO WHILE loop involves making the condition DO WHILE .NOT. EOF(). This condition combined with a SKIP in the program causes dBASE to go through the file record by record. If an index is in effect, the file is looked at in index order, otherwise it is accessed in the physical order of the file. The following program shows the use of a DO WHILE loop to look at each record in a file and print out duplicates.

```
SET DELE ON
USE new INDEX ssn
SET PRINT ON
DO WHILE .NOT. EOF()
    memvar=ssn
    SKIP
    IF memvar=ssn
        ? memvar
        DISP
    ENDIF
ENDDO
SET PRINT OFF
```

What This Program Does

The best time to check for duplicates is at input time to insure that duplicates are not added to the file. However, another approach is to take a file and use a program such as the one above to look for duplicates.

This program takes a file named *new*, which is indexed on ssn, goes through the file, and looks at each record. The index key is social security number. Because the file is indexed, all of the records with a common index key value appear to be clustered together. Thus whenever two contiguous records have the same key value, a duplicate exists. The value of ssn for the first record is stored to a memory variable call *memvar*. A SKIP is then executed to go to the next record and a comparison done to see if the second record has the same social security number as the first. If this is the case, a duplicate exists and the record is printed out.

THE STRUCTURE OF A PROGRAM—USING SUBROUTINES

The hierarchy chart in Figure 11-1 shows how dBASE programs are structured. Starting at the dot prompt an instruction is given such as DO main to execute

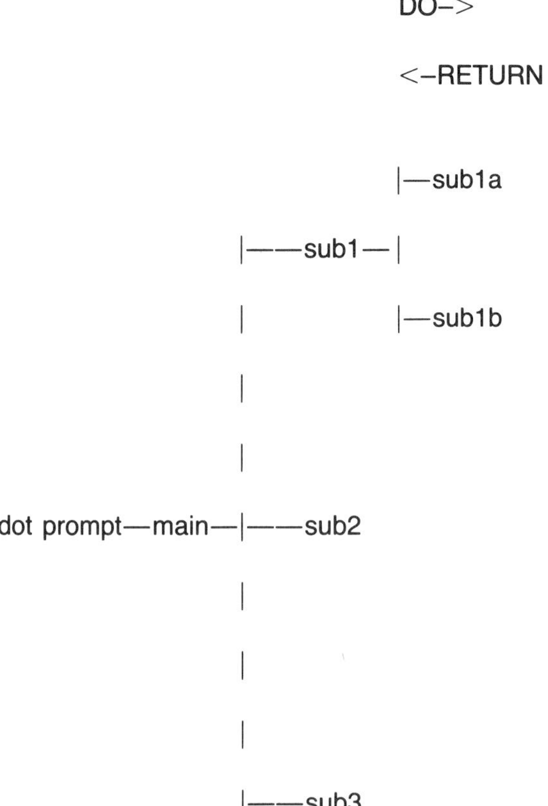

Figure 11-1. Hierarchical structure of dBASE program.

a program called main. main.prg generally consists of a main menu which in turn, based on a menu selection, allows calling one of three programs: sub1.prg, sub2.prg, or sub3.prg.

Program sub1.prg in turn calls two other programs: sub1a.prg and sub1b.prg.

In the chart, control moves to the right with a DO statement. Each time a RETURN is encountered in a program control returns to the left.

dBASE appears to be a modular programming language. However, in contrast to Pascal or C, in which there is virtually no overhead for calling a subroutine, there is a very high overhead for calling another program. Each program that is called in dBASE III PLUS is a separate file on the disk, and the overhead of opening that file will be incurred.

In a modular language, such as Pascal or C, each separate subroutine or function does not generally exceed one page of code. Since dBASE severely penalizes the user for programming in a modular fashion, subroutines are generally longer. For instance, it is common to implement each menu option with one or two subroutines, each of which may be several pages long.

STRUCTURING PROGRAMS

When you structure a dBASE program it is generally useful to implement each menu option with a separate .prg file that is called from the menu program.

The syntax for calling a program is

DO *<program name>*

This command gives program control to the first instruction in the program named. When a RETURN instruction is encountered, control is returned to the program line after the DO statement. If no RETURN statement is encountered in the program, the end-of-file marker is interpreted as a RETURN.

As a true data base management system, dBASE separates data and programs. RETURNING from or closing a program file has no impact on the data base files opened in that program.

CLOSING .dbf FILES

If the intent is to close .dbf files, one of the following commands must be used.

USE closes the .dbf file opened in the currently selected work area.

CLOSE DATA closes all .dbf files in all work areas except a catalog file in work area 10.

CLEAR ALL closes all .dbf and .ndx files, releases all memory variables, and selects work area 1.

CLOSING .prg FILES

The RETURN statement closes the current .prg file with no impact on the .dbf files opened in it.

The DO statement causes control to move to the right on the structure tree in Figure 11-1. A RETURN statement closes the .prg file that is being executed and returns control to the calling program. The RETURN statement has no effect on open .dbf files.

RULES FOR MEMORY VARIABLE AVAILABILITY

dBASE defaults to its own special brand of private memory variable. By default dBASE memory variables are only available in the subroutine in which they are created or in subroutines called by that subroutine. Thus a memory variable defined in sub1 in the diagram in Figure 11-1 would be available in sub1a or sub1b, but not in main, sub2, or sub3 or in programs called by sub2 or sub3.

This default can be overridden by declaring a memory variable public by using the PUBLIC declaration. Memory variables declared as PUBLIC are available to all modules as well as at the dot prompt. If an explicit declaration such as PUBLIC is used, defining a memory variable becomes a two-step process.

```
PUBLIC memvar
memvar=0
```

After the declaration PUBLIC memvar, memvar is a logical variable set to False. By setting it equal to 0, it becomes a numeric variable equal to 0.

Declaring memory variables as PUBLIC is useful when they are to be passed to higher level routines.

Conversely, variables can be hidden from higher level definitions that use the same variable name by declaring them PRIVATE. Variables declared explicitly as PRIVATE are still available to subroutines called by the program in which they were created.

Variables created in the main program are available to all programs that are called by main. Thus they appear to be public even though they are actually private. Variables created in the main module will be available to all sub modules but will disappear when control is returned to the dBASE dot prompt. All memory variables created at the dot prompt are public.

If programming is done in a structured fashion in which memory variables are initialized in a higher level routine that calls lower level routines when they are used, it is rarely necessary to worry about public and private memory variables. However, they must be considered when writing general-purpose subroutines that will be called from many different programs.

1. Declare variables used in the routine as PRIVATE to hide memory variables from higher level definitions.

2. To return values to higher level routines, declare the variables as PUBLIC or use parameter passing as described below.

When debugging programs, it is important to know that when a program is canceled, all memory variables created by the program are erased from memory. Here, the SUSPEND option is useful to preserve and review memory variable contents. This process is discussed in the chapter on debugging.

Syntax for Hiding a Memory Variable

To hide a memory variable from higher level definitions of variables with the same name, the syntax is

```
PRIVATE memvar
memvar=0
```

Variables cannot be declared PRIVATE at the dot prompt.

Passing Parameters

When writing subroutines that will be called from various parts of a program, it is sometimes useful to pass parameters. The syntax is

```
DO sub1 WITH param1,param2,param3
```

Parameters can be literal values or memory variables. For instance, this example could be implemented as

```
DO sub1 WITH 1,2,mvar
```

The first two values are literals and the third is the name of a numeric memory variable.

The program or procedure sub1 must start then in the following manner:

```
* sub1.prg
PARAMETERS p1,p2,p3
p3=p2+p1
RETURN
```

The first noncomment line in the program must be a PARAMETERS statement that defines the parameters being passed. The parameters can be assigned different names in the program being called. dBASE looks at the ordering in the PARAMETERS statement to see which one goes with which.

In this simple example, the only purpose of the routine is to add the two numbers together. While it would be imprudent to use a separate subroutine for this purpose, this example illustrates how passing parameters works. In this routine the third parameter is assigned the value of the sum of the first two parameters. That result is then passed back in the third parameter.

This routine could be invoked in the following way.

```
mvar=0
DO sub1 WITH 10,12,mvar
? 'The sum of 10 and 12 is ' +STR(mvar)
```

Summary of Memory Variable Conventions

The upshot of these memory variable conventions is that, for the most part, programmers do not need to be concerned about whether a memory variable is public or private so long as they follow a simple rule: Declare each memory variable in the subroutine in which it is used, or in a higher level subroutine.

The only times when a programmer has to worry about whether a memory variable is public or private is when writing general-purpose modules to be called by a variety of programs.

THE PROBLEM WITH HAVING EACH SUBROUTINE AS A SEPARATE FILE

The problem with having each subroutine as a separate file is that the overhead of calling a subroutine is greatly increased when compared with compiled languages. The time required to find and open a file can be up to several seconds, depending on the type of system used. The other disadvantage of having each subroutine as a separate file is that each time a subroutine is called, one file is used up against the total limit of fifteen files open in dBASE III PLUS.

PROCEDURE FILES

To overcome the overhead of storing each subroutine in a separate file, dBASE III implemented procedure files that contain multiple command files in one large file. This approach means that the overhead of opening one file only is incurred for up to 32 procedures that can be contained in a procedure file. A procedure file looks like:

```
PROCEDURE   proced1
<program instructions>
RETURN

PROCEDURE  proced2
<program instructions>
RETURN
```

Each procedure starts with the key word PROCEDURE and ends with a RETURN. It is opened with SET PROCED to filename.

INLINE CODE VS. SEPARATE SUBROUTINES

Due to the cost of calling subroutines, programmers must make trade-offs about when to include code in a program or to call it as a separate subroutine. The following guidelines apply.

1. If the function is to be performed more than once in different parts of the program, it is best to write it as a subroutine and call that subroutine each time the function is to be performed. In other words, if duplicate lines of code occur in a program, it is best to put them in a subroutine and call the subroutine each time that function is to be executed.

2. When code is embedded in a DO CASE statement, if the time required by the dBASE interpreter to read through the code is greater than the time required to open a file, the code should be put in a separate subroutine. For instance, in a menu example as shown below, if pressing a wrong response causes a significant delay in redisplaying the menu, the probable cause is putting too many instructions within the DO CASE construct rather than calling a separate subroutine for each case.

A MENU EXAMPLE

A typical menu provides a good example of using a DO CASE inside a DO WHILE and calling subroutines.

```
ap.prg 12/31/88
** ap.prg
** accounts payable system main menu
** check system date
CLEAR
mchoice=' '
@ 2,1 SAY 'Is today '+DTOC(DATE())+ ' ? y or n' GET mchoice
READ
IF UPPER(mchoice)='N'
    RUN date
ENDIF
```

```
* reset function keys except 1 which can't be reset
SET FUNCTION 2 TO ' '
SET FUNCTION 3 TO ' '
SET FUNCTION 4 TO ' '
SET FUNCTION 5 TO ' '
SET FUNCTION 6 TO ' '
SET FUNCTION 7 TO ' '
SET FUNCTION 8 TO ' '
SET FUNCTION 9 TO ' '
SET FUNCTION 10 TO ' '
SET TALK OFF
SET STATUS OFF
SET DELETED ON
* main menu loop
DO WHILE .T.
     CLEAR
     CLOSE DATA
     SET DEVICE TO SCREEN
     @ 2,60 SAY date()
     @ 4,28 SAY 'ACCOUNTS PAYABLE PROGRAM'
     @ 6,20 SAY '<E> Enter check'
     @ 7,20 SAY '<V> Edit/review vendors'
     @ 8,20 SAY '<A> Edit/review chart of accounts'
     @ 9,20 SAY '<R> Review checks entered '
     @ 10,20 SAY '<P> Print checks'
     @ 11,20 SAY '<O> Reports menu '
     @ 12,20 SAY '<C> Edit checks before they are printed'
     @ 13,20 SAY '<I> Recreate indexes'
     mch=' '
     @ 16,20 SAY 'Enter choice' GET mch PICTURE '!'
     @ 20,0 SAY 'Press Return to exit'
     READ
```

```
DO CASE
  CASE mch= ' '
      @ 20,0 SAY 'Are you sure you want to exit? (Y/N)' GET mch
      READ
      IF UPPER(mch)='Y'
            quit
      ENDIF

  CASE mch='E'
          DO enter
  CASE mch='V'
          DO vendor
  CASE mch='A'
          DO account
  CASE mch= 'R'
            USE aptemp
            CLEAR
            DISP off DATE,CVENDNAME,AMT ALL
            ?
            ? 'End of listing'

            WAIT
            USE

  CASE mch='C'
      DO edit

    CASE mch='O'
          DO reports
    CASE mch='P'

        DO writeche

    CASE mch='I'
        CLEAR
        SET SAFETY OFF
        ? 'Indexing—Please wait'
        USE vendor
        INDEX ON vendno TO vendor
        USE account
```

```
 94              INDEX ON acctno TO account
 95
 96
 97
 98
 99      ENDCASE
100
101 ENDDO while t
```

What This Program Does

Lines 4–13 allow the user to verify the system date and, if it is incorrect, to correct it.

Lines 17–26 reset the function keys. This approach averts the problem of users accidentally leaning the manual against the function key for APPEND and having a blank record accidentally appended to the end of the file.

Lines 29–31 set the environment to set TALK and STATUS off and to SET DELETED ON. Resetting critical parts of the system environment is important because one never knows how previously executed programs have set the system environment.

Lines 35–101 contain a DO WHILE .T. loop. It is this loop that causes the menu to be redisplayed on the screen after each choice is made. This loop causes control to return to the menu after each choice is executed. Note that DO WHILE .T. means do forever. The only way to exit this loop is to press enter at the menu prompt.

At the beginning of the DO WHILE loop is a CLEAR statement to clear the screen. Next is a CLOSE DATA to close all open .dbf files. Note that it is important to not keep .dbf files open when they are not needed. A user may leave the menu on the screen for a long period of time. For this reason it is best to close all .dbf files while a menu is displayed on the screen. SET DEVICE TO SCREEN makes sure that @...SAY...GET output is directed to the screen. This command is included to cover the possibility that a printing of @...SAY was aborted abnormally. If that had occurred, the menu would then be displayed on the printer unless the SET DEVICE command was issued.

Lines 39–48 display the menu choices on the screen. This could be accomplished optionally by using a TEXT...ENDTEXT statement and simply including each line of text on a separate line.

In line 49 the memory variable mch is initialized as being one blank long. Line 50 contains the command to get the menu choice, and the READ on line 52 activates the GET.

The DO CASE statement from lines 54–99 directs program control according to the menu choice made. Note that in most cases control goes to a separate program using the DO command. In a few cases where the instructions can be executed in a few lines, the actual code is embedded in the DO CASE, as in the case of reindexing and listing the checks in the temporary file.

Note in particular menu option 'I', reindexing. This option serves to rebuild the indexes if they should become corrupted. It also includes documentation of the index keys right in the program.

If an invalid menu choice is made, the menu is redisplayed on the screen.

DESIGN CONSIDERATIONS

This is a list of elements that should be included in all programs:

1. Routine to recreate indexes. As shown in the example above, a reindex routine serves both a documentation purpose and offers users a menu option to recreate indexes if they should become corrupted.

2. A routine to force backup whenever any data is changed. For small-to-medium applications, calling dBASE from a batch file and using the DOS backup command works well. The contents of the batch file might look like the following.

```
dBASE main
\dos\backup *.dbf a:
```

This approach will force users to backup whenever they exit the program and will prompt them to insert the proper number of disks. For larger applications, other backup media may be required.

3. A routine to check the diskspace whenever the program is started:

```
IF DISKSPACE() < 500000
   ? 'less than half a meg of disk space is left'
   ? 'plan on deleting some files'
   WAIT
ENDIF
```

4. A routine to reset the function keys. Nothing is more annoying than having a user lean a manual on the function keys and go into the APPEND mode.

```
SET FUNCTION 2 TO ''
SET FUNCTION 3 TO ''
SET FUNCTION 4 TO '  '
SET FUNCTION 5 TO '  '
SET FUNCTION 6 TO '  '
SET FUNCTION 7 TO '  '
SET FUNCTION 8 TO '  '
SET FUNCTION 9 TO '  '
SET FUNCTION 10 TO '  '
```

5. Commands that reset the environment to the desired values. Previously called programs may have set environmental variables to values that are not desired for the current program.

```
SET STATUS OFF
SET TALK OFF
SET ECHO OFF
SET DEVICE TO SCREEN
SET STEP OFF
```

6. Within the menu loop
   a. CLEAR to clear the screen
   b. CLOSE DATA
   Having a CLOSE DATA command inside the menu loop insures that .dbf files are never open when the menu is displayed on the screen. Users often leave the computer with the menu displayed on the screen for long periods of time. If a power outage occurs or some other event to interrupt power, the computer will be turned off with files open. Index corruption and/or corruption of the data files can occur in this instance.
   c. SET DEVICE TO SCREEN
   If a print routine in which device was sent to print aborts abnormally, the menu may be displayed on the printer. Thus it is a good idea to have a SET DEVICE TO SCREEN command within each menu loop.

7. Routine to check the index. It prevents problems to check the validity of all indexes as the program is started up and to rebuild corrupted indexes. The time required to check each index using the techniques described in chapter 7 only requires two or three seconds per index and represents a good investment of time.

Considerations in Application Modules

The following should be observed in designing applications modules.

1. Give users a chance to change their minds. Users may select a menu option to add a record or to do something else they really didn't want to do. They need to be given an opportunity to back out of their choices.

2. Warn users when significant events will occur and allow them to change their minds. For instance, if a menu option posts a temporary file to a master file, warn the user that after the option is executed it will be too late to add or edit any of the data.

3. Use letters for menu choices rather than numbers. It is easier to remember to press *A* to add, *E* to edit, *R* for report, etc., than to look at the menu each time to see the number of the selection. In addition, a one-character character memory variable can have 10 values if used as a number vs. 26 values for letters.

4. Provide as much on-line help as feasible. Users hate consulting manuals and in well-designed programs it should rarely be necessary to consult the manual.

BRANCHING BASED ON KEYSTROKES

Another type of program control available in dBASE involves branching based on keystroke using the following commands:

```
ON ESCAPE DO progname
ON KEY DO progname
```

ON ESCAPE

Normally when the Escape key is pressed during program execution, if a SET ESCAPE OFF has not been executed, a prompt appears asking whether to cancel, suspend, or resume the program. The ON ESCAPE command allows the programmer to substitute a program or dBASE command to be executed when the Escape key is pressed. This command executes like inserting a DO statement after the instruction that happens to be executing when the Escape key is pressed.

This approach could be used to pause program execution at any point, as in the following example

```
ON ESCAPE WAIT
```

If this command were in effect, when the Escape key was pressed the WAIT command would be executed and the program would pause until any key was pressed. If Escape were pressed with this command in effect during execution of a command such as LIST, the LIST would be aborted and the message *Press any key to continue* would appear on the screen.

It is possible to use this approach in program debugging, with the following short program.

```
* stepecho.prg
SET ECHO ON
SET TALK ON
SET STEP ON
```

If the main program contains the command

```
ON ESCAPE DO stepecho
```

When a problem area of the program is executing, pressing the Escape key will turn on talk, echo, and step so that debugging can take place.

ON KEY

This program causes a command to be executed when any key is pressed. This command is useful for stopping a printing operation in progress. For example,

```
* stopprin.prg
SET DEVICE TO SCREEN
CLOSE DATA
RETURN
```

In the print routine the following commands would be used:

```
ON KEY DO stopprin
? 'Press any key when printer is ready'
? 'During printing, press any key to abort'
WAIT
```

Trapping Errors under Program Control

When errors occur in programs, program execution is halted and an error message such as the following appears.

```
*** Unrecognized command verb.
          ?
FFAAFAF
Called from - C:JUNK.prg

Cancel, Ignore, or Suspend? (C, I, or S)
```

The user is given the choice of pressing *C* to cancel, *I* to ignore, or *S* to suspend program execution. Using the ON ERROR command, the programmer can override the default dBASE and error message and generate error messages of his own.

The syntax of ON ERROR is as follows:

ON ERROR DO <*program name*>

In other words, programmers can write their own program that is activated when an error condition arises. Some cautions should be observed in using this feature of dBASE. It would be possible to write an ON ERROR program that ignores the fact that an error has occurred and continues program execution as if nothing had happened. This would not be a good idea, since unpredictable results might follow.

dBASE III PLUS provides two functions that are especially useful in error routines. These functions are

ERROR() which returns the number of the error
MESSAGE() which returns the error message

Using these functions, the simplest type of error routine might be

```
* error.prg
* program to be activated when an error occurs
? STR(ERROR())+'  '+MESSAGE()
WAIT
```

This program does basically what the default dBASE error handling routine does—it displays the error message, pauses, and then gives the option to proceed to the next instruction.

The only differences are: the error number as well as the message is displayed, and the user is not given a choice to suspend or cancel.

This program could be modified so that the error message is displayed using an @...SAY so that it is always displayed on the same line of the screen.

If an ON ERROR routine is in effect, errors from commands typed at the dot prompt will also be trapped by the routine. The ON ERROR routine can be canceled by simply typing ON ERROR.

dBASE is somewhat inconsistent about which errors are trapped and which are not. For instance, system level errors such as *printer not ready* or *drive not ready* are still trapped by dBASE itself regardless of the ON ERROR status. This limitation makes ON ERROR routines of questionable value in many applications.

If not sure whether an ON ERROR routine is in effect, type DISPLAY STATUS.

The following more complete error routine assumes that the programmer has done routine debugging of the program and that user-correctable errors are checked for. It can be invoked with the command

```
ON ERROR DO error1.

* error1.prg
merror=ERROR()
@ 20,0

DO CASE
    CASE merror=6
        @ 20,0 SAY MESSAGE()
        @ 21,0 SAY 'Check config.sys for files =20 and reboot'
    CASE merror=15
        @ 20,0 SAY MESSAGE()
        @ 21,0 SAY 'Files may be corrupted. Call programmer.'
    CASE merror=19
        @ 20,0 SAY MESSAGE()
        @ 21,0 SAY 'Possible index corruption—Run reindex option'
    OTHERWISE
        @ 20,0 SAY MESSAGE()+ ' ' +DBF()
        @ 21,0 SAY 'Print screen and call programmer'

ENDCASE

WAIT
```

What This Program Does

This program traps three specific error conditions:

1. Error 6 is *too many files open*. One cause for this error message is that a config.sys file containing FILES=20 is not present.

2. Error 15, *Not a dBASE database*, is an error message that occurs when an attempt is made to open a corrupted .dbf file. In this case the user is advised to contact the programmer.

3. Error 19 is *Index file does not match database*, which can occur if index corruption has taken place. This error message advises the user to run the reindex option that should be included in the program.

For all other error message, the message is displayed on the screen with a message to print the screen and call the programmer.

dBASE IV: COMPILER VS. INTERPRETER

One of the main enhancements of dBASE IV is its pseudocompiled approach vs. the interpreted approach used in earlier versions of dBASE. In dBASE IV before a .prg file is executed, it is pseudocompiled to a file with the name file name as the .prg file, but with a .dbo extension. This means that there is now less overhead for calling subroutines, and more than one procedure can be included in a single program file.

When more than one procedure is included in a .prg file, every procedure after the first one must be assigned a name and begin with the declaration PROCEDURE *<procedure name>*. The first procedure in the file is assigned the name of the .prg file.

When a DO *<filename>* is executed, a check is made to see if a .dbo file exists. If one does not exist, the .prg file called is compiled into a .dbo object file before the file is executed.

If SET DEVELOPMENT ON is in effect, the date and time stamp of the .dbo file is compared to the date and time stamp of the .prg file. If the .prg file has been modified since the last compilation, the .prg file is recompiled prior to execution. To force recompilation of a .prg file, the command COMPILE *<filename>* can be used.

In dBASE IV when a DO *<filename>* command is issued, dBASE checks for the existence of the file in the following order.

1. As a procedure in the current .dbo file
2. As a procedure in file named with SET PROCEDURE TO
3. As a separate .prg file

Much of the increased speed of compilers comes from the ability to execute DO WHILE loops more quickly. In an interpreted environment, when a DO WHILE loop is executed, each instruction in the loop must be be interpreted or translated during each pass through the loop. In a compiled environment, that translation process only occurs once. DO WHILE loops in dBASE IV are executed significantly faster than those in dBASE III PLUS.

HOTKEYS IN dBASE IV

dBASE IV has expanded the ON KEY function to trap specific key strokes. This feature might be useful in allowing the user to press a *hotkey* to see a listing of valid vendor codes, for instance, before entering the vendor code. The following program fragment will accomplish that function.

```
* hotkey.prg
mvendor=SPACE(5)
DEFINE WINDOW vendors FROM 12,1 TO 20,79
ON KEY LABEL F2 DO vendlist
@ 20,0 SAY 'Press F2 for list of vendors'
@ 10,5 SAY 'Vendor code ' GET mvendor FUNCTION '!'
READ
RETURN

PROCEDURE vendlist
@ 20,0
USE vendor INDEX vendor
ACTIVATE WINDOW vendors
DISP ALL vendno,vendname
USE
DEACTIVATE WINDOW vendors
RETURN
```

Note that the ON KEY function is actually a program control feature. By simply pressing a key, program control can be transferred to an entirely new routine. It makes most sense to allow activation of an ON KEY while a READ is being executed as shown in the example above.

The ON KEY LABEL command can also be used in conjunction with the menu options described below. For instance to disable the left arrow and right arrow keys from exiting from a pop-up menu, the following code could be added to the beginning of the program that defines the menu.

```
ON KEY LABEL LEFTARROW DO nothing
ON KEY LABEL RIGHTARROW DO nothing
```

At the end of the .prg file this procedure could be added

```
PROCEDURE nothing
RETURN
```

NEW MENUING OPTIONS

A variety of new menuing options are included that can enhance the appearance of applications.

Pop-up Menus

Note that dBASE IV includes a number of new menuing options. The menu example for the accounts payable example shown above could be rewritten as a series of pop-up menus. Pop-ups are menus that show each option on a line on the screen. They can be made to appear anywhere on the screen.

```
* pop-up menus for accounts payable example
CLEAR
* step 1: define pop-up name and location on screen
DEFINE POPUP ap from 1,40 to 12,79
* step 2: define the prompt for each bar of the light bar menu
DEFINE BAR 1 OF ap PROMPT 'Enter check'
DEFINE BAR 2 OF ap PROMPT 'Edit/review vendors'
DEFINE BAR 3 OF ap PROMPT 'Edit/review chart of accounts'
DEFINE BAR 4 OF ap PROMPT 'Review checks entered'
DEFINE BAR 5 OF ap PROMPT 'Print checks'
DEFINE BAR 6 OF ap PROMPT 'Reports menu'
DEFINE BAR 7 OF ap PROMPT 'Edit checks before they are printed'
DEFINE BAR 8 OF ap PROMPT 'Recreate indexes'
DEFINE BAR 9 OF ap PROMPT 'Quit'
* step 3: specify the procedure or program which will be executed
*         when a selection is made
```

```

ON SELECTION POPUP ap DO apsel

* step 4: activate the popup

ACTIVATE POPUP ap


PROCEDURE apsel


    DO CASE


       CASE BAR()=1
             DO enter
       CASE BAR()=2
             DO vendor
       CASE BAR()=3
             DO account
       CASE BAR()=4
               USE aptemp
               CLEAR
               DISP OFF date,pvendno,amt ALL
               ?
               ? 'End of listing'

               WAIT
               USE

       CASE BAR()=5
           DO writeche

         CASE BAR()=6
             DO reports
         CASE BAR()=7

             DO edit

```

```
60        CASE BAR()=8
61            CLEAR
62            SET SAFETY OFF
63            ? 'Indexing—Please wait'
64            USE vendor
65            INDEX ON vendno TO vendor
66            USE account
67            INDEX ON acctno TO account
68
69        CASE BAR()=9
70          mch=' '
71          @ 20,0 SAY 'Are you sure you want to exit? (Y/N)' GET mch
72          READ
73          IF UPPER(mch)='Y'
74              quit
75          ENDIF
76
77
78
79
80    ENDCASE
81    CLEAR
```

NOTE: This example is meant to demonstrate menu structure. Not all of the programs that are called by the menu are included in this book. The above program takes advantage of dBASE IV's ability to have multiple procedures in a single .prg file. The first part of the program takes the name of the .prg file, appop. The second procedure, apsel, is declared using the PROCEDURE declaration.

What This Program Does

This program replicates everything from line 35 on in the prior menu program. Note that lines 1–34 must stay intact. The steps for defining a pop-up menu are as follows:

1. In line 5 a DEFINE POPUP statement defines the pop-up. Note that the space allocated must be large enough to display all the menu options with a separate option on each line. If the space defined is too small, only some of the options will be shown. The *arrow* keys can be used to scroll through the other options.

2. Step 2 is to define each bar. This is done in lines 9–17 where nine bars are defined. Note that when used in a pop-up, the Quit option must be defined explicitly. For each bar, its position and prompt are defined. Optionally, a help message that would be displayed at the bottom of the screen can be added for each bar by adding 'MESSAGE <message string> to the DEFINE BAR statement.

3. Step 3 defines the procedure that will be executed when a selection occurs. This is done in line 22.

4. Step 4 is to activate the pop-up with an ACTIVATE POPUP command, as in line 26. Note that this command performs the same function as the DO WHILE .T. loop in the previous example. The ACTIVATE POPUP command assures that after each command is executed, control is returned to the menu.

The procedure to be executed based on the menu choice is defined in PROCEDURE apsel. Note that the procedure apsel contains the DO CASE structure from the previous example with two changes:

1. The CASE condition is based on which bar is selected using the BAR() function.

2. In CASE BAR()=9, the memory variable mch must be defined explicitly because it isn't used to store memory selections as in the prior example.

Note that when a menu is displayed, the up and down *arrow* keys are used to move between choices and Enter must be pressed to select a choice.

Pull-down Menus

The menu could also be created as a pull-down menu by using the following code. Pull-down menus list menu options across the top of the screen. Since the menu prompts must be listed across the top of the screen, menus must be broken down into objects so that the menu prompts for a single application fit across the top of the screen. dBASE IV uses the length of the prompt plus three extra spaces for each prompt. In this accounts payable application, the prompts required for the menu, using the previous two approaches, would be too long to fit across the top of the screen. For that reason, we break down our menus into the following options, each of which will have its own submenus

1. Checks
2. Vendors
3. Accounts
4. Reports

Each of these options will be listed on the top bar and have a pull-down menu. The code required to implement this is as follows; three separate program files are shown.

```
* pull-down menus for accounts payable example

* define pop-up menu checks
DO checks

CLEAR
* step 1: define menu name with optional message
DEFINE MENU ap MESSAGE 'Accounts Payable Menu'

* step 2: define the prompt for each pad of the pull down menu

DEFINE PAD checks OF ap PROMPT 'Checks'
DEFINE PAD Vendors OF ap PROMPT 'Vendors'
DEFINE PAD Accounts OF ap PROMPT 'Accounts'
DEFINE PAD Reports OF ap PROMPT 'Reports'
DEFINE PAD Indexes OF ap PROMPT 'Indexes'
DEFINE PAD Quit OF ap PROMPT 'Quit'

* step 3: specify the procedure or program which will be executed
*         when a selection is made

ON PAD Checks OF ap ACTIVATE POPUP checks
ON SELECTION PAD Vendors OF ap DO vendor
ON SELECTION PAD Accounts OF ap DO Account
ON SELECTION PAD Reports OF ap DO Reports
ON SELECTION PAD Indexes OF ap DO Buildndx
ON SELECTION PAD Quit OF ap DO Exit

* step 4: activate the menu
```

```

ACTIVATE MENU ap PAD checks



PROCEDURE buildndx
        CLEAR
        SET SAFETY OFF
        ? 'Indexing—Please wait'
        USE vendor
        INDEX ON vendno TO vendor
        USE account
        INDEX ON acctno TO account
        CLEAR
RETURN

PROCEDURE exit

      mch=' '
      @ 20,0 SAY 'Are you sure you want to exit? (Y/N)' GET mch
      READ
      IF UPPER(mch)='Y'
         QUIT
      ENDIF


RETURN
```

```
* checks.prg
* pop-up menus for accounts payable example

CLEAR
* step 1: define pop-up name and location on screen

DEFINE POPUP checks FROM 1,1 to 7,27

* step 2: define the prompt for each bar of the light bar menu

DEFINE BAR 1 OF checks PROMPT 'Enter check'
```

```
12 DEFINE BAR 2 OF checks PROMPT 'Edit checks before printing'
13 DEFINE BAR 3 OF checks PROMPT 'Review checks entered'
14 DEFINE BAR 4 OF checks PROMPT 'Print checks'
15
16 * step 3: specify the procedure or program which will be executed
17 *         when a selection is made
18
19 ON SELECTION POPUP checks DO check
```

Three separate program files are shown here. The first, appull.prg, defines the menu bar for the ap menu. The first instruction, on line 4, DO checks, will call the program checks that define a pop-up menu that will appear when 'Checks' is selected from the menu bar at the top of the screen.

Line 8 has the DEFINE MENU statement that defines the *menu ap*. The MESSAGE clause defines the message that will appear at the bottom of the screen.

Lines 12–17 define the various pad names that appear across the top of the screen. Note that each pad is identified by a pad name that does not appear in quotes. This pad name will be used to identify the pad.

Lines 22–27 use the ON SELECTION PAD statement to define the action that will be taken when each pad is selected. Note that in line 22 if the checks pad is selected, the pop-up named checks that was defined in the program checks.prg will be activated. In the remaining lines 23–27 a procedure or program file will be executed.

Note that in line 22 the syntax ON PAD rather than ON SELECTION PAD is used because the action involves activating a pop-up menu which is used as a pull-down menu. Using the ON PAD syntax results in the pull-down menu being shown without pressing Enter when that pad option is highlighted.

In line 31 the ACTIVATE MENU command actually ACTIVATEs the menu. The PAD modifier tells dBASE which pad to highlight first.

The rest of this file contains two procedures, buildndx and exit, referenced in the ON SELECTION command. Buildndx rebuilds the indexes. Exit exits the program. Note that each program or procedure that is called as a menu option and returns control to the menu should end with a CLEAR to clear the screen. We can no longer use the approach of including a CLEAR statement in the DO WHILE loop.

Users should be informed that, in this case, they can exit from the pull-down menu by pressing escape. As in Lotus 1-2-3, the Escape key can be used to backup one step in menu selections.

Next is the checks program that defines, but does not activate the checks pop-up menu. As discussed, the menu is defined in line 7. Each bar is defined in lines 11–14. In line 19, the ON SELECTION POPUP command is used to give control to the program check.prg to evaluate the selections made.

```
1 * Check.prg
2
3
4    DO CASE
5
6
7      CASE BAR()=1
8              DO enter
9
10     CASE BAR()=2
11             DO edit
12     CASE BAR()=3
13               USE aptemp
14               CLEAR
15               DISP off date,pvendno,amt ALL
16               ?
17               ? 'End of listing'
18
19               WAIT
20               USE
21               CLEAR
22       CASE BAR()=4
23
24             DO writeche
25
26
27   ENDCASE
28   CLEAR
29 RETURN
```

The last program in this group is check.prg, which branches based on the selection made from the checks pop-up menu. This program must be a separate .prg file, as it does not work as a procedure in checks.prg.

A DO CASE structure is used to evaluate the BAR that is highlighted. In CASEs 1, 2, and 4, separate .prg files are executed. In CASE 3 the actual code is embedded in the DO CASE statement. The CLEAR in line 28 insures that the screen is cleared before control is returned to the menu.

Comparison of Menu Types

FUNCTION	*HORIZONTAL BAR MENU*	*POP-UP*
Naming menu	DEFINE MENU	DEFINE POPUP
Naming prompts	DEFINE PAD	DEFINE BAR
Defining actions	ON PAD ON SELECTION PAD	ON SELECTION POPUP
Opening menu	ACTIVATE MENU	ACTIVATE POPUP
Showing inactive menu	SHOW MENU	SHOW POPUP
Closing menu	DEACTIVATE MENU	DEACTIVATE POPUP
Releasing menu definitions	CLEAR MENUS RELEASE MENUS	CLEAR POPUPS RELEASE POPUPS
Returning menu name	MENU()	POPUP()
Returning number option selected	PAD()	BAR()

Note that after menus are understood, they can be generated with the Applications Generator and then the code modified as needed. One caution to observe is that if the code is modified, the menu can no longer be worked with in the Applications Generator.

SCAN...ENDSCAN: A NEW PROGRAM CONTROL STRUCTURE

dBASE IV includes a new program control structure called SCAN...ENDSCAN. It really adds no new functionality to the language. The following two code fragments are equivalent.

```
USE <file name>
SCAN WHILE .NOT. EOF()
    DISPLAY
ENDSCAN
```

```
USE <file name>
DO WHILE .NOT. EOF()
    DISPLAY
    SKIP
ENDDO
```

SCAN...ENDSCAN is a special case of a DO WHILE statement that includes an implied SKIP with every iteration of the loop. The SCAN condition can be either a FOR or WHILE clause. Note that if a WHILE clause is used as the condition for SCAN...ENDSCAN, the WHILE condition must be made true before the loop is executed or else the loop will not execute. If a FOR clause is used, the record pointer is automatically positioned to search for matching records in a manner similar to LIST FOR <condition>.

The execution time appears to be approximately equal for the DO WHILE and the SCAN...ENDSCAN. However, surprisingly, the SCAN...ENDSCAN construct with a FOR clause is quicker than a DISPLAY FOR <condition>.

ON ERROR

Two new functions have been added for inclusion in ON ERROR routines.

PROGRAM() returns the name of the program that was executing when the error occurred.

LINENO() returns the line number where the error occurred.

Chapter 12

DEBUGGING PROGRAMS AND PROGRAM DEVELOPMENT

It ain't finished 'til it's finished.
—Disgruntled programmer

In many applications approximately half of the development time is spent testing and debugging the system. Despite the best attempts of programmers and users, bugs creep into a system for the following reasons:

1. Simple syntax errors
2. Errors in logic caused by faulty programming
3. Errors in logic caused by incomplete communication between users and programmers

Part of the testing process is an extension of the design process. Some users don't fully understand how a program works until they use it for actual production such as generating reports under tight deadlines. At this point it is not uncommon for the programmer to learn about features that the user wanted but did not articulate until the program was being tested.

For large-scale projects it is possible to do extensive feasibility studies to anticipate these problems in advance. However, for the kind of projects undertaken on microcomputers using high-level languages, it is often more efficient to understand that the testing process will uncover aspects of the problem that the user had not previously communicated to the programmer. It is the programmer's job to design the system flexibly enough to incorporate anticipated as well as unanticipated changes.

dBASE provides various tools to assist in the debugging process.

THE DESIGN PROCESS

The design process begins with discussions between user and programmer. Using the techniques discussed in chapter 2, the logical design process can begin. However, users are often unclear about what they want. For this reason it is best to develop a program in stages, meeting with the users frequently. As each individual part of the program is shown to the users, they will become aware of changes that need to be made.

In the final stages of program testing, it is helpful to have someone with minimal familiarity with the program use it. Since the programmer knows what the program is expecting, the programmer in a sense is the worst person to test the program. An inexperienced user will make unanticipated entries and check the program's error trapping capabilities.

TRAPPING SYNTAX ERRORS

The dBASE III PLUS interpreter will catch misspelled command words, unterminated strings, and undefined memory variables. More subtle problems such as unmatched DO WHILES and ENDDOs will tend to cause obscure problems and will not necessarily be trapped directly by the dBASE III PLUS interpreter. Various third-party programs go through and format dBASE programs and catch unmatched program control structures such as missing ENDDOs.

USING ESCAPE TO SUSPEND, RESUME, AND CANCEL

At any time during a program, so long as SET ESCAPE OFF has not been executed, the program can be stopped to generate a prompt that says

```
*** INTERRUPTED ***
Called from - C:ap.prg
Cancel, Ignore, or Suspend? (C, I, or S)
```

This prompt allows execution of the options

1. C cancels execution of the program.

2. I ignores the fact that the Escape key was pressed and continues execution of the program.

3. S suspends the program and goes to the dot prompt to enter commands. If commands are entered at the dot prompt, the cautions below about commands that can be entered while a program is suspended should be followed. After entering commands, the program execution can be continued by typing RESUME.

SET TALK ON

SET TALK ON echoes to the screen the values of memory variables as they are changed. It shows the progress of indexing a file, etc. SET TALK ON can be useful while the program is being debugged but is an annoyance when the program is in final form. SET TALK OFF is generally included in the environmental commands at the beginning of the main module.

SET ECHO ON

SET ECHO ON displays command lines on the screen as they are executed. While showing the command lines makes a total mess of the screen, it can be useful in debugging in the following cases.

1. When a program is not executing properly, SET ECHO ON will show the commands in the order that they are executed.

2. If a program is inexplicably slow in a certain part, SET ECHO ON can be used to determine which instruction or instructions are causing the slowness. Simply SET ECHO ON and watch the time required to execute each instruction.

SET STEP ON

SET STEP ON in conjunction with SET ECHO ON and SET TALK ON constitute the most powerful features dBASE III PLUS offers for debugging. This command allows stepping through the program one instruction at a time and stopping whenever desired between instructions to do such things as check the values of memory variables and the record to which the record pointer is pointing.

The command is invoked in the following manner:

SET ECHO ON
SET STEP ON
SET TALK ON
DO <program name>

The display will appear on the screen for each line in the program such as the following where CLEAR is the command to be executed:

CLEAR
Press SPACE to step, S to suspend, or Esc to cancel...

Three options are offered:

1. Space to execute the next instruction

2. S to suspend back to the dot prompt. If this approach is used, the program will be suspended and the dot prompt will appear on the screen. Various commands such as DISPLAY and DISPLAY MEMORY can be executed safely at this point. Observe the cautions below about entering commands when the program is suspended. To return to executing the program at this point, type *RESUME.*

3. Escape to cancel. Note that SET STEP ON will be in effect if another program is executed. To turn off the debugging features, the following commands must be executed at the dot prompt or be included at the beginning of the next program that is called.

SET ECHO OFF
SET STEP OFF
SET TALK OFF

This approach to debugging offers several advantages:

1. If a problem is encountered in a certain part of the program, SET STEP ON, SET ECHO ON, and SET TALK ON will allow the programmer to step through each instruction and see the impact of each instruction. This allows the user to see the sequence in which instructions are executed, whether DO WHILE loops are executed, etc. If a problem occurs with a certain instruction, the program can be suspended and commands can be entered to see which record the record pointer is pointing to (DISPLAY) and to see what values memory variables have been set to (DISPLAY MEMORY).

2. If the record pointer is pointing to the wrong record, a command can be issued to insure that the record pointer is pointing to the correct record and *RESUME* typed to continue with the program. If the program then executes correctly, the program code can be changed so that the record pointer will be pointing to the proper record.

3. SET STEP ON and SET ECHO on together allow the programmer to see a visual display of how dBASE executes instructions. Stepping through programs can give the new programmer a visceral feel for how DO WHILE loops execute, for instance.

CAUTIONS ON ENTERING COMMANDS WHEN A PROGRAM IS SUSPENDED

If a program is suspended so that certain conditions can be checked before the program is resumed, certain cautions must be observed.

1. Don't enter commands that move the record pointer unless they are explicitly needed to make the program execute properly. Commands such as LIST or DISPLAY ALL will move the record pointer to end of file which would then cause the program, when it resumes, to assume that it is pointing to a record position that is different from the position of the record pointer based on program logic. Safe commands are

DISPLAY MEMORY   displays the contents of memory variables.
DISPLAY   displays the record to which the record pointer is pointing.

2. Be careful about changing the selected area. If a SELECT command is issued to change the selected area, be sure that another SELECT command is issued to return to the area that was selected by the program.

LIMITATIONS OF SET STEP

One limitation of SET STEP is that full line comments beginning with an * are not displayed. This means that it is possible to get lost in the program.

To overcome this limitation, partial line comments can be used. && can be used to include a comment at the end of a line. In addition lines after ENDDO or ENDIF can be used as comments as long as at least one blank is skipped. (Note: In dBASE IV, && should be included for comments after ENDIF or ENDDO.)

Another limitation of SET STEP in dBASE III PLUS is the manner in which the screen is cluttered as the command lines are echoed to the screen.

dBASE IV

dBASE IV makes a number of changes that can change the way program development must take place. However, dBASE III PLUS programs may be run in dBASE IV without modification. Modifications are only necessary to take advantage of the extensions provided in dBASE IV.

dBASE IV works in a pseudocompiled environment. This means that programs are first pseudocompiled or *tokenized* before they are executed. There are now two types of errors that must be dealt with.

1. Compile errors. Examples of compile errors are illegal syntax and unmatched parentheses. These are errors that can be detected at compile time.

2. Run-time errors are errors that can only be detected when the program is executed. This type of error might be a missing .dbf file or index tag, or it might be division by zero caused by variables taking on unanticipated values.

The source file for compilation is a .prg or .prs file. Files with a .prg extension contain regular dBASE commands, while files with a .prs extension contain SQL commands. The compile process creates a .dbo file that is a tokenized file that must be interpreted by the dBASE interpreter. Multiple procedures can now be contained in a single .prg.

dBASE IV offers more alternatives for development and debugging than dBASE III PLUS. The default development mode is a pseudocompiled one. This means that the programmer creates a source file with a .prg (for normal dBASE code) or .prs (SQL code) extension. dBASE then tokenizes the file to create a .dbo file. When a program is executed, dBASE checks for the existence of a .dbo file. If a .dbo file is not present, the .prg or .prs file is compiled to create a .dbo file. If editing changes have been made to the program, and SET DEVELOPMENT ON is in effect, dBASE must recompile the source file to create a new .dbo file.

dBASE IV defaults to only compiling program files as they are executed. Thus when a main file and many subroutines are present in separate .prg files, only the main file is compiled when it is called. The subroutines are not compiled until they are executed. This approach can cause a noticeable delay as each program is called.

While debugging is taking place, the command SET DEVELOPMENT ON can be executed to insure that dBASE IV will check the system time and date of the source file and compare it to the .dbo file to see whether recompilation is necessary.

One advantage of the dBASE IV approach is that syntax errors are trapped whether the command lines are executed or not. In the dBASE III PLUS environment, if a command line is buried in an IF...ENDIF construct that is rarely executed, the syntax error will not be trapped until the command is executed. In dBASE IV the syntax error is trapped in the compile process.

In a sense dBASE IV goes *too* far in trapping syntax errors. For instance, in all previous versions of dBASE, it was possible to use the remainder of the line after an ENDIF or ENDDO for a comment line if a space was inserted between the ENDIF or ENDDO and the comment. In dBASE IV, this approach generates a warning unless && is included in front of the comment. However, even if the warning is generated, the program will run fine.

TO DEVELOP OR NOT TO DEVELOP

There is some confusion as to what is included in the regular version of dBASE IV versus the developer's release. Basically, the regular version of dBASE IV contains everything with the exception of the template language and the ability to develop stand-alone run-time modules.

LINKING

All of the source files can be linked together and pseudocompiled into one giant .dbo file, using the DBLINK utility of dBASE IV. Such an approach is a good idea if the run-time facility is to be used.

DESIGN STRATEGIES

In dBASE IV virtually any program file can be like a procedure file. Multiple procedures can be contained in a single .prg file because the file is pseudocompiled. All procedures after the first procedure need a PROCEDURE declaration and a procedure name.

DEBUGGING

dBASE IV includes a full screen debugger as shown in Figure 12-1. The debugger includes several windows:

1. The Code window or Edit window in the upper left shows the actual code. The line of code to be executed next will be highlighted. When E (for edit) is pressed, this window can be entered and code edited. Changes entered

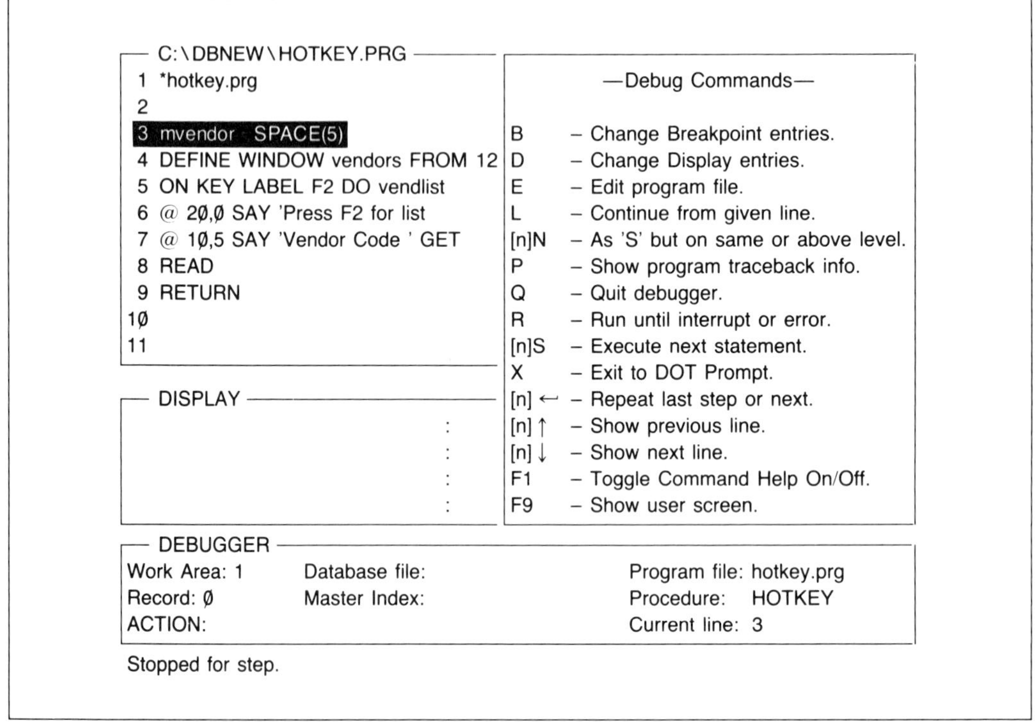

Figure 12-1. The dBASE IV full screen debugger.

into the Edit window are saved to the file but are not executed until the file is recompiled. To exit, press Ctrl-End. If code is changed in the Edit window, the following steps must be taken to execute the new code.

a. Ctrl-End to exit from editing session
b. Q to exit debugger
c. Cancel to close file being debugged
d. Compile <filename>
e. Debug <filename>

2. At the bottom of the screen is the Status window that shows the work area selected, the .dbf file that is opened, the master index, etc.

3. Below the Code window is the Display window. This window can be entered by pressing *D*. In this window, specifications can be entered for conditions that are to be displayed. Possible conditions might be RECNO() to display the current record number.

4. To the right of the Display window is the Breakpoint window, where conditions can be entered that cause the program to halt execution if that condition becomes true. This window can be entered by pressing *B* for Breakpoint.

5. The Help window is superimposed on the right side of the Code window. Pressing F1 toggles the Help window on and off.

6. The screen the user sees can be toggled on and off by pressing F9.

The debugger can be activated in either one of these ways:

1. SET TRAP ON—causes the debugger to be activated whenever an error condition occurs or when Escape is pressed.

2. DEBUG <*program name*>

Note that in the development environment of dBASE IV, syntax errors are caught as part of the compile process. It is run-time errors and logic errors for which the debugger is most useful.

The DEBUG commands are as follows:

B Change the breakpoints. Breakpoints are logical conditions that cause the program to pause.

D Change Display entries.

E Open the Edit window to edit a program file.

L Continue program execution from a given line—the programmer will be prompted for the line number.

<*n*>N Execute the next *n* lines.

P Show program traceback information—the current program, procedure, and line number as well as the programs which called it.

Q Quit debugger and go to dot prompt.

R Run the program until a breakpoint or error is encountered.

S Start stepping through the program one instruction at a time.

<*n*>S Execute *n* lines and then begin stepping.

X Suspend program execution and exit to dot prompt. By typing RESUME, control returns to the debugger.

<CR> Execute the highlighted line of code.

<*n*><up arrow> Move highlight up *n* lines of code.

<*n*><down arrow> Move highlight down *n* lines of code.

F1 toggles the Help menu on and off.

F9 toggles between the debugger and the screen that the user sees.

NEW ENVIRONMENTAL FUNCTIONS

dBASE IV includes two new environmental functions that can be useful for program development.

MEMORY() returns the amount of RAM available in the system. When developing a program involving memory-intensive activity, you may find it useful to use this function to check the amount of RAM available.

```
. ? MEMORY()
        72
```

SET('<*set condition*>') The SET function now accepts the name of ON/OFF set conditions as an argument.

```
. ? SET('ECHO')
OFF
```

Some SET commands that are set to integers can also be accessed in this manner.

```
. ? SET('MEMOWIDTH')
        50
```

This feature is useful when writing general-purpose subroutines to check the environmental variables and reset them at the conclusion of the subroutine.

Chapter 13

dBASE IV AND SQL

In fact, it cannot be denied that SQL in its present form leaves rather a lot to be desired—even that, in some respects it fails to realize the full potential of the relational model.

—*C. J. Date,* A Guide to the SQL Standard

Structured Query Language (SQL) was developed by IBM as a relational language in the mid-1970s and later incorporated into their mainframe data base management products.

This chapter covers some of the highlights of SQL, emphasizing how it interfaces with dBASE IV.

SQL is not a full programming language in that it has no program control structures and limited I/O capabilities. Rather, it consists of a Data Definition Language (DDL) and Data Manipulation Language (DML).

SQL, like dBASE, is used in multiple ways:

1. It can be used interactively by entering commands at a prompt.

2. SQL commands can be embedded into a program written in another language. Embedded SQL has historically been combined with such languages as C.

WHY dBASE AND SQL

dBASE and SQL complement each other. Where dBASE is strong, SQL is weak and vice versa. One significance of dBASE IV is that it combines the dBASE programming language with SQL. SQL is good at performing complex retrievals based on multiple files. Such queries often take significant programming time in dBASE. SQL is weak at controlling input and output, while dBASE is quite strong in this area.

Ashton-Tate's long-term strategy for networked applications involves using dBASE as a front end for an SQL server. SQL also feels comfortable to mainframe users who are accustomed to using it.

SQL's strength lies in making complex queries on multiple files relatively easy.

In version 1.0 of dBASE IV, the implementation of SQL involves translating the SQL query into dBASE IV command language. Execution is slow because of the time required for the translation process and the time required to execute the code.

BASIC PHILOSOPHY OF SQL

The basic philosophy and design of SQL is somewhat different from dBASE. In dBASE each table or physical data file is stored separately in a physical DOS file. Users sometimes refer to each .dbf file as a data base. In SQL each .dbf file is called a table in a data base catalog. Each record is called a row and each field refers to a column.

SQL tries to separate the user from the physical implementation of the system. In SQL data is always viewed in tables. Two types of tables exist: base tables and virtual tables. Base tables are where the data is actually stored. Virtual tables can be created at any time as views to contain data from one or more base tables. A data base can contain many tables.

HOW SQL IS IMPLEMENTED IN dBASE

SQL can be accessed in either one of two ways from within dBASE:

1. At the dot prompt, SET SQL ON allows SQL commands to be entered interactively. When SQL is set ON, many dBASE command verbs and SET commands become inactive. Those commands are listed in the manual.

2. SQL commands can be embedded in program files. SQL commands must be in separate program files with a .prs extension. Commands from dBASE mode and SQL mode can be mixed together in a single program, using the following conventions. Commands that follow the dBASE rules must be in a file with a .prg extension. Commands that follow the SQL rules must be in a file with a .prs extension.

Note that in a .prs file, it is important to watch the semicolons (;). For SQL commands such as SELECT, the parts of the commands can be on separate lines with a semicolon terminating the command. With dBASE commands allowed in SQL mode, a semicolon indicates the extension of a line.

DATA DEFINITION LANGUAGE

The Data Definition Language (DDL) is used to create tables and data base catalogs. Creating and modifying file structures under program control is possible in dBASE, but it can be a nightmare involving the use of such esoteric commands as CREATE FROM and COPY TO EXTENDED.

Creating a Data Base

Before any tables can be created, a data base catalog must be created. The command in dBASE SQL is

```
CREATE DATABASE <data base name>;
```

This command creates a new subdirectory as a child of the current subdirectory and sets up the system files in that subdirectory that will keep track of tables and other information about the data base.

To use a data base that has previously been created, the command is

```
START DATABASE <data base name>;
```

Creating Tables within a Data Base

In SQL the command to create a table within a data base comes after the data base has been STARTed:

```
CREATE TABLE <table name>
(<column1> <type>,
 <column2> <type>,
 .....
 <column> <type>);
```

After the table name is specified, each column or field must be specified with its type. For example,

```
CREATE TABLE address
    (lname char(15), fname char(12),
     straddr char(20), city char(15),
     state char(2), zip char(5));
```

In the context of dBASE, this capability can be useful for modifying a file structure under program control. Occasionally it is necessary to modify a file structure under program control, such as when trying to add additional fields to accumulate subtotals.

SQL Data Types

Each field or column must be assigned a data type. The data types supported by SQL are slightly different from data types traditionally supported by dBASE. The following data types are supported by dBASE's implementation of SQL.

Character Types

char(*n*) The length of the character field, up to 254, must be specified when it is defined.

Numeric Types

smallint Stores an integer of up to six digits including sign.
integer Stores an integer of up to 11 digits including sign.

The following numeric types require the specification of the total digits (x) including sign and decimal points and the number of digits to the right of the point (y).

decimal(x,y) Stores a fixed decimal value. x may be up to 19.
float(x,y) Stores a signed floating point number. x may be up to 20.
numeric(x,y) Stores a signed fixed decimal number. x may be up to 20.

Date

date Similar to a dBASE date field with a default format of mm/dd/yy. Literal values may be equated to a date field by using {mm/dd/yy}.

Logical

logical Similar to dBASE logical: holds value of True or False
Note that no equivalent of dBASE memo fields are supported.

ADDING DATA

SQL's method of allowing data entry might be called the brute force method. The basic command is

INSERT INTO <*table name*> [(<*column list*>)]
    VALUES (<*value list*>);

In this command all the data to be entered has to be physically hard-coded into the INSERT INTO command. This primitive method of data entry is why SQL is generally used in conjunction with another language. The I/O routines are written in the other language. Since dBASE has relatively strong I/O capabilities, it makes a lot of sense to combine it with SQL, which is stronger at manipulating data that involves complex relations.

For example,

```
INSERT INTO ADDRESS (lname,fname) VALUES
('Smith','John');
```

After each successful INSERT command, the following message is displayed.

```
1 row(s) inserted
```

MODIFYING STRUCTURE UNDER PROGRAM CONTROL

The SQL ALTER TABLE command is roughly equivalent to the dBASE MODIFY command. One main difference is that MODIFY STRUCTURE is designed for changing the data base structure interactively, while ALTER TABLE is geared to changing the structure under program control. The following is the syntax for adding a column.

ALTER TABLE <*table name*> ADD (<*column name*> <*column type*>)

Surprisingly, dBASE implementation of SQL only allows using an ADD clause with ALTER TABLE to add a column. Most SQLs include the following syntaxes of the ALTER TABLE command, none of which are supported in dBASE IV SQL.

1. Deleting a column

```
ALTER TABLE <table name> DROP <column name>
```

2. Renaming a table

```
ALTER TABLE <table name> RENAME TABLE <new table name>
```

3. Renaming a column

```
ALTER TABLE <table name> RENAME <old col name> <new col name>
```

4. Change the length of a column

```
ALTER TABLE <table name> MODIFY <col name> <new length>
```

In dBASE IV SQL to modify the structure of a table other than by adding a column, a new table must be created with the desired structure and then data inserted from the desired columns of the old table.

CHANGING DATA

Standard SQL provides an UPDATE command for changing data in a record. UPDATE is somewhat similar to the REPLACE command. The syntax of the UPDATE command is:

```
UPDATE <table name>
    SET <column name> = <new value>
    [,<column name> = <new value>...]
    [<WHERE clause>];
```

If the WHERE clause is omitted, all rows are updated. The following is an example of updating a single row.

```
UPDATE address SET fname='Frank' WHERE lname='Smith';
```

QUERYING

The mainstay of the SQL query language is the SELECT command. In some ways, it is used in a manner similar to that of the dBASE LIST command. However, instead of simply generating screen or printer output, the SELECT command takes a table or tables and creates another table that meets the specified conditions. The syntax of that command is

```
SELECT     [DISTINCT] <columns list>
FROM       <file name name(s)>
WHERE      <condition>
GROUP BY <column expression> [HAVING <condition]
ORDER BY
```

The SELECT clause names the columns or column expressions to be shown. The FROM lists the table or tables to be accessed. The WHERE clause is used to eliminate rows that do not meet the desired condition. The GROUP BY is used to arrange the resulting table into groups for such purposes as subtotals. The ORDER BY is used to arrange the resulting table in the specified order.

When you write a SELECT statement, the following questions must be addressed.

1. SELECT: What are the desired columns or column expressions?
2. FROM: In what tables are these columns?
3. WHERE: What are the conditions that link the tables?
4. WHERE: What are the selection criteria to eliminate unwanted data?
5. GROUP BY: What values are to be aggregated for such purposes as subtotals?
6. HAVING: What conditions must each group meet to be included in the results table?
7. ORDER BY: In what order should the results be presented?

The following SQL command extracts data from a single table named addrlist.

```
SELECT name,address
FROM   addrlist
WHERE  zip='94704'
```

It would be roughly equivalent to the following dBASE commands.

```
USE addrlist
LIST name, address FOR zip='94704'
```

A more complex example of the SQL select statement using multiple files is shown in the chapter on SET RELATION TO.

AGGREGATE FUNCTIONS

Various aggregate functions are included with SQL to allow calculating subtotals, subaverages, subcounts, etc., based on the WHERE clause.

These functions include

```
COUNT()
SUM()
MIN()
MAX()
AVG()
```

and can be applied to the whole table.

```
SELECT COUNT(*)
FROM region
```

would return the number of rows in the region table. An asterisk (*) in SQL generally stands for *all*.

The following command would return the sum of the sales fields for all rows in the table.

```
SELECT SUM(sales)
FROM region
```

Examples of using these functions with a WHERE clause to generate subtotals, subcounts, etc., are shown in the examples below.

PAGING SCREEN OUTPUT

The SELECT command defaults to displaying all output on the screen without pausing at the end of each screen. SET PAUSE ON causes a pause at the end of each screen similar to that caused by the dBASE DISPLAY ALL command.

JOIN CONDITIONS

When a query is to be generated based on two or more files, a join condition must be specified. If a join condition is not specified, the resulting table will be the Cartesian product of the two files. This means that each record in file1 will be joined with each record in file2. The resulting file will have a number of records equal to the number of records in file1 multiplied by the number of records in file2. The join condition usually specifies which key field in table1 matches with which key field in table2. For instance, when there is an invoice file and a line item file, the join condition is specified in the WHERE clause and might be as follows

```
WHERE invoice.invnum = line_item.invnum
```

This join condition tells the SQL interpreter to match the record in the line_item file with the records in the invoice file based on the contents of the field invnum. If the files were designed correctly, there will be many records in the line_item file for each invoice record in the invoice file. The syntax used is the file name followed by a period (.) followed by the field name.

SUBQUERIES: NESTED QUERIES

Another approach in SQL is to execute a nested query. In a nested query, an intermediate table is created from which the final query is performed. The two queries can be linked by conditions such as the following:

=,>,< If only one record is generated by the first query, the outer query can be based on a field condition being equal to (=), greater than (>), or less than (<) the result of the first query.

IN If the first query generates multiple records, the IN predicate can be used to select a row from the inner query.

ALL Allows applying a criteria against ALL of the rows in the first query. Such as greater than ALL of the results of the first query.

INDEXES

Indexes can be created to speed up the execution of SELECT commands using the syntax

```
CREATE [UNIQUE] INDEX <index name>
    ON <table name>
        (<column name> [ASC/DESC]
        [,<column name> [ASC/DESC]);
```

Deleting an Index

DROP INDEX <*index name*>

TRANSACTION ROLLBACK

Many implementations of SQL allow changes of mind by rolling back transactions that have been made. Transactions are not saved to disk until a COMMIT command is issued. In these implementations, to cancel transactions before a COMMIT command is issued, the ROLLBACK command can be used.

However, in dBASE SQL, ROLLBACK is only possible when transactions are bracketed by the BEGIN TRANSACTION...END TRANSACTION control structure. In this case the END TRANSACTION acts as a COMMIT.

VIEWS

Views are virtual or temporary tables that are created for output purposes based on the underlying or base tables. The syntax is

CREATE VIEW <*view name*> [(<*column list*>)]
AS <*subselect*> [WITH CHECK OPTION];

Subselect in this syntax means that the results of a SELECT statement can be used to create a view. In many cases views cannot be updated or changed by using commands such as UPDATE.

```
CREATE VIEW Chicago AS SELECT * FROM address
    WHERE city='Chicago';
```

HOW DATA IS STORED

For each SQL data base, dBASE sets up a number of .dbf files, including the following in a separate subdirectory, with the same name as the data base, to keep track of catalog information about the data base. If a dBASE DIR is run, these files are shown as NOT being dBASE IV files. However, in dBASE mode they can be USEd and their contents LISTed.

SYSTABLS Contains a list of all tables and the number of columns in each.

SYSCOLS Contains a list of all columns and the associated table.
SYSIDXS Contains a list of all indexes.
SYSVIEWS Contains a list of all views in the data base.
SYSKEYS Contains a list of index keys.

EXTRACTING DATA FROM SYSTEMS FILES

The SELECT command can be used to extract data about the data base from system files.

```
SELECT name,colcount,remarks
FROM systabls;
```

Lists the name, number of columns, and remarks for all tables in the data base.

```
SELECT name,tbname
FROM sysidxs;
```

Lists all the column names in all the tables in the data base.

```
SELECT * FROM sysviews;
```

Lists all the views. Note that * means all columns.

```
SELECT * FROM sysidxs WHERE tbname=<table name>;
```

List all the indexes for a given table name.

```
SELECT * FROM syscols WHERE tbname=<table name>;
```

List all the columns in a given table.

STRUCTURE OF FILES

The structures of two of the files, syscols and systabls, are shown below:

Structure for database: C:\DB4\SAMPLES\SYSCOLS.DBF
Number of data records: 121
Date of last update : 12/22/88

Field	Field Name	Type	Width	Dec	Index
1	COLNAME	Character	10		N
2	TBNAME	Character	10		N
3	TBCREATOR	Character	10		N
4	COLNO	Numeric	3		N
5	COLTYPE	Character	1		N
6	COLLEN	Numeric	3		N

7	COLSCALE	Numeric	2		N
8	NULLS	Character	1		N
9	COLCARD	Numeric	10		N
10	UPDATES	Character	1		N
11	HIGH2KEY	Character	8		N
12	LOW2KEY	Character	8		N
** Total **			68		

Structure for database: C:\DB4\SAMPLES\SYSTABLS.DBF
Number of data records: 16
Date of last update : 07/25/88

Field	Field Name	Type	Width	Dec	Index
1	TBNAME	Character	10		N
2	CREATOR	Character	10		N
3	TBTYPE	Character	1		N
4	COLCOUNT	Numeric	3		N
5	CLUSTERRID	Numeric	10		N
6	INDXCOUNT	Numeric	3		N
7	CREATED	Date	8		N
8	UPDATED	Date	8		N
9	CARD	Numeric	10		N
10	NPAGES	Numeric	10		N
** Total **			74		

NOTE: Because each of the system tables is created as a .dbf file, the file name must follow the DOS constraint of an eight-character file name. Thus systables in a standard SQL becomes systabls in dBASE IV SQL.

Since the system tables are .dbf files, any of them can be opened as a .dbf file when SQL is set OFF and the structure and contents reviewed. However, it is not a good idea to change the contents of these files and thus corrupt the data base catalog information.

SYSDBS

The .dbf file sysdbs.dbf in the sqlhome subdirectory, a child of the directory in which dBASE resides, keeps track of the last SQL data base used. When SET SQL ON is executed, this file is checked and an attempt made to open the SQL data base last used. If, for some reason, that data base was deleted since the last use, the entry must be deleted from the SYSDBS file or it will be impossible to SET SQL ON. The file is flagged as *read only*.

FROM dBASE TO SQL AND BACK

The first thing to understand is the difference between the traditional dBASE concept of a data base and the SQL concept. dBASE has referred traditionally to a single table that is stored in a .dbf file as a data base. In SQL terms, a data base is a collection of tables. In SQL many tables can be created as part of a single data base. Extracting information from multiple tables within a single data base is relatively easy.

Rough Equivalents of Commands

dBASE	*dBASE SQL*
USE <file name>	START DATABASE *<file name>*
DISP STRU	SELECT * FROM syscols
LIST	SELECT *
	FROM *<table name>*
MODI STRU	ALTER TABLE *<table name>*
CREATE	CREATE TABLE
	CREATE VIEW
INDEX ON *<field>* TO file	CREATE INDEX *<name>* ON table (*field*)
DIR	SELECT * FROM systabls
USE	STOP DATABASE

ENTERING COMMANDS

Several differences exist between entering dBASE commands and SQL commands.

1. With SQL set on, all command lines that use SQL commands must end with a semicolon. Command lines that use allowable dBASE commands should not end with a semicolon unless the command is to be extended to the next line.

When SQL is set on, open .dbf files are *not* closed. It is therefore a good idea to execute a CLOSE DATA prior to SET SQL ON.

2. SQL commands may NOT be abbreviated by using the first four letters of the command, as in dBASE.

3. Commands may be typed at the dot prompt or in the Editor. To access the Editor press Control-Home from the dot prompt.

4. To change the command executed previously, press up arrow so that the command appears at the dot prompt. Then, if the command is too long to be edited as a single line, press Control-Home to load it into the Editor so that it can be modified. When finished making changes, press Control-End to exit the Editor.

5. When you reference fields of the same name from two or more tables, the name of the table must become part of the field name. The table name, a period (.), and the field name comprise the full field name. For example

```
items.part_no = inventry.part_no
```

6. If a date value is specified, the dBASE IV convention of enclosing the date in {} must be followed. Many implementations of SQL allow a date to be entered in the form mm/dd/yy. However, for dBASE SQL, it must be entered as {mm/dd/yy}.

7. If more than one table is referenced in a SELECT command, a link field must be specified in the WHERE clause.

8. Generally, dBASE functions can be used as part of SQL commands.

INTERFACING dBASE AND SQL

How does dBASE SQL interact with native dBASE? Since dBASE is relatively strong at I/O where SQL is weak, and SQL is stronger at extracting data from multiple tables involving complex relations, the logical interaction of dBASE and SQL might be

1. Input data to tables in dBASE mode.
2. Use SQL to extract data from multiple tables.
3. Send the data back to dBASE for generation of reports.

Since data is stored somewhat differently in dBASE mode, to implement the above approach, data would have to be first entered into .dbf files in dBASE mode and then transferred to SQL mode. The data is extracted in SQL mode and then sent back to dBASE.

FROM dBASE TO SQL

Several methods exist to transfer data from dBASE mode to SQL mode.

Before transferring data, think through the problem and remember the difference between the way dBASE treats a data base and the way sql does. dBASE stores each table in a separate physical DOS file. SQL's concept of a data base includes multiple tables or .dbf files.

Using DBDEFINE

One method is to use the DBDEFINE command. When you use this approach, an SQL data base must first be created and then the contents of the .dbf files read into it.

1. If the data base to be used doesn't already exist, create the data base.

SQL. CREATE DATABASE test;

This command creates a subdirectory named *test* containing the .dbf files that track an SQL data base contained in it.

2. To add to an existing data base, copy the .dbf and associated .dbt file into the subdirectory created in the step above or into the subdirectory of an existing data base.

SQL. RUN COPY testsql.* test

3. Start the data base created in step 1 or the existing data base to be used.

SQL. START DATABASE test;

4. DBDEFINE

DBDEFINE with no arguments adds all .dbf files contained in the given subdirectory as tables in the data base.

DBCHECK

If a file is used both in dBASE and SQL mode, it is helpful to run DBCHECK prior to each use in SQL mode. This command insures that the SQL catalog files are updated to reflect any changes made to the file while in dBASE mode.

Loading Data from Other Formats into SQL

The LOAD command can be used to import data from a file to an SQL table that has previously been created. The syntax is

LOAD DATA FROM <[<*path*>] *file name*>
    INTO TABLE <*table name*>
        [[TYPE] {SDF/DIF/WKS/SYLK/FW2/RPD/dBASEII/
        DELIMITED WITH {BLANK/<*delimiter*>}}];

LOAD DATA inserts data from a source file into an existing SQL table in a data base that has been STARTed. If TYPE is not specified, a .dbf source file is assumed. Other source file types may include

SDF (Standard Data Format-ASCII fixed length fields)
DIF (Visicalc)
WKS (LOTUS 1-2-3)
SYLK (MultiPlan)
FW2 (Framework II)
RPD (RapidFile)
dBASEII (dBASE II)

Unloading Data

The opposite result can be achieved by exporting data from an SQL table to an external file type. The syntax of the UNLOAD command is

```
UNLOAD DATA TO <[<path>] file name>
    FROM TABLE <table name>
        [[TYPE] {SDF/DIF/WKS/SYLK/FW2/RPD/dBASEII
        /DELIMITED WITH {BLANK/<delimiter>}}];
```

UNLOAD DATA reads data from an SQL table into a non-SQL file. If TYPE is not specified, a .dbf file is assumed. The non-SQL file TYPE may be specified using the file types listed under LOAD.

OVERHEAD OF EXTRACTING INFORMATION

Each type of query has overhead. Each SELECT statement can use more than one of the ten work areas provided by dBASE IV.

1. Each table referenced in the FROM clause of a SELECT statement requires one work area.

2. For each OPEN CURSOR command one work area is required.

3. A work area is required for each GROUP BY or ORDER BY clause.

4. Another work area is required for each SAVE TO TEMP clause.

5. If the SQL statements are bracketed with a BEGIN TRANSACTION...END TRANSACTION construct, one work area is required for each system catalog table opened.

The following SELECT statement requires four work areas.

```
SELECT ordnum,part,qty
FROM invoice,line_item
WHERE invoice.ordnum = line_item.qty
GROUP BY ordnum
SAVE TO TEMP orders
```

Two work areas would be required for the two tables referenced in the FROM clause, one for the GROUP BY and one for the SAVE TO TEMP clause.

ERROR TRAPPING

dBASE SQL provides two system memory variables that are useful for trapping errors.

SQLCODE is set to the following:

0	operation successful
−1	error code
+100	warning that no rows were returned

SQLCNT returns the number of rows affected by the last SQL operation.

GETTING IT BACK TO dBASE

Various options exist for getting data back to dBASE from SQL mode.

SAVE TO TEMP

One option involves adding a SAVE TO TEMP <*file name*> [KEEP] to the SELECT command. This option has the effect of sending the results of a SELECT query to a .dbf file that can be manipulated in dBASE.

The command

```
SELECT * FROM syscols SAVE TO TEMP columns KEEP;
```

creates a new .dbf file named *columns* containing the contents of the syscols file. columns.dbf could be opened and manipulated after SQL is set OFF.

Transferring to Memory Variables

The results of a select query can be saved to memory variables, using the INTO switch of the SELECT statement. This approach is most useful when a SELECT statement will return one row of data.

```
SELECT colno,colname,coltype,collen
INTO mcolno,mcolname,mcoltype,mcolength
FROM syscols
WHERE tbname='VENDORS' AND colname='VENDOR';
```

Note that if the SELECT statement returns no rows, the memory variables will not be defined. For this reason, either the value of the memory variable sqlcnt should be tested before testing the values of the memory variables or the memory variables should be created as blanks or zeroes first and a test done to determine whether or not the SELECT statement changed their values.

Cursors

Cursors are the traditional way of transferring data between SQL and its host language. Cursors can be used when more than one row is returned by a SELECT statement. The SQL cursor points to a row in the SELECT statement's result table.

The statements effecting cursors are

1. DECLARE <*cursor name*> The DECLARE statement is used prior to the SELECT to associate the named cursor with the results table of the SELECT statement.
2. OPEN <*cursor name*> opens the cursor.
3. FETCH <*cursor name*> INTO <*memory variable list*> gets the next row from the results table and puts it into the named memory variables.
4. CLOSE <*cursor name*> closes the cursor.

The following simple program uses a SELECT to generate a results table. The DO WHILE loop in conjunction with the FETCH is used so that in each iteration of the loop one row from the results table is read into memory variables and those memory variables output on the screen. When the end of the results table is reached, the system memory variable sqlcode will be equal to zero and the loop will be EXITed.

```
* cursor.prs

* step 1: declare the cursor for the select statement
DECLARE test CURSOR FOR
SELECT region,officename,sales
FROM region;

* step 2: open the cursor
OPEN test;

* step 3: use a DO WHILE loop to fetch rows one at a time
DO WHILE .T.
  FETCH test INTO mregion,moffice,msales;
  * test if any more rows in result table
    IF sqlcode=0
        ? mregion+' '+moffice+STR(msales)
    ELSE
        EXIT
    ENDIF
ENDDO

* step 4:close the cursor
CLOSE test;
```

CAUTION: When using embedded SQL code in a .prs file, all lines of SQL code must end with a semicolon. If they do not, the compiler will not necessarily generate an error message, and the program will *NOT* run correctly.

EXAMPLES OF USING SQL

The following shows the solutions to the problem for extracting data from a single file, discussed in chapter 8. These examples are given to compare native dBASE syntax with SQL syntax.

Since the intent of SQL is to isolate the end user from the data, SQL gives users very little ability to optimize their queries. Generally the SQL approaches shown in this chapter will be much slower in execution than the optimized dBASE approaches shown in the chapter on extracting summary data from a file. One of the few types of optimizing that can be done involves the creation of indexes using the approach described above.

In this section the term *field* is used interchangeably with *column*, and *file* is used interchangeably with *table*.

Assume a file with the following structure and indexed on region:

```
Structure for database: C:region.dbf
Number of data records:          5
Date of last update    : 12/06/87
Field      Field Name        Type          Width      Dec
   1       REGION            Character         2
   2       OFFICENAME        Character        15
   3       SALES             Numeric          10
   4       NUM_EMPL          Numeric           6
** Total **                                   34
```

With sample records such as the following:

Record#	REGION	OFFICENAME	SALES	NUM_EMPL
1	AT	Atlanta Main	1100000	98
2	AT	West Side	1800000	105
3	BO	Boston Main	3400000	210
4	CH	Downtown	3900000	280
5	CH	Evanston	1500000	110

What is the most efficient way to do the following?

NOTE: For these queries to work, the DBDEFINE command described earlier in this chapter must be used to convert the .dbf file to an SQL table.

1. Show the total sales for each region.

```
SELECT region,SUM(sales)
FROM region
GROUP BY region;
```

This command essentially subtotals sales by region. The GROUP BY region clause is used in conjunction with the SUM(sales) in the SELECT clause to cause sales to be subtotaled on region. Note that in the SELECT clause, region is the same field or column as the GROUP BY, and SUM(sales) is a command that aggregates sales figures for each region.

2. Show the number of employees for each region.

```
SELECT region,SUM(num_empl)
FROM region
GROUP BY region;
```

This example uses the same approach as number 1, but subtotals number of employees by region.

3. Show the sales per employee for each office.

```
SELECT officename,sales/num_empl
FROM region;
```

This example uses a SELECT to list the contents of the office name field and the result of the sales field divided by number of employees for each record.

4. Show the average sales per employee for each region.

```
SELECT region,AVG(sales/num_empl)
FROM region
GROUP BY region;
```

This example uses the same principle as example 1, but substitutes the function AVG for SUM.

5. Show the average sales per office for each region.

```
SELECT region,AVG(sales)
FROM region
GROUP BY region;
```

This example uses the AVG() function to aggregate the average sales per office by region.

6. Show the offices in the Chicago region with sales greater than $1 million.

```
SELECT officename,sales
FROM region
WHERE sales > 1000000 AND region='CH';
```

This example shows a simple listing of all rows that meet the selection criteria of sales greater than 1,000,000 and region ='CH'.

7. Show the office in the Chicago region with the highest sales/employee.

```
SELECT officename,sales/num_empl
FROM region
WHERE region='CH' AND
```

```
sales/num_empl >=ALL(SELECT sales/num_empl
                     FROM region
                     WHERE region='CH');
```

This example uses a subquery to find the office in the Chicago region where sales/num_empl is greater than or equal to *sales/num_empl* for any office in the Chicago region.

8. Show the office in the Chicago region with the lowest sales per employee.

```
SELECT officename,sales/num_empl
FROM region
WHERE region='CH' AND
sales/num_empl <=ALL(SELECT sales/num_empl
                     FROM region
                     WHERE region='CH');
```

This example uses the same approach as the previous one except that the *greater than* (>) sign is replaced with a *less than* (<) sign.

9. Show the offices in the Chicago region with above-average sales.

```
SELECT officename,sales
FROM region
WHERE region='CH' AND sales >=(SELECT AVG(sales)
                               FROM region
                               WHERE region='CH');
```

This approach again makes use of a subquery. First a subquery is done to calculate the average sales for offices in the Chicago region. Then an outer query is done to select the offices with sales greater than or equal to the average previously calculated.

10. Show the offices in the Chicago region with below-average sales.

```
SELECT officename,sales
FROM region
WHERE region='CH' AND sales >=(SELECT AVG(sales)
                               FROM region
                               WHERE region='CH');
```

The solution is the same as the previous example except the greater than sign is replaced with a less than sign.

11. Show the offices by region in order of ascending sales.

```
SELECT region,officename,sales
FROM region
ORDER BY region,sales;
```

This command uses the ORDER by clause to order by concatenated fields. The fields to be ordered by are separated by commas. Ascending order is assumed.

12. Show the offices by region in order of ascending sales per employee.

```
SELECT region,officename,sales/num_empl
FROM region
ORDER BY 1,3
```

This example shows another syntax of the ORDER BY clause. In this case *1,3* means to order by the first column name in the SELECT clause plus the third column name in the SELECT clause.

NOTE: If the *num_empl* field is zero for any record, a *numeric overflow* error message will be generated.

13. Generate a list of offices alphabetically by region.

```
SELECT region,officename
FROM region
ORDER BY region,officename
```

This approach uses an ORDER BY clause to order by two character fields.

Chapter 14

dBASE FILES AND OTHER FILE TYPES

I've never seen an ASCII file I couldn't import into dBASE.
—Unidentified dBASE programmer

THE dBASE FILE HEADER

This section covers how a dBASE file is stored on the disk. It is helpful to understand how dBASE actually stores data in a .dbf file to understand how to interface a dBASE file with other file types. Also, sometimes dBASE files become corrupted and it is helpful to be able to look directly at the file.

When the DISPLAY STRUCTURE command is executed, this display appears:

```
Structure for database: C:addrlist.dbf
Number of data records:        4
Date of last update:    01/06/89
Field   Field Name   Type        Width   Dec
    1   LNAME        Character      15
    2   FNAME        Character      12
    3   STRADDR      Character      20
    4   CITY         Character      15
    5   STATE        Character       2
    6   ZIP          Character       5
    7   AMT          Numeric        10     2
    8   DATE         Date            8
** Total **                         88
```

The contents of the file are shown in Figure 14-1.

Using a disk editor, we can see how the data is actually stored on the disk. Each dBASE .dbf file begins with a file header that contains information about the file. After the file header the actual data is stored in the file.

Figure 14-2 contains the beginning of the dBASE file header. The first byte contains 03 hex to indicate that it is a dBASE III file without a memo field. If the file had a memo field, this byte would contain 83 hex.

The byte assignments are

byte 0	dBASE version number 02 dBASE II 03 dBASE III or IV without memo field 83 dBASE III with memo field 8B dBASE IV with memo field
bytes 1–3	Date of last update yy mm dd expressed in hex
bytes 4–7	Number of records in the file
bytes 8–9	Length of file header in bytes
bytes 10–11	Length of each record
bytes 12–31	Reserved
bytes 32–*n*	Listing of fields

NOTE: dBASE IV files with SQL tables will have other values in byte 0.

```
Record#  LNAME           FNAME  STRADDR            CITY      STATE
 ZIP          AMT  DATE
      1  Smith           John   123 Main           Berkeley  CA
 947Ø4     123.12  Ø1/31/88
      2  Jones           Frank  234 Third Street   Oakland   CA
 947ØØ      9Ø.ØØ  Ø1/31/88
      3 *Anderson        Mary   5678 Third Street  Berkeley  CA
 947Ø6      75.ØØ  Ø1/31/88
      4  Howard          John   981 Center Street  Berkeley  CA
 947Ø4      66.ØØ  Ø1/31/88
```

Figure 14-1. LIST of file contents.

```
                                                                    Vol Label=None
 ------------------------------- File View/Edit Service ------------------------------
Path=C:\DBNEW\A*.DBF
File=ADDRLIST.DBF      Relative sector being displayed is: 0000000

Displacement  ----------------- Hex codes ------------------         ASCII value
 0000(0000)   03 59 01 06 04 00 00 00 21 01 58 00 00 00 00 00   ♥Y☺♠♦      !☺X
 0016(0010)   00 00 00 00 00 00 00 00 00 00 00 00 00 00 00 00
 0032(0020)   4C 4E 41 4D 45 00 00 00 00 00 00 43 09 00 A7 57   LNAME        G°  ºW
 0048(0030)   0F 00 00 00 01 00 00 00 00 00 00 00 00 00 00 00   ╪     ☺
 0064(0040)   46 4E 41 4D 45 00 00 00 00 00 00 43 18 00 A7 57   FNAME        C↑  ºW
 0080(0050)   0C 00 00 00 01 00 00 00 00 00 00 00 00 00 00 00   ♀     ☺
 0096(0060)   53 54 52 41 44 44 52 00 00 00 00 43 24 00 A7 57   STRADDR      C$  ºW
 0112(0070)   14 00 00 00 01 00 00 00 00 00 00 00 00 00 00 00   ¶     ☺
 0128(0080)   43 49 54 59 00 00 00 00 00 00 00 43 38 00 A7 57   CITY         C8  ºW
 0144(0090)   0F 00 00 00 01 00 00 00 00 00 00 00 00 00 00 00   ╪     ☺
 0160(00A0)   53 54 41 54 45 00 00 00 00 00 00 43 47 00 A7 57   STATE        CG  ºW
 0176(00B0)   02 00 00 00 01 00 00 00 00 00 00 00 00 00 00 00   ☻     ☺
 0192(00C0)   5A 49 50 00 00 00 00 00 00 00 00 43 49 00 A7 57   ZIP          CI  ºW
 0208(00D0)   05 00 00 00 01 00 00 00 00 00 00 00 00 00 00 00   ♣     ☺
 0224(00E0)   41 4D 54 00 00 00 00 00 00 00 00 4E 4E 00 A7 57   AMT          NN  ºW
 0240(00F0)   0A 02 00 00 01 00 00 00 00 00 00 00 00 00 00 00   ◙☻    ☺

Home=beg of file/disk   End=end of file/disk
ESC=Exit  PgDn=forward  PgUp=back  F1=toggle mode  F2=chg sector num  F3=edit
```

Figure 14-2. dBASE file header.

CHANGES IN dBASE IV

dBASE IV does not change the structure of the file header except to use the reserved bytes for various flags. Bytes 12–31, which are reserved in dBASE III PLUS, are used in the following manner in dBASE IV:

bytes 12–13	Reserved
bytes 14	Incomplete transaction flag
byte 15	Encryption flag
bytes 16–27	Used by dBASE on LAN
bytes 28	Flag for production index, 01 if production .mdx exists, 0 if not
bytes 29–31	Reserved

Because dBASE IV uses only bytes that are reserved in dBASE III PLUS, .dbf files can be passed between dBASE III PLUS and dBASE IV if they do not have a memo field or floating point field.

In a dBASE IV .dbf file, the first byte(03) is the same as dBASE III PLUS for .dbf files that do not contain memo fields. .dbf files that do not contain memo fields can be interchanged between dBASE III PLUS and dBASE IV. For dBASE IV .dbf files with memo fields, the first byte is 8B hex so that they can't be used in dBASE III PLUS.

dBASE IV .dbf files with memo fields can be converted to files readable by dBASE III PLUS using the commands

```
USE <file name>
COPY TO <new file name> DBMEMO3
```

In dBASE IV files containing floating point fields but not memo fields, the first byte is set to 03 so that dBASE III PLUS can open the file. However, dBASE III PLUS does not know how to handle the floating point field.

HEXADECIMAL NUMBERS

To understand a dBASE file header, it is useful to understand the hexadecimal number system. The hexadecimal, or base 16, numbering system is used to conveniently represent a single 8-bit byte with 2 digits. The base 10 number system counts from 0 to 9, and the hexadecimal system counts from 0 to 15.

Decimal	*Hex*
0	0
1	1
2	2
3	3
4	4
5	5
6	6
7	7
8	8
9	9
10	A
11	B

12	C
13	D
14	E
15	F

The letters *A–F* are used to represent *10–15* in the base 10 system.

By comparing the dBASE file header with the output of the DISP STRUCTURE command, we can understand how dBASE stores information on the disk.

Bytes 1–3 contain the date of last update year, month, and day; 59 is the hex equivalent of 89, 01 represents the month, and 06 represents the day.

Bytes 4–7 contain the number of records in the file. Notice from the DISP STRUCTURE that there are four records in the .dbf file and that four appears in byte four. Notice that the least significant part of the number appears first.

Bytes 8–9 contain the number of bytes in the file header. dBASE supports variable length file headers dependent on the number of fields.

Bytes 10–11 contain the number of bytes per record. From the DISPLAY STRUCTURE output there are 88 bytes in this record. Fifty hex is equal to eighty decimal.

Byte 32 begins the information about the individual fields. First the field name is listed (up to ten characters).

Thirty-two bytes are reserved for each field:

The first row of bytes for each field

0–10	field name
11	field type in ASCII: C,N,L,M,D (F in dBASE IV)
12–15	reserved

The second row of bytes

16	length of field in binary
17	number of decimal places if numeric field
18–19	reserved
20	work area id
21–31	reserved bytes

Next the actual data is stored as shown in Figure 14-3.

Note that the data is stored in fixed length field format with fields being padded with blanks. A byte is left at the beginning of each record for the deletion flag.

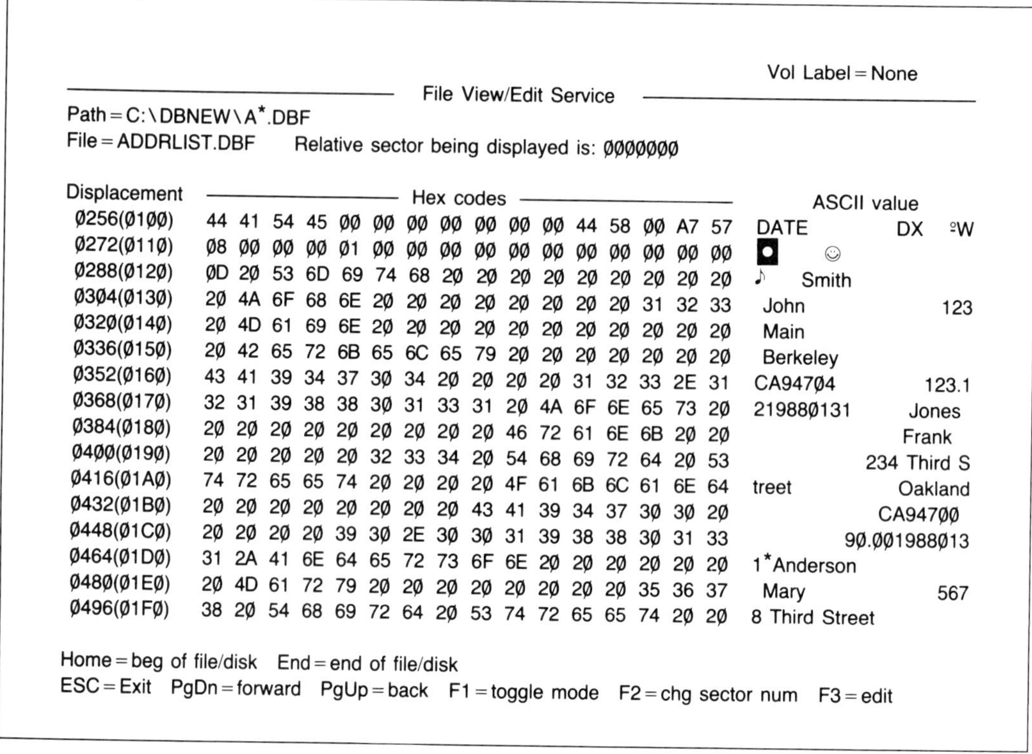

```
                                                                         Vol Label=None
 ______________________________________ File View/Edit Service ____________________________________
Path=C:\DBNEW\A*.DBF
File=ADDRLIST.DBF     Relative sector being displayed is: ØØØØØØØ

Displacement  ______________ Hex codes ______________________            ASCII value
 Ø256(Ø1ØØ)   44 41 54 45 ØØ ØØ ØØ ØØ ØØ ØØ ØØ 44 58 ØØ A7 57   DATE            DX  ºW
 Ø272(Ø11Ø)   Ø8 ØØ ØØ ØØ Ø1 ØØ ØØ ØØ ØØ ØØ ØØ ØØ ØØ ØØ ØØ ØØ   ◘     ☺
 Ø288(Ø12Ø)   ØD 2Ø 53 6D 69 74 68 2Ø 2Ø 2Ø 2Ø 2Ø 2Ø 2Ø 2Ø 2Ø   ♪  Smith
 Ø3Ø4(Ø13Ø)   2Ø 4A 6F 68 6E 2Ø 2Ø 2Ø 2Ø 2Ø 2Ø 2Ø 2Ø 31 32 33    John              123
 Ø32Ø(Ø14Ø)   2Ø 4D 61 69 6E 2Ø 2Ø 2Ø 2Ø 2Ø 2Ø 2Ø 2Ø 2Ø 2Ø 2Ø    Main
 Ø336(Ø15Ø)   2Ø 42 65 72 6B 65 6C 65 79 2Ø 2Ø 2Ø 2Ø 2Ø 2Ø 2Ø    Berkeley
 Ø352(Ø16Ø)   43 41 39 34 37 3Ø 34 2Ø 2Ø 2Ø 2Ø 31 32 33 2E 31   CA947Ø4          123.1
 Ø368(Ø17Ø)   32 31 39 38 38 3Ø 31 33 31 2Ø 4A 6F 6E 65 73 2Ø   219880131    Jones
 Ø384(Ø18Ø)   2Ø 2Ø 2Ø 2Ø 2Ø 2Ø 2Ø 2Ø 2Ø 46 72 61 6E 6B 2Ø 2Ø                Frank
 Ø4ØØ(Ø19Ø)   2Ø 2Ø 2Ø 2Ø 2Ø 32 33 34 2Ø 54 68 69 72 64 2Ø 53           234 Third S
 Ø416(Ø1AØ)   74 72 65 65 74 2Ø 2Ø 2Ø 2Ø 4F 61 6B 6C 61 6E 64   treet        Oakland
 Ø432(Ø1BØ)   2Ø 2Ø 2Ø 2Ø 2Ø 2Ø 2Ø 2Ø 43 41 39 34 37 3Ø 3Ø 2Ø                CA947ØØ
 Ø448(Ø1CØ)   2Ø 2Ø 2Ø 2Ø 39 3Ø 2E 3Ø 3Ø 31 39 38 38 3Ø 31 33            9Ø.ØØ1988Ø13
 Ø464(Ø1DØ)   31 2A 41 6E 64 65 72 73 6F 6E 2Ø 2Ø 2Ø 2Ø 2Ø 2Ø   1*Anderson
 Ø48Ø(Ø1EØ)   2Ø 4D 61 72 79 2Ø 2Ø 2Ø 2Ø 2Ø 2Ø 2Ø 2Ø 35 36 37    Mary              567
 Ø496(Ø1FØ)   38 2Ø 54 68 69 72 64 2Ø 53 74 72 65 65 74 2Ø 2Ø   8 Third Street

Home=beg of file/disk   End=end of file/disk
ESC=Exit  PgDn=forward  PgUp=back  F1=toggle mode  F2=chg sector num  F3=edit
```

Figure 14-3. How data are stored.

INTERFACING WITH FOREIGN FILES

dBASE allows easy interfacing with ASCII files that have certain field structures. Files can be exported from dBASE to another application by using variants of the COPY TO command. Conversely, dBASE can be imported from other applications by using variants of the APPEND FROM command.

To see the effect of various variants of the COPY TO command, we execute the commands

```
USE addrlist
COPY TO address.txt SDF
TYPE address.txt
```

When the address.txt file is typed, it will appear as shown in Figure 14–4.

Smith	John	123 Main	Berkeley	CA94704	123.12
Jones	Frank	234 Third Street	Oakland	CA94700	90.00
Anderson	Mary	5678 Third Street	Berkeley	CA94706	75.00
Howard	John	981 Center Street	Berkeley	CA94704	66.00

Figure 14-4. An ASCII file with fixed length fields.

In dBASE, SDF refers to fixed length fields. Each field is fixed length and padded with blanks. The disk image of this file is shown in Figure 14-5.

Note that the structure of this file is very similar to the way data is stored in a .dbf file. The SDF file differs from a .dbf file in that it has no file header and there is a carriage return and line feed between each record.

Another variant of the COPY TO command involves using the DELIMITED option.

```
USE addrlist
COPY TO addrdel.txt DELIMITED
TYPE address.txt
```

In this sequence of commands, the SDF at the end of the COPY command is changed to DELIMITED. The results of this type command are shown in Figure 14-6.

Note that fields are not padded with blanks, but instead the content of each field is contained in quotes and separated by commas. Users of the MailMerge feature of Micropro's WordStar will recognize this as the format for a MailMerge address list file.

Users of MailMerge may wish to take their MailMerge file, import it into dBASE for indexing or sorting, and then export it back to MailMerge.

IMPORTING FOREIGN FILES

Importing foreign files is done through using variations of the APPEND FROM command. APPEND FROM is used most frequently to APPEND FROM a .dbf file. When APPENDing FROM a .dbf file, dBASE looks at the field names of the open file and of the file being APPENDED from. If the field names match, data is transferred from the file being APPENDED FROM to the dBASE file that is in use.

To import data from the fixed length field file shown in Figure 14-4 above, the following steps can be taken.

```
                                                                    Vol Label = None
 ________________________________ File View/Edit Service ________________________________
Path = C:\DBNEW\A*.TXT
File = ADDRLIST.TXT     Relative sector being displayed is: ØØØØØØØ

Displacement  ---------------- Hex codes ----------------------    ASCII value
ØØØØ(ØØØØ)  53 6D 69 74 68 2Ø 2Ø 2Ø 2Ø 2Ø 2Ø 2Ø 2Ø 2Ø 2Ø 4A  Smith              J
ØØ16(ØØ1Ø)  6F 68 6E 2Ø 2Ø 2Ø 2Ø 2Ø 2Ø 2Ø 2Ø 31 32 33 2Ø 4D  ohn              123 M
ØØ32(ØØ2Ø)  61 69 6E 2Ø 2Ø 2Ø 2Ø 2Ø 2Ø 2Ø 2Ø 2Ø 2Ø 2Ø 2Ø 42  ain                  B
ØØ48(ØØ3Ø)  65 72 6B 65 6C 65 79 2Ø 2Ø 2Ø 2Ø 2Ø 2Ø 2Ø 43 41  erkeley             CA
ØØ64(ØØ4Ø)  39 34 37 3Ø 34 2Ø 2Ø 2Ø 2Ø 31 32 33 2E 31 32 ØD  947Ø4           123.12♪
ØØ8Ø(ØØ5Ø)  ØA 4A 6F 6E 65 73 2Ø 2Ø 2Ø 2Ø 2Ø 2Ø 2Ø 2Ø 2Ø 2Ø  ◙Jones
ØØ96(ØØ6Ø)  46 72 61 6E 6B 2Ø 2Ø 2Ø 2Ø 2Ø 2Ø 2Ø 32 33 34 2Ø  Frank             234
Ø112(ØØ7Ø)  54 68 69 72 64 2Ø 53 74 72 65 65 74 2Ø 2Ø 2Ø 2Ø  Third Street
Ø128(ØØ8Ø)  4F 61 6B 6C 61 6E 64 2Ø 2Ø 2Ø 2Ø 2Ø 2Ø 2Ø 2Ø 43  Oakland              C
Ø144(ØØ9Ø)  41 39 34 37 3Ø 3Ø 2Ø 2Ø 2Ø 2Ø 2Ø 39 3Ø 2E 3Ø 3Ø  A947ØØ           9Ø.ØØ
Ø16Ø(ØØAØ)  ØD ØA 41 6E 64 65 72 73 6F 6E 2Ø 2Ø 2Ø 2Ø 2Ø 2Ø  ♪◙Anderson
Ø176(ØØBØ)  2Ø 4D 61 72 79 2Ø 2Ø 2Ø 2Ø 2Ø 2Ø 2Ø 2Ø 35 36 37   Mary              567
Ø192(ØØCØ)  38 2Ø 54 68 69 72 64 2Ø 53 74 72 65 65 74 2Ø 2Ø  8 Third Street
Ø2Ø8(ØØDØ)  2Ø 42 65 72 6B 65 6C 65 79 2Ø 2Ø 2Ø 2Ø 2Ø 2Ø 2Ø   Berkeley
Ø224(ØØEØ)  43 41 39 34 37 3Ø 36 2Ø 2Ø 2Ø 2Ø 2Ø 37 35 2E 3Ø  CA947Ø6           75.Ø
Ø24Ø(ØØFØ)  3Ø ØD ØA 48 6F 77 61 72 64 2Ø 2Ø 2Ø 2Ø 2Ø 2Ø 2Ø  Ø♪◙Howard

Home = beg of file/disk   End = end of file/disk
ESC = Exit  PgDn = forward  PgUp = back  F1 = toggle mode  F2 = chg sector num  F3 = edit
```

Figure 14-5. Disk image of ASCII file with fixed length fields.

1. Create a .dbf file with the fields in the same order as in the fixed length field file and with the lengths *exactly* equal to the lengths of the fields in the SDF file.

2. USE the file created in step 1 above.

3. APPEND FROM address.txt SDF

```
"Smith","John","123 Main","Berkeley","CA","947Ø4",123.12,1988Ø131
"Jones","Frank","234 Third Street","Oakland","CA","947ØØ",9Ø.ØØ,1988Ø131
"Anderson","Mary","5678 Third Street","Berkeley","CA","947Ø6",75.ØØ,1988Ø131
"Howard","John","981 Center Street","Berkeley","CA","947Ø4",66.ØØ,1988Ø131
```

Figure 14-6. An ASCII file in delimited format.

NOTE: dBASE likes to see a .txt extension on the file being imported with the SDF or DELIMITED option.

When this APPEND FROM command is executed, dBASE looks at the field length of the the first field in the .dbf file and reads that number of bytes from the fixed length field file into that field. Thus it is critically important that the field structure of the .dbf file exactly match the field structure of the file being imported.

IMPORTING A DELIMITED FILE

To import the contents of the delimited file shown in Figure 14-6 the following steps must be performed.

1. Create a .dbf file with the fields in the same order as in the fixed length field file and with the field lengths equal to the maximum length of the contents of the fields in the delimited file.

2. USE the file created in step 1 above.

3. APPEND FROM address.txt DELI

When this form of the APPEND FROM command is executed, dBASE takes the characters found between the first two quotes and puts them into the first field of the .dbf file. If what is contained between the quotes is too long for the field in the .dbf file, the excess is truncated.

GENERIC TRANSFER OF A SPREADSHEET FILE TO dBASE

Spreadsheets created in Lotus 1-2-3, Release 1A, can be imported into dBASE III PLUS after creating a .dbf file with a field for each column in the spreadsheet, by using the command

APPEND FROM <*spread sheet file name*> WKS

If a spreadsheet other than Lotus, or a version of Lotus that is not supported by dBASE, is used, the following method will work to transfer a spreadsheet file to dBASE. It uses the approach of printing a spreadsheet to a file, which will create an ASCII file with fixed length fields. A dBASE file can be created with the appropriate structure, and an APPEND FROM SDF can be used to import the contents of the ASCII file into dBASE.

In Lotus or Other Spreadsheet

1. Go into the Print menu and set the left and top margins to 0. If this step is not performed, blank records will appear at the beginning of the file and blank spaces at the left will effect which data is put into which field.
2. Print the spreadsheet to a file.

In dBASE

3. Create a file with the proper structure and each field equal to the width of the spreadsheet column.
4. Use the newfile.
5. APPEND FROM sprd.txt SDF.

Now list the records in the new file to make sure that each is positioned in the proper field.

CHANGES IN dBASE IV

dBASE IV adds several new options to the COPY TO and APPEND FROM commands that allow importing and exporting other types of files.

Supported in dBASE III PLUS	
Delimited	Delimited as shown above
SDF	Fixed length fields
DIF	VisiCalc format
SYLK	Multiplan Spreadsheets
WKS	Lotus release 1A
Added in dBASE IV	
DBASEII	dBASE II
FW2	Framework II
RPD	RapidFile

THE IMPORT AND EXPORT COMMANDS IN dBASE IV

The IMPORT and EXPORT commands have been greatly enhanced in dBASE IV. In dBASE III PLUS they were used only for interfacing with PFS file type files. In dBASE IV numerous file types are supported. The advantage of using IMPORT instead of APPEND FROM is that IMPORT automatically creates a dBASE IV .dbf file with the structure of the file being imported. The APPEND FROM requires that the file be created before the APPEND FROM is executed.

File types supported in dBASE IV include

PFS	PFS file
DBASEII	dBASE II
FW2	Framework II
RPD	Rapid File
WK1	Lotus release 2 (IMPORT only)

Note that IMPORT supports a WK1 format for Lotus release 2, while the APPEND FROM options support WKS for release 1 of Lotus. The syntax for importing a dBASE II file is

```
IMPORT FROM dbii.dbf DBASEII
```

Be sure that the extension of the file being imported is explicitly stated. This import command will do the following:

1. Read the structure of the dBASE II file and create a dBASE IV file with the same structure.

2. Append the records from the dBASE II file into the new file.

Chapter 15

SELECTED TOPICS

Next year will be the year of the LAN.
—Bill Gates from speech given in 1984

INTERFACING WITH DOS

It is helpful to understand how dBASE interfaces with DOS and how DOS type functions can be performed within dBASE.

They Say That Backing Up Is Hard to Do

To avoid possible loss of data, users must be forced to backup the appropriate files at the end of each work session. The necessity for backing up can be explained as insurance—a small investment of time to prevent a longer time spent re-entering data if the hard disk fails.

dBASE applications consist primarily of these types of files:

.dbf files in that the actual data is stored
.ndx files that contain indexes
.prg files that contain programs

The only files that need to be backed up on a daily basis are the .dbf files (and .dbt files if memo fields are used). It is a waste of time to backup index files. A better approach is to have a menu option to recreate all indexes. This option not only allows for recreating indexes when necessary, but it also forces the program to include documentation for all index names and keys within the program. The programmer can backup .prg files when changes are made.

The programmer must insure that users are forced to backup their data after each posting session.

Forcing Backup by Using the DOS Utility

One approach to backup is to call the dBASE program from within a DOS batch file, which then forces backup as the program is exited. The batch file might look like this:

```
dBASE main
\dos\backup *.dbf a:
```

This approach would force users to backup their .dbf files at the conclusion of each session. Users would be prompted by the backup command to insert as many floppy disks as necessary to accomplish the backup.

Always Keep at Least Two Backup Copies

To provide greater insurance against hard disk problems as well as floppy disk failure, users must maintain two sets of sequentially numbered floppy disks. One set is labeled *even*, the other set is labeled *odd*. Users are instructed to backup to the *even* set on even days and to the *odd* set on odd days. The procedure insures that should both a hard disk failure occur and a bad floppy disk be present in one set of disks, the other set of disks will be at most one day behind.

Recovering from a Hard Disk Crash

Should a hard disk crash occur, the following steps can be used to recover.

1. Recreate the subdirectory for the application
2. Recopy the program files onto the disk
3. Use the DOS command

```
RESTORE a: c:*.dbf
```

4. Execute recreate index option written in the program

Limitations of the DOS Backup Utility

The DOS backup utility is best used in cases where there are relatively few floppies required to backup the data. For a project requiring many floppy disks to backup, it makes sense to use a faster commercial program to backup to floppies or to use some other media such as tape for a backup.

Using DOS Subdirectories to Separate Projects

If multiple projects are being worked on at the same time, it is important to separate those projects so that program crashes do not unnecessarily corrupt data and so there is no possibility of overwriting files with the same name. To accomplish this result, the subdirectory structure shown in Figure 15-1 can be used.

For each project being worked on, create a subdirectory that is a child of the subdirectory containing dBASE. Then perform the following steps in DOS.

1. Make the subdirectory for the project being worked on the current subdirectory.

```
C> cd \dbase\proj2
```

2. Set a path to the \dbase subdirectory

```
C> path=\dbase
```

3. Enter the dBASE program

```
C> dBASE
```

Now dBASE will interpret all commands involving files as if they refer to the subdirectory proj2. Any files that are created will be created in proj2.

```
                \proj1

\dbase          \proj2

                \proj3
```

Figure 15-1. Subdirectory structure.

Note that this approach is significantly different from using the SET PATH TO command in dBASE. If \dbase were the current DOS subdirectory and a SET PATH TO \proj2 was executed in dBASE, any files that were created would be created in the subdirectory \dbase. The SET PATH TO command in dBASE only tells dBASE where to look if a file cannot be found in the current DOS subdirectory. SET PATH TO does not change the subdirectory where files are created.

Running DOS Programs from within dBASE

dBASE provides the option of running DOS programs from dBASE using the RUN command. Two requirements must be observed to use the RUN command.

1. The RUN command works by loading a second copy of command.com into RAM memory. Thus command.com must be available to load. This can be a problem on floppy disk systems if the program disk does not contain command.com.

2. Sufficient RAM must be available in order to load a second copy of command.com.

Examples of Using RUN:

1. Change the system date

```
RUN date
```

2. Change the system time

```
RUN time
```

3. Get a DOS directory of the currently logged drive

```
RUN dir /p
```

4. Copy all .prg files to a floppy disk

```
RUN copy *.prg a:
```

The DOS Default Drive vs. the dBASE Default Drive

SET DEFAULT TO D: can be used to define the default drive to use for finding files. A path cannot be specified as part of the drive specification with this command. This command determines where any new files will be created and where files will be looked for before using the path established with SET PATH. The dBASE default supersedes the DOS default drive.

The DOS Path vs. the dBASE Path

Both dBASE and DOS can have separate paths set. The path is where DOS or dBASE looks for a file if it isn't found in the current subdirectory. When a file is created, it is always created in the current subdirectory. The path is only relevant when searching for files.

A path can be set to a separate drive. If most of the files to be used are in the logged directory on the hard disk but some files are on drive A SET PATH TO A: can be used to specify that drive A is to be searched for files not found on the hard disk.

DOS Functions from within dBASE

Some DOS type functions such as copying files can be performed from within dBASE without using the RUN command. However, the syntax of these commands is annoyingly different from the DOS syntax.

Directories

The dBASE DIR command defaults to displaying a listing of all .dbf files in the currently logged drive, showing the number of records in the file and the size of the file. DIR *.* shows the names of all files as does the DOS DIR command, but the dBASE version does not show the size of each file. DIR *.prg shows all .prg files but not their sizes. The dBASE DIR command does not show the file size or date of last update except for .dbf files.

Typing a File

The TYPE command displays the contents of a text file on the screen. The output can be directed to the printer by adding TO PRINT. Thus from within dBASE the program file main.prg can be printed out using the syntax

```
TYPE main.prg TO PRINT
```

Copying Files

The dBASE COPY TO command copies the currently open .dbf file to another file, record by record in index order, if an index is open. From within dBASE, whole files can be copied using the COPY FILE command.

```
COPY FILE file1 TO file2
```

Note that in contrast to the DOS COPY command, the TO must be explicitly specified. If safety is set on, a warning will appear if an attempt is made to copy to a file name that already exists.

Renaming Files

Files may be renamed from within dBASE by using the syntax

```
RENAME file1 TO file2
```

Erasing Files

Files may be deleted by using the ERASE command

```
ERASE file1
```

Speeding Up Opening Files

Part of the overhead of opening a file is the time required by DOS to find the file in the subdirectory, so removing all extraneous files from a subdirectory can speed up access time.

MACROS

All versions of dBASE have supported some level of macro substitution. Macro substitution allows substituting one value for another in a command line. Before a command line is parsed, the dBASE interpreter checks for a single ampersand. If one exists, it looks for a character type memory variable based on the name after the &. If a valid memory variable is found, it substitutes the contents of that memory variable into the command line.

Ashton-Tate has traditionally disliked the use of macros, presumably because it gives programmers too much power. For instance, in dBASE II macros could be nested two levels deep by using &&<memvar name>. In dBASE III PLUS the double ampersand symbol was used for in-line comments, signaling that nested macros would not be supported. In dBASE IV, users are warned that using & macros will slow down program execution. In dBASE IV another kind of macro—enclosing a memory variable name in parentheses—was introduced. In many cases, & macros are no longer needed, but in some cases they still are useful.

Some common uses of macros have been the following:

1. Using the contents of a memory variable as the argument for a FIND command.

```
mlname='Smith'
FIND &Smith
```

The SEEK command was introduced in dBASE III so that it wouldn't be necessary to use macros in this manner.

2. To create memory variable arrays.

```
ctr=1
DO WHILE ctr < 11
    dum='element'-LTRIM(STR(ctr))
    &dum=0
    ctr=ctr+1
ENDDO
```

This program will create 10 memory variables named *element1* through *element10* with each variable set to 0. The memory variable *ctr* is initialized as 1. With each pass through the DO WHILE loop, the memory variable *dum* is used to create the name of the next array element. The *macro*, *&dum*, is used to set each element to 0. The memory variable *ctr* is then incremented. This approach was needed to create memory variable arrays prior to dBASE IV. In dBASE IV real arrays are supported, so this approach is no longer needed.

3. To pass values to subroutines. In some cases general-purposes subroutines exist that must be executed in different contexts and then another program called. The following approach could be used.

```
DO proced1 WITH 'prog1'

PROCEDURE proced1
PARAMETERS prog
* <series of instructions>

DO &prog
```

This approach would result in doing the specified program, in this case prog1, at the conclusion of procedure proced1. This case would still require the use of macros in dBASE IV.

4. To test for the existence of a file. The FILE() command allows testing for the existence of a file. In dBASE III PLUS, the syntax required when the file name was stored in a memory variable was

```
memvar='file.dbf'
? FILE('&memvar')
```

In dBASE IV, the following syntax is supported:

```
? FILE(memvar)
```

meaning that & macros no longer have to be used in this instance.

INKEY

The dBASE INKEY function allows trapping input one keystroke at a time. However, one problem is that some keys such as the *left arrow* key are not always trapped properly. This bug makes the INKEY() function of limited value. The following program illustrates how the INKEY function works.

```
* inkey.prg
SET TALK OFF
* selected key values returned
* F1=28
* F2= -1
* F3= -2
* UP ARROW=5
* L ARROW= 19 SPORADIC
* R ARROW= 4
* D ARROW= 24
* INS=22
* display value of each key pressed on the screen
i=0
DO WHILE .NOT. i=27
    i=0
    @ ROW(),26 SAY 'INKEY() = '
```

```
    DO WHILE i=0
        i=INKEY()
    ENDDO
    ?? STR(i,3)
ENDDO
```

LOADING ASSEMBLY LANGUAGE MODULES

dBASE allows loading assembly language modules with the LOAD command and executing them with the CALL command. This approach applies only to binary files. .exe or .com files should be executed using the RUN command.

A simple example of a binary module involving a single DOS interrupt is a program to print the screen. The program can be created using the DOS debug utility in the following manner.

```
C:\DBNEW>debug
-n prscreen.bin
-e 100 cd 05 cb
-r cx
CX 0000
:3
-w
Writing 0003 bytes
-q
```

In dBASE the module can be loaded by typing

```
LOAD prscreen
```

To execute it within a program, the command is

```
CALL prscreen
```

When the module is no longer needed, it can be released with the command

```
RELEASE MODULE prscreen
```

NETWORKING

Companies often outgrow single-user applications and want to undertake networking, which involves sharing of data among users. Several elements must be present for networking to take place.

1. Physical linking among computers.
2. Systems software to manage the interchange of information among computers.
3. Applications software that supports networking.

Networking configurations are of several types:

1. Peer-to-Peer: Peer-to-peer networking allows users to share files on various hard disks.
2. Server: In this system a single computer is designated as the server. All the other computers on the network can access the files contained on the hard disk of the server.

This section will deal with server networks in which multiple work stations can access files on the server.

Advantages of Networking

Networking allows real-time updating of files by many users. A hotel reservation system might be thought of as one example. Each reservation agent on the system must be able to simultaneously sell rooms for any given day. However, if there is only one room left for a given day, multiple agents should not be allowed to sell the same room. Thus once one agent *locks* it, it should either be unavailable to other agents or flagged as being changed by another user.

dBASE III PLUS and Networks

Several types of locking are available in a data base system to make sure that information is not updated simultaneously by multiple users.

1. File locking locks an entire file. Ideally the entire file should be locked only when major updates are performed on the whole file, since individual records are not available to other users until the file is unlocked.
2. Record locking locks only a single record so that other users may access other records in the file.
3. Field locking locks only a single field of a single record.

Neither dBASE III PLUS nor dBASE IV supports field locking. However, both support record and file locking.

dBASE III PLUS provided facilities for networking at the applications software level. This was done through two main functions.

1. File locking in which an entire file could be locked by a single user while it was being processed.

2. Record locking in which a single record of a file could be locked. This type of locking is generally the most useful because many users could be accessing a single file at the same time, each accessing a single record one at a time.

A check could be performed on whether or not a record was locked by using the following syntax:

```
IF RLOCK()
    REPLACE <field1) WITH <mvar1>
    UNLOCK
ENDIF
```

RLOCK() returns a True if the record is not already locked and if it can be locked at this time. It then proceeds to lock the record. It returns a False if it is currently locked by another user.

The network environment is entered by using the SET command

```
SET EXCLUSIVE OFF
```

There were many problems with the way dBASE III PLUS handled networking.

1. If a user locked a record and forgot to unlock it, it was impossible to tell which user had locked it, and all other users would be shut out. The only alternative is to use the RETRY command to retry the operation until the record is unlocked.

2. Implementing certain common commands such as APPEND BLANK causes the entire file to be locked.

3. If a record was locked it was not only not possible to know who locked it, but it was also not possible to read it.

Network = Sharing + Security

The problem with networking is to allow a certain amount of data sharing but not too much sharing. Some of the situations to be avoided are

1. Two users trying to update the same record at the same time.
2. One user getting and relying on the information contained in a record while another user is changing that information.
3. Two users trying to lock the same record at exactly the same time—deadly embrace.
4. Users accessing information that they do not have authorization to access; for example, a clerk trying to access the record containing the president's compensation information.

Applications software that supports networking should address all of these problems.

Real Time vs. Batch

Computer applications are often divided into two types: real time and batch. In a real-time application all data must be updated instantaneously. One example is an airline or hotel reservation system, where it is critical to know at any given time how many seats are available on any flight or if a certain room is available on a specified night.

By contrast, accounting applications are often done in batch mode. When a month is closed all the transactions from that month are accumulated and the financial statements prepared. Payroll is a batch application—at the end of each pay period, all of the payroll data is accumulated and the checks are issued. If employees take orders, it is often possible for clerks to accumulate their orders into temporary files and to have the temporary files posted to the master file overnight, if it is not critical to know the status of an order placed the same day.

Generally, real time applications are much more difficult to implement than batch applications.

In a true batch system, some level of data sharing can be accomplished without a local area network. For instance, in the order taking example, each work station could generate a temporary file for that day's orders. Each night the temporary files are posted to the master file, which is then transferred back to each work station to allow checking on the status of orders. The actual transfer of data is accomplished by transferring floppy disks between machines. This *sneaker network* approach is utilized by many smaller companies.

Design gets more difficult when multiple users will be reading and writing to the same records at the same time. If all updates are batched and multiple users are reading the same records at once, design is not a problem.

Access Levels

The question of which user can access which records is addressed through the assignment of an access level, using the PROTECT command. Each user is assigned an access level including levels of access to given files. The access level can be tested by using the ACCESS() function before a given user is allowed access to a given record.

Changes in dBASE IV

dBASE IV locks a record automatically when it is being accessed in multi-user mode. However, this default lock does not keep other users from accessing the record in read only mode. In fact, if user 1 is changing the record and user 2 is looking at it, the contents of user 1's changes can appear on user 2's screen. The command SET REFRESH TO <*n*> determines how often (in seconds) the updates made by user 1 are written to the file so that they will appear on user 2's screen.

dBASE IV gives the programmer more flexibility in the level of locking to be used. In dBASE III PLUS once a record was locked, no other user could even look at it. In dBASE IV, if it is locked by one user, it can be looked at by another user.

With such an approach, however, what happens if one user is changing a record while another user is generating a report? How accurate will the report be? The default in dBASE IV allows the report to be generated while users are changing records, meaning that the report may be out of date by the time it is generated.

The SET LOCK ON/off command controls whether automatic locking takes place when read only commands such as AVERAGE, SUM, CALCULATE, COPY, and REPORT are executed.

SET REFRESH TO

SET REFRESH works with the BROWSE and EDIT commands in multi-user modes. One user could be BROWSEing records while another user is changing records. SET REFRESH TO specifies the number of seconds between checks to see if data have been changed. The range is 1 to 3600 seconds and the default is 0.

CONVERTing Files

dBASE IV offers a new CONVERT command that adds a field named *_dbaselock* to a file. If this field is added, various other functions can be used to get the lock status of each record.

CHANGE() Returns a logical True if the contents of the current record in the open .dbf file in the currently selected area have been changed since they were read from disk.

LKSYS(<*n*>) Returns either the time of the record lock, date of lock, or the ID of the user who last locked the record or file based on the passed argument:

0	Time the lock was placed
1	Date the lock was placed
2	Name of user who placed lock

Since in dBASE IV users can view records locked by another user, if a file is CONVERTed, the LKSYS() function can be used to determine if the record is being changed by another user.

BEGIN TRANSACTION...END TRANSACTION

The BEGIN TRANSACTION...END TRANSACTION construct discussed in the chapter on transaction processing is useful in a multi-user environment. If a transaction is in progress on a file, another user looking at the file can be informed that the file is being changed and may not be quite up to date. Also, if a transaction aborts abnormally, the ROLLBACK command allows the file to be returned to its previous condition.

COMPLETED() Tests whether a transaction has been successfully completed.

ISMARKED([alias]) Returns a True if a transaction is in progress.

Since, in a multi-user environment different, stations can be performing different transactions on the same file, the ISMARKED() function can be used to check whether a given .dbf file has the transaction flag set, meaning that another user is in the process of changing it.

Ashton-Tate seems to express doubt about the reliability of the ROLLBACK command by suggesting in the manual that all files be backed up prior to initiating a transaction.

If a transaction aborts abnormally and the ROLLBACK command is not issued, the RESET command should be used to reset the transaction flag in the .dbf file header.

Other Network Functions

NETWORK() Returns a logical True if dBASE is currently running on a network and a logical False if it is not.

LOCK() Now allows locking multiple records with a single line command. Fifty simultaneous locks are now possible. LOCK() does not prevent a locked record from being read while locked. If a record number list is not specified, then an attempt is made to lock the current record.

USER() Returns the name of the user logged into PROTECT.

Chapter 16

USING THE NEW dBASE IV FEATURES

Nothing quite new is perfect.
—*Cicero,* Brutus

dBASE IV provides various menuing options to help the programmer design "flashy"-looking front ends. Chapter 11 presented the basics of the new menuing options and compared them with the old-fashioned dBASE menu. This chapter shows how to use the new menuing options to access records and how to use other features of dBASE IV presented in earlier chapters.

USING POP-UP MENUS TO POINT AND SHOOT AT RECORDS

This section will show how to use dBASE IV pop-up menus so that the menu options are records in a file. A record can be selected by highlighting it on the menu and pressing Enter. The example will make use of this .dbf file.

```
Structure for database: C:\DBNEW\VENDOR.DBF
Number of data records:         135
Date of last update:     12/09/88
Field    Field Name     Type        Width     Dec     Index
   1     VENDNO         Character       5                 Y
   2     VENDNAME       Character      26                 N
```

3	DEFAUAMT	Numeric	10	2	N
4	DEFAUACCT	Character	5		N
5	STRADDR	Character	25		N
6	CITY	Character	15		N
7	STATE	Character	2		N
8	ZIP	Character	5		N
** Total **			94		

It is possible with pop-up menus to allow users to select records by using the point and shoot technique. This feature allows programmers to design their own front ends for programs. This program shows how.

```
* vendpop.prg
USE vendor
DEFINE WINDOW show FROM 17,0 TO 22,79
DO showvend WITH 10,20
PROCEDURE showvend
* popup menus for accounts payable example
PARAMETERS start,number
CLEAR
* step 1: define pop-up name and location on screen
DEFINE POPUP vendor FROM 1,40 TO 12,79
* step 2: define the prompt for each bar of the light bar menu
N=1
GOTO start
DO WHILE N <=NUMBER .AND. .NOT. EOF()
    DEFINE BAR n OF vendor PROMPT STR(RECNO())+vendno+" ";
    vendname
    SKIP
    n=n+1
ENDDO
* step 3: specify the procedure or program that will be executed
*          when a selection is made
ON SELECTION POPUP vendor DO vendsel
```

```
27
28 * step 4: activate the popup
29
30 ACTIVATE POPUP vendor
31
32
33 PROCEDURE vendsel
34
35        ACTIVATE WINDOW SHOW
36        skipno=BAR()
37        GOTO start+skipno-1
38        disp
39        WAIT
40        DEACTIVATE WINDOW show
41
42 RETURN
```

What This Program Does

The main program first uses the vendor file. It then defines a window named Show from 17,0 to 22,29. This window will be used to display the selected record. It then calls the procedure *showvend* with parameters of 10 and 20 as the starting and ending physical record numbers to be displayed. Note that further restrictions could be set on the record to be accessed with a SET FILTER TO instead of passing parameters using physical record numbers.

The PARAMETER statement in *showvend* defines the first parameter as the starting record number in the memory variable *start*, and the second parameter is the number of records to look at in the memory variable *number*. Next a pop-up menu called Vendor is defined from 1,40 to 12,79.

In the loop in lines 17–21, each individual bar of the pop-up is defined as being equal to the contents of two fields from a given record. It does not matter if the number of records defined is greater than the size of the pop-up window. dBASE allows scrolling through records if there are too many to fit into the window.

Line 26 defines the procedure *vendsel* as the procedure to be looked at to determine the action to be taken based on the bar selected.

Line 30 activates the pop-up.

The procedure *vendsel* uses the number of the bar selected as the offset from the starting record number to select the record to be displayed. Note that in this example the record is simply displayed. Other actions could be taken such as copying the contents of that record to an array.

After the record is looked at, control is returned to the menu. To exit from the menu, press Escape as long as Escape is not set OFF.

Using DEFINE POP-UP PROMPT FIELDS

The above program could be rewritten slightly to take advantage of the PROMPT FIELDS switch of the DEFINE POPUP command. This approach has the advantage of eliminating step 2: defining each prompt as a separate step. However, the cost is that each prompt can only be a single field.

```
* vendpop1.prg
* program to set up menu to point and shoot at records
* using PROMPT FIELD option of DEFINE POPUP
USE vendor
DEFINE WINDOW show FROM 17,0 TO 22,79
DO showvend WITH 10,20

PROCEDURE showvend
* pop-up menus for accounts payable example
PARAMETERS START,NUMBER
CLEAR
* step1: define pop-up name and location on screen
DEFINE POPUP vendor FROM 1,40 TO 12,79 PROMPT FIELD vendname

* step2: define the prompt for each bar of the light bar menu
* this step is now taken care of by the PROMPT FIELD vendname
* switch on the command above
* step 3: specify the procedure or program that will be executed
*         when a selection is made

ON SELECTION POPUP vendor DO vendsel

* step 4: activate the pop-up

ACTIVATE POPUP vendor

PROCEDURE vendsel

    ACTIVATE WINDOW SHOW
    skipno = BAR()
    GOTO start + skipno-1
    disp
```

```
    WAIT
    DEACTIVATE WINDOW show
RETURN
```

By comparing the two programs above, vendpop and vendpop1, the difference between the two approaches can be seen.

Selecting Records and Editing

The next program shows how to to use pop-up menus to select a record for editing. This program uses the approach shown in access.prg in chapter 7. Users are prompted to enter a last name, and all records having that last name are shown in a pop-up menu. Users then can use the up and down *arrow* keys to select the desired record and edit it. Note that since EXACT is set OFF, the leftmost part of the name can be entered. This means that to see all of the cases with a last name beginning with *S*, enter an *S* for last name.

Note the dBASE IV approach of including multiple procedures in a single file is used. The first procedure requires no procedure statement and is called by the name of the .prg file. The second procedure, namesel, is declared with the PROCEDURE declaration. Similarly, the third procedure, editrec, is also named in a PROCEDURE declaration.

```
* accesspu.prg
* program to access based on multiple last names
SET EXACT OFF
CLEAR WINDOWS
SET TALK OFF
SET HEADING OFF
DEFINE WINDOW edit FROM 14,1 TO 23,79
SELECT a
USE address INDEX name
DO WHILE .T.
          mlname=SPACE(15)
          CLEAR
          @ 2,10 say 'Enter last name to search for '
          @ 3,10 SAY 'Press Return to exit'
          @ 4,10 GET mlname PICTURE '@!'
          READ
          IF mlname=' '
```

```
            RETURN
          ENDIF
          SEEK TRIM(mlname)
          IF EOF()
            ? 'No employees found for last name ' +mlname
              WAIT
              LOOP
          ELSE
              EXIT
          ENDIF
          CLEA
          N=1
ENDDO     && WHILE .T.
CLEAR
* step 1: define pop-up name and location on screen
DEFINE POPUP names FROM 1,40 TO 12,79 ;
            MESSAGE 'Press Escape to exit'
* step 2: define the prompt for each bar of the light bar menu
N=1
DO WHILE TRIM(lname)=TRIM(mlname) .AND. .NOT. EOF()
      DEFINE BAR n OF names PROMPT STR(RECNO())+lname+'+;
      fname
      SKIP
      n=n+1
ENDDO
* step 3: specify the procedure or program that will be executed
*         when a selection is made
ON SELECTION POPUP names DO namesel
* step 4: activate the popup
ACTIVATE POPUP names
PROCEDURE namesel
```

```
        skipno = BAR()
        SEEK TRIM(mlname)
        IF EOF()
            return
        ENDIF
        @ 24,0
        ACTIVATE WINDOW edit
        SKIP skipno - 1
        DO editrec
        DEACTIVATE WINDOW edit

PROCEDURE editrec

mlname = lname
mfname = fname
mtitle = title
mcompany = company
mstraddr = straddr
mcity = city
mstate = state
mcity = city
mzip = zip
mphone = phone
medit = 'Y'
DO WHILE UPPER(MEDIT) = 'Y'

          @ 1,5 SAY 'Last name' GET mlname PICTURE '@!'
          @ 1,28 SAY 'Fname    ' GET mfname PICTURE;
          '!XXXXXXXXXXXXXX'
          @ 2,5 SAY 'Title     ' GET mtitle
          @ 3,5 SAY 'Company ' GET mcompany
          @ 4,5 SAY 'Address  ' GET mstraddr
          @ 5,5 SAY 'City      ' GET mcity PICTURE
                                  '!XXXXXXXXXXXXXX'
          @ 5,30 SAY 'State     ' GET mstate PICTURE '!!'
          @ 5,50 SAY 'Zip ' GET mzip PICTURE '99999'
          READ
```

```
94            @ 7,5 SAY 'Do you want to make changes? Y/N' GET medit
95            READ
96            @ 7,0
97 ENDDO &&edit loop
98
99 mpost='N'
100 @ 7,0 SAY 'Ok to post? Y/N' GET mpost
101 READ
102 IF UPPER(MPOST)='Y'
103      REPLACE lname WITH mlname
104      REPLACE fname WITH mfname
105      REPLACE title WITH mtitle
106      REPLACE company WITH mcompany
107      REPLACE straddr WITH mstraddr
108      REPLACE city WITH mcity
109      REPLACE state WITH mstate
110      REPLACE zip WITH mzip
111 ENDIF
112 DEACTIVATE WINDOW edit
```

What This Program Does

The DO WHILE loop in lines 10–32 allows the user to enter a last name to search for. If an invalid name is entered, the user is prompted again for the name.

When a valid name is entered, control goes to line 25 where a pop-up menu is defined. The DO WHILE loop from lines 40–44 defines the prompts of the pop-up menu as each record with a matching last name.

When a selection is made, control goes to PROCEDURE namesel, where the record pointer moves to select the record that was chosen by the user from the menu.

Next the PROCEDURE editrec is executed. The contents of each field are stored to memory variables and the memory variables displayed on the screen in an Edit window. After the user enters changes, a prompt is provided to allow editing of the changes. Then another prompt allows confirmation of the changes before they are posted back to the file.

This approach of storing the contents of fields to memory variables and then editing the memory variables before saving them back to the file allows the user to see and verify the changes before they are recorded.

Adding Search Options

If the program above does not find a match on last name, it simply prompts the user to enter another name. However, this approach could be amplified by adding the following options:

1. If an exact match on last name is not found, use the dBASE IV SET NEAR ON option to find the nearest match.

2. Give the user the option to use the dBASE IV SOUNDEX() feature to search based on the sound of the name.

3. If no match is found, allow the user to add a new record.

```
* multacce.prg
* program to access based on multiple last names
  or leftmost characters of name

CLOSE DATA
SET STATUS OFF
CLEAR WINDOWS
SET TALK OFF
SET HEADING OFF
DEFINE WINDOW edit FROM 14,1 TO 23,79
DEFINE WINDOW menu FROM 14,1 TO 23,50
SELECT a
USE address INDEX name
DO WHILE .T.
          SET NEAR OFF
          mlname=SPACE(15)
          CLEAR
          @ 2,10 say 'Enter last name to search for '
          @ 3,10 SAY 'Press Return to exit'
          @ 4,10 GET mlname PICTURE '@!'
          READ
          IF mlname=' '
               RETURN
          ENDIF
          SEEK TRIM(mlname)
          IF EOF()
               ACTIVATE WINDOW menu
```

```
            ? 'No employees found for last name ' +mlname
            ? '<S> Soundex search'
            ? '<C> Closest match'
            ? '<A> Add new address'
            ?

              WAIT 'Enter choice 'TO msch
              DEACTIVATE WINDOW menu
              DO CASE
                CASE UPPER(msch)='S'
                  DO soundsearch
                  LOOP
                CASE UPPER(msch)='C'
                  SET NEAR ON
                  SEEK TRIM(mlname)
                  IF EOF()
                    @ 20,0 SAY 'No matches found for '+mlname
                    WAIT
                    @ 20,0
                  ELSE
                    CLEAR
                    ? 'Closest match is: '+lname+' '+fname
                    WAIT
                    LOOP

                  ENDIF &&EOF()
                CASE UPPER(msch)='A'
                  Do addrec
              ENDCASE
              LOOP
        ELSE
              EXIT
        ENDIF &&EOF()
        CLEA
        N=1

ENDDO     && WHILE .T.
CLEAR
* step 1: define pop-up name and location on screen
DEFINE POPUP names FROM 1,40 TO 12,79 ;
```

```
                MESSAGE 'Press Escape to exit'
* step 2: define the prompt for each bar of the light bar menu
N=1
DO WHILE TRIM(lname)=TRIM(mlname) .AND. .NOT. EOF()
     DEFINE BAR n OF names PROMPT STR(RECNO())+lname+" +
     fname
     SKIP
     n=n+1
ENDDO
* step 3: specify the procedure or program that will be executed
*         when a selection is made
ON SELECTION POPUP names DO namesel
* step 4: activate the popup
ACTIVATE POPUP names
RETURN
PROCEDURE namesel
        skipno=BAR()
        SEEK TRIM(mlname)
        IF EOF()
              return
        ENDIF
        @ 24,0
        ACTIVATE WINDOW edit
        SKIP skipno-1
        DO editrec
        DEACTIVATE WINDOW edit
PROCEDURE editrec
mmlname=lname
mfname=fname
```

```
mtitle=title
mcompany=company
mstraddr=straddr
mcity=city
mstate=state
mcity=city
mzip=zip
mphone=phone
medit='Y'
DO WHILE UPPER(MEDIT)='Y'

        @ 1,5 SAY 'Last name' GET mmlname PICTURE '@!'
        @ 1,28 SAY 'Fname    ' GET mfname PICTURE;
        '!XXXXXXXXXXXXXX'
        @ 2,5 SAY 'Title     ' GET mtitle
        @ 3,5 SAY 'Company   ' GET mcompany
        @ 4,5 SAY 'Address   ' GET mstraddr
        @ 5,5 SAY 'City      ' GET mcity PICTURE;
                               '!XXXXXXXXXXXXXX'
        @ 5,30 SAY 'State    ' GET mstate PICTURE '!!'
        @ 5,50 SAY 'Zip ' GET mzip PICTURE '99999'
        READ
        @ 7,5 SAY 'Do you want to make changes? Y/N' GET medit
        READ
        @ 7,0
ENDDO &&edit loop

mpost='N'
@ 7,0 SAY 'OK to post? Y/N' GET mpost
READ
IF UPPER(MPOST)='Y'
    REPLACE lname WITH mmlname
    REPLACE fname WITH mfname
    REPLACE title WITH mtitle
    REPLACE company WITH mcompany
    REPLACE straddr WITH mstraddr
    REPLACE city WITH mcity
    REPLACE state WITH mstate
    REPLACE zip WITH mzip
ENDIF
```

```
DEACTIVATE WINDOW edit

* procedure to do SOUNDEX() search
PROCEDURE soundsearch
* check if any names beginning with same letter
SEEK SUBSTR(mlname,1,1)
IF EOF()
    ? 'No matches found for names beginning with '+;
    (SUBSTR(mlname,1,1)
    WAIT
    RETURN
ENDIF && EOF()
CLEAR

* step 1: define pop-up name and location on screen
DEFINE POPUP names FROM 1,40 TO 12,79 ;
                MESSAGE 'Press Escape to exit'

* step 2: define the prompt for each bar of the light bar menu
* read in matches based on first letter being equal and SOUNDEX()
* equal
N=1
DO WHILE SUBSTR(lname,1,1)=SUBSTR(mlname,1,1) .AND. .NOT;
EOF()
    IF SOUNDEX(lname)=SOUNDEX(mlname)
      DEFINE BAR n OF names PROMPT STR(RECNO())+lname+''+;
      fname
      n=n+1
    ENDIF
      SKIP

ENDDO

* step 3: specify the procedure or program that will be executed
*         when a selection is made

ON SELECTION POPUP names DO namesound
@ 13,40 SAY 'Soundex matches for ' +mlname

* step 4: activate the popup
```

```
ACTIVATE POPUP names
PROCEDURE namesound
          skipno=BAR()
          SEEK SUBSTR(mlname,1,1)
          IF EOF()
                  RETURN
          ENDIF
          SET FILTER TO SOUNDEX(lname)=SOUNDEX(mlname)
          IF SOUNDEX(lname) <> SOUNDEX(mlname)
               SKIP
          ENDIF
          @ 24,0
          ACTIVATE WINDOW edit
          SKIP skipno-1
          IF .NOT. EOF()
               DO editrec
          ENDIF
          DEACTIVATE WINDOW edit
          SET FILTER TO
RETURN
PROCEDURE addrec
* procedure to add a new record
ACTIVATE WINDOW EDIT
* initialize memory variables
mmlname=SPACE(20)
mfname=SPACE(15)
```

```
mtitle=SPACE(15)
mcompany=SPACE(20)
mstraddr=SPACE(20)
mcity=SPACE(15)
mstate=SPACE(2)
mzip=SPACE(5)

* get input
mflag=.T.
CLEAR
DO WHILE mflag
          @ 0,5 SAY 'Last name ' GET mmlname PICTURE '@!'
          @ 0,45 SAY 'First name 'GET mfname

          @ 1,5 SAY 'Title      ' GET mtitle
          @ 2,5 SAY 'Company name ' GET mcompany
          @ 3,5 SAY 'Street address ' GET mstraddr
          @ 4,5 SAY 'City ' GET mcity
          @ 4,35 SAY 'State ' GET mstate PICTURE '@!'
          @ 4,47 SAY 'Zip ' GET mzip PICTURE '99999'
          READ
@ 7,2 SAY 'Do you want to edit? (Y/N)' GET mflag PICTURE 'Y'
          READ
   @ 7,2
      ENDDO
@ 7,2
* check if valid name entered
IF mfname=' ' .OR. mmlname= ' '
          RETURN
ENDIF

* get names in proper format
mfname=LTRIM(mfname)
mfname=UPPER(SUBSTR(mfname,1,1))-LOWER(SUBSTR(mfname,2,14))

mpost='N'
@ 7,2 SAY 'OK to post? (Y/N)' GET mpost
READ
IF UPPER(mpost)='Y'
        APPEND BLANK
```

```
262             REPL fname WITH mfname
263             REPL lname WITH mmlname
264             REPL title WITH mtitle
265             REPL company WITH mcompany
266             REPL straddr WITH mstraddr
267             REPL city WITH mcity
268             REPL state WITH mstate
269             REPL zip WITH mzip
270 ENDIF &&post
271 DEACTIVATE WINDOW edit
272
```

What This Program Does

The program above is contained in a single file named multacce.prg. This takes advantage of the dBASE IV ability to include multiple procedures in a single file. The screen display generated by this program is shown in Figure 16-1.

As in the previous example, the user is prompted in lines 18–21 to enter the last name to search for. Also, as in the previous program, the leftmost

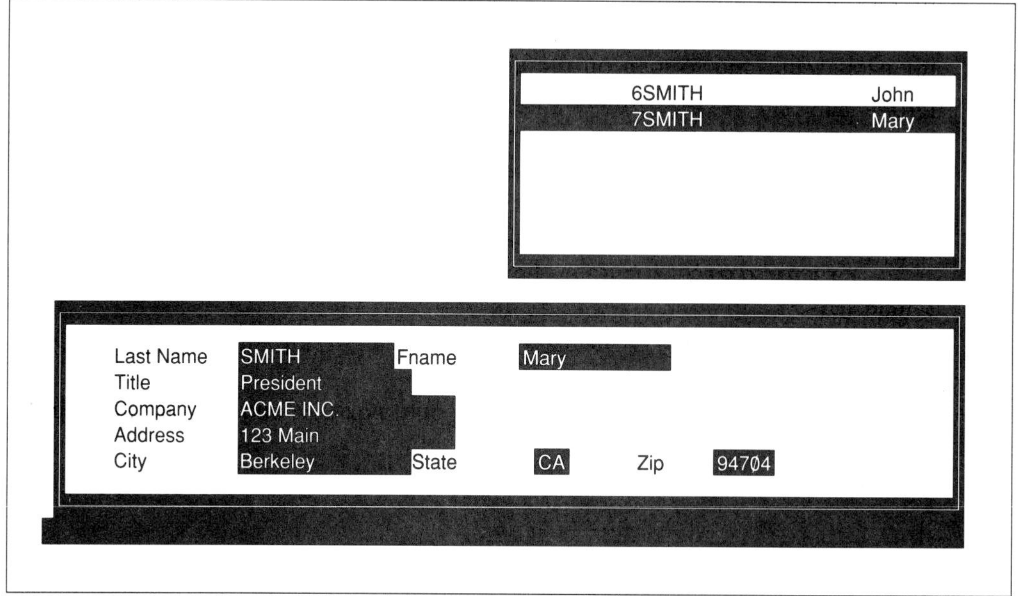

Figure 16-1. Edit screen using a pop-up menu and window.

characters of the last name can be entered, since EXACT is set OFF. For instance, S could be entered to see all records for last names beginning with *S*. The SEEK on line 25 checks the index to see if a match is found. If it is, then control goes to line 65 where a pop-up menu is set up to show all of the matching records. The user can then use the *arrow* keys to select the desired record. Once a record is selected, control goes to the editrec routine on line 103 to allow editing of the record.

However, if a match is not found, a menu appears, giving options to add a new record, find the closest match, or to perform a soundex search.

If add a new record is selected, control goes to the procedure addrec on line 216. This is a simple add routine.

If closest match is selected, the command SET NEAR ON is executed on line 41. The SEEK is again performed on line 42. If EOF() is encountered, no matches are found. If EOF() is not true, the record after where the desired record would be is displayed.

If SOUNDEX is selected, control goes to the procedure soundsearch on line 148. This procedure looks for all the records in which the SOUNDEX() value of the last name is equal to the SOUNDEX() value of the name sought. Since the SOUNDEX() algorithm keeps the first letter of the name, the SEEK SUBSTR(mlname,1,1) on line 150 goes to the first record in which the first letter of the last name is equal to the first letter of the desired last name.

The DO WHILE loop in lines 166–173 looks at all the records in which the first letter of the last name equals the first letter of the desired last name. The IF statement in lines 167–170 checks whether the SOUNDEX() values match. If they do, they are put into the menu.

The user then selects the desired record and the procedure namesound moves the record pointer to that record. This is done by again doing a SEEK to position the record pointer to the first record in which the first letter of the last name is equal to the first letter of the desired last name. Then the SET FILTER command on line 195 is used to filter out records in which the SOUNDEX values do not match.

Remember that SET FILTER does not position the record pointer. The IF statement in lines 196–198 checks whether or not the first record with the first letter of the last name equal to the first letter of the desired last name matches the filter. If it does not, a SKIP is performed to find the next record that matches. The SKIP skipno-1 in line 202 then skips the desired number of records. Note that with the filter in effect, only records that match the filter are looked at in SKIPping. Finally, if EOF() is not true, the procedure editrec is executed to allow editing of the record.

USING dBASE IV ARRAYS

Why Use Arrays?

dBASE IV finally includes arrays. There are several possible reasons for using arrays in the context of dBASE.

1. To copy the contents of selected fields of a whole file to a memory variable array, to manipulate more quickly the data. This is not really feasible in dBASE IV because of the limits on the number of array elements. The maximum number of elements in an array is 1170. To calculate how many records can be read into an array, use the formula

```
numfields=<number of fields in a record>
numrecs=1170/numfields
```

Then dimension an array in this way:

```
DECLARE farray[numrecs,numfields]
```

This command sets up the prescribed number of array elements as logical values set to False. To get the contents of the records from the file to the array, the following command can be used.

```
USE <file name>
COPY TO ARRAY farray
```

2. To copy a single record to an array for editing or moving between files. An example is shown below.

Syntax for Creating Arrays

One- or two-dimensional arrays can be declared with the DECLARE statement.

```
DECLARE <array name> [r,c]
```

Each array element is treated as a separate memory variable. Although up to 2,048 memory variables are allowed, arrays seem to allow up to only 1170 elements, which severely limits their use for larger files.

When an array is DECLAREd, each element is defined as a logical value set to False.

To declare an array public, the following syntax could be used.

PUBLIC ARRAY <*array name*> [r,c]

To create an array that will hold only one record, a one-dimensional array with the number of elements equal to the number of fields in the array can be created.

DECLARE <*array name*> [<*number of fields*>]

CAUTION: If an array is declared with the same name as an array or memory variable that already exists, the existing array or memory variable will be wiped out.

Generic Edit Routine

The following generic edit routine uses arrays to allow editing the contents of a single record by first storing the record contents to an array and then editing the contents of the array and posting back the contents.

```
* edit.prg
* generic edit program using arrays
* file to be edited must be open in current work area
* and record pointer pointing to record to be edited

SET TALK OFF
* get number of fields
numfields=1
DO WHILE LEN(FIELD(numfields)) <> 0
        numfields=numfields+1
ENDDO
DECLARE edit[numfields-1]
COPY NEXT 1 TO ARRAY edit
CLEAR
f=1
DO WHILE f <numfields .AND. f <20
    @ f+2,1 SAY FIELD(f) GET edit[f]
```

```
18     f=f+1
19 ENDDO
20 READ
21 mpost=' '
22 @ 22,0 SAY 'OK to post changes? Y/N ' GET mpost
23 READ
24
25 IF UPPER(MPOST)='Y'
26       f=1
27       DO WHILE f < numfields
28         mfield=field(f)
29         REPLACE &mfield WITH edit[f]
30         f=f+1
31       ENDDO
32 ENDIF
33
34
35
36
```

What This Program Does

This program generates an Edit screen by first creating an array with one element for each field in the file. The code in lines 8–11 calculates the number of fields in the file. This is done using the FIELDS() function. The memory variable counter *numfields* is incremented until LEN(FIELDS(numfields))=0, indicating that the previous field was the last field. When the DO WHILE loop is exited, numfields is equal to one more than the number of fields in the file.

The DECLARE statement on line 12 declares an array with one element for each field in the file. This program assumes that the record pointer is positioned at the record to be edited. The copy statement in line 13 copies the contents of the current record to the array.

The code in lines 14–19 paints the screen with one field appearing on each line. This approach assumes that the field names plus the field contents will fit on a single line. The DO WHILE loop uses the memory variable f as a field pointer. In line 17 the FIELDS() function is used to extract the name of the field and the appropriate array element referenced with GET edit[f]. The read on line 20 activates the gets.

The prompt in line 22 allows the user to indicate whether it's all right to post the changes to the file. If an affirmative answer is given, the code in lines 25–32 actually posts the contents of the array back to the fields. For each pass through the loop, the memory variable mfield contains the name of the field. Macro substitution is used in the replace statement to generate the name of the field to be replaced. The field contents are replaced with the contents of the corresponding array element.

Appendix 1

dBASE III PLUS QUICK REFERENCE SUMMARY

This appendix lists the most useful syntaxes of the dBASE commands that are essential for programming purposes. A complete listing can be found in the Ashton-Tate dBASE III PLUS manual. This listing includes only the most useful syntaxes of the most useful commands.

This reference section contains three types of entries

1. dBASE key words or command verbs are identified in upper case without parentheses at the end.

2. dBASE functions are identified in upper case with parentheses at the end. Note that functions can not be used as stand-alone commands: they must be used in conjunction with a command verb.

3. dBASE concepts are identified in upper and lower case.

SYNTACTICAL NOTES

Command modifiers appearing within square brackets ([]) are optional.

If a SET command has an ON or OFF option, the default option is displayed in upper case.

BASIC SYNTAX OF dBASE COMMANDS

The basic syntax of a dBASE command is

<*command verb*> [<*expression list*>] [<*scope*>]
[FOR <*condition*>] [WHILE <*condition*>] [TO FILE/
TO PRINT]

The typical command has these elements:

1. Command verb. All dBASE command lines must start with a command verb such as LIST, except for assignment statements in which a memory variable can be set equal to an expression.

2. Expression list. The field, list of fields, or any valid dBASE expression to which the command is to apply.

3. Scope. Indicates the records to which the command verb is to be applied. Typical scopes include

RECORD <*n*> To specify a record, such as DISPLAY RECORD 3

NEXT <*n*> To apply the command to the next *n* records, such as LIST NEXT 10

ALL To apply the command to all records in the file

REST To apply the command to all records from the current one to the end of file.

4. FOR clause. Supported by many dBASE commands. It implies sequential access. Each record must be checked to see if the FOR clause is true.

5. WHILE clause. Most often used in conjunction with an index. The WHILE clause must be true for the current record or the command will not execute. As soon as the WHILE clause is not true, the command stops executing.

6. TO. The output of many commands can be directed to the printer, using the TO PRINT switch, or to a file by using TO FILE <*file name*>.

This reference includes the commands and features of dBASE most frequently used by programmers.

&<character variable name> An ampersand followed by the name of a character memory variable indicates macro substitution. Before the syntax of the command is parsed by the interpreter, the contents of the character memory variable are substituted into the command line. This syntax results in using a .dbf file named test.

```
. mvar='test'
test
. USE &mvar
```

&& <comment> Double ampersands in a command line indicate that the rest of the line contains a comment.

*** <command line>** An asterisk (*) at the beginning of a command line indicates that the entire line is a comment line.

? <*expression*> The question mark command is used for simple output. A carriage return and line feed is sent prior to printing the expression indicated. To suppress the leading carriage return and line feed, the double question mark can be used. Data types must match: if a numeric and character variable are to be output with the same *?*, the number must be converted to a character using the STR function. PICTURE clauses can be used in conjunction with a *?* statement, using the TRANSFORM function.

```
? 'the answer is '+STR(mnum)
? TRANSFORM(mnum,'999,999.99')
```

<*str1*> $ <*str2*> The $ operator returns a logical True if string 1 is contained in string 2 and a logical False if it is not.

@ *r,c* [SAY <*expression*>] [PICTURE <*expression*>] [GET <*expression*>] [PICTURE <*expression*>] [RANGE<*exp1*>,<*exp2*>] In its simplest form, @ *r,c* SAY is used to output a single variable or literal value. *r* is the row coordinate and *c* is the column coordinate. Data types must match: if a numeric and character variable are to be output with the same @...SAY, the number must be converted to a character by using the STR function. A SAY displays the contents of a variable but does not allow the user to change it.

@ r,c	clears row r starting at column c
@ r,c CLEAR	clears from r,c to end of screen
@ r,c TO r1,c1	draw box from r,c to r1,c1
@ r,c CLEAR TO r1,c1	erase box above

By contrast, a GET shows the current contents of the variable and allows the user to change it. A GET is not activated until a READ is executed. For example,

```
mzip=SPACE(5)
@ 10,1 SAY 'Enter zip code ' GET mzip
READ
```

The output of the @...SAY command can be directed to the printer with SET DEVICE TO PRINT and back to the screen with SET DEVICE TO SCREEN.

CAUTION: When you direct output to the printer with @...SAY, the row and column coordinates must be sequential or extraneous page ejects will be generated. *See also:* PICTURE and READ.

ABS(*n*) Returns the absolute value of the numeric argument.

ACCESS() Returns the access level of the last user to log on to a multiuser system or a 0 in a single-user environment.

APPEND By itself, puts dBASE into a full screen editing mode to append a new record to the currently open file. APPEND is generally not used in programs because it does not give the programmer enough control over how data is entered.

APPEND BLANK Appends a blank record to the currently open .dbf file and allows the contents of the fields of the new record to be changed under program control using the REPLACE command.

When a blank record is appended, all character fields are set to blanks, numeric fields to 0, date fields to a blank date, and logical fields to False.

APPEND FROM <*file name*>] [FOR <*expression*>] Adds the contents of one file to the physical end of another .dbf file. A FOR clause can be used to selectively append only records that meet a specified condition.

APPEND FROM as it is most commonly used takes the following forms. All forms of the APPEND FROM command append the specified file to the end of the currently open .dbf file.

APPEND FROM <*file name*> Appends the contents of the file filename-.dbf to the .dbf file currently open in the selected area. Matching is done based on field name. Only the contents of the fields in the file being appended *from* that match the field names in the file being appended *to* are appended.

When you append from a file with deleted records, the following conventions apply. If SET DELETED ON, the deleted records are not appended. If SET DELETED OFF, the deleted records are appended but are not still flagged for deletion.

If it is necessary to keep track of whether the deletion flag has been set for appended records, create a one-character field that can be used for your own deletion flag prior to the APPEND operation.

```
REPLACE ALL delflag WITH .T. FOR DELETED()
```

APPEND FROM <*file name*> SDF Append the contents of an ASCII file with fixed length fields to a .dbf file. If the first field in the .dbf file is *n* characters long, the first *n* characters from the ASCII file are put in that field for the records added.

dBASE expects the SDF file to have a .txt or similar extension that must be specified. If the file has no extension, use the filename followed by two periods(.).

```
APPEND FROM test..SDF
```

APPEND FROM <*file name*> DELIMITED Appends the contents of an ASCII file with delimited fields to a .dbf file. In each record, the contents of everything up to the first delimiter that fits into the first field of the .dbf file are put in that field, etc.

dBASE expects the delimited file to have a .txt or similar extension that must be specified. If the file has no extension, use the file name followed by two periods.

```
APPEND FROM test..DELI
```

APPEND FROM <*file name.wks*> WKS Imports a Lotus 1-2-3 release 1A spreadsheet into a .dbf file. First a .dbf file must be created with fields corresponding to each column in the spreadsheet. The field widths must be greater than or equal to the contents of the spreadsheet columns.

ASC(<*character*>) Returns the decimal ASCII value of the first character in a character string

```
. ? ASC('A')
  65
```

AT(<*string1*>,<*string2*>) Returns a number equal to the starting position of string1 within string2. If string1 is not contained in string 2, a zero is returned.

```
. ? AT('A','dBASE')
      3
```

AVERAGE [<*scope*>] [<*expression list*>] [FOR <*condition*>] [WHILE <*condition*>] [TO <*memvar list*>] Calculates the average values contained in numeric fields. Typing the verb AVERAGE will default to averaging all the numeric fields in a given .dbf file and displaying those averages on the screen if TALK is set on. Under program control, AVERAGE can be used to store averages to memory variables.

```
AVERAGE sales TO avsales
```

When you average multiple fields, it is best to use a single AVERAGE statement that results in a single pass through the file by using the syntax

```
AVERAGE qty,sales TO avqty, avsales
```

BOF() Evaluates to a logical True when an attempt is made to do a negative SKIP to a record before the beginning of file.

BROWSE [FIELDS <*field list*>] Enters a full screen editing mode to access the records in a file. This command is generally not used under program control because it allows the user too much leeway in changing data.

CALL <*module name*> WITH <*expression*> CALL is used to execute a binary program that has been loaded into memory with the LOAD command.

CANCEL Causes the currently running program to be exited. It closes all open .prg files except the currently open procedure file and returns control to the dot prompt.

CDOW(<*date*>) Returns the character name of the day of the week of the specified date.

```
. ? CDOW(CTOD('01/01/88'))
Friday
```

CHR(*n*) Returns the character associated with the decimal ASCII value of the argument.

```
. ? CHR(65)
A
```

CMONTH(<*date*>) Returns the character value of the month of the date specified.

```
. ? CMONTH(CTOD('01/01/88'))
January
```

CLEAR Clears the screen.

CLEAR ALL Closes all open .dbf and .ndx files and releases all memory variables.

CLEAR FIELDS Cancels a field list established with SET FIELDS TO *<field list>*.

CLEAR GETS Clears all pending GETs. This command can be used in place of a READ if the intention is to display field contents in inverse video without allowing the user to change the contents of the field.

CLEAR MEMORY Releases all memory variables.

CLEAR TYPEAHEAD Deletes all characters in the TYPEAHEAD buffer. This is a useful command to insert prior to eliciting a keyboard response for users who tend to lean on the keyboard.

CLOSE ALTERNATE Closes the current alternate file. It is equivalent to SET ALTERNATE TO.

CLOSE DATA Closes all .dbf and .ndx files except for a catalog file.

CLOSE FORMAT Closes the format file open in the current work area.

COL() Returns the current horizontal cursor position on the screen, so that @...SAY output can be specified at the next column position.

```
@ 2,COL()+1 SAY 'This is the next column'
```

config.sys To allow dBASE III PLUS to open its full quota of 15 files of all types, the root directory of the hard disk must have a config.sys file containing FILES =20. A BUFFERS =15 may also be used to attempt to speed up execution time by allocating more RAM for buffering. The number of buffers allocated can be varied based on experimentation.

config.db A text file located in the same directory with dBASE that dBASE III PLUS checks every time it is started so that the operating environment can be configured. Most SET commands can be included in the config.db file in a slightly different format. Instead of typing SET HELP OFF at the dot prompt, the following can be contained in the config.db file.

```
HELP = OFF
```

CONTINUE Used in conjunction with the LOCATE command. After a LOCATE is executed to find the first occurrence of a condition, the CONTINUE command can be used to find subsequent occurrences of the LOCATE condition. The following code segment uses the LOCATE command to look for the first occurrence of a record with lname='Smith'. If one is found, EOF is not true and the record is displayed. The CONTINUE command looks for the next occurrence and displays each additional occurrence found until EOF() is true.

```
LOCATE FOR lname='SMITH'
    DO WHILE .NOT. EOF()
        DISPLAY
        CONTINUE
    ENDDO WHILE NOT EOF
```

COPY FILE <*file1*> TO <*file2*> Similar to the DOS copy command. It allows copying a file without opening it in dBASE. The syntax is different from the DOS COPY command in that the word FILE and the word TO must be included in the syntax. (*See* RUN to access the DOS copy command from within dBASE.) This command is generally faster than USEing the file and executing a COPY TO <*file name*>.

COPY STRUCTURE TO <*file name*> Used to copy the structure of the currently open .dbf file to a new .dbf file. This command is useful for creating temporary files with the same structure as the original file.

COPY TO <*file name*> STRUCTURE EXTENDED Creates a file with this field structure.

```
Structure for database: C:struc.dbf
Number of data records:         8
Date of last update     : 08/29/88
Field       Field Name       Type          Width      Dec
    1       FIELD_NAME       Character        10
    2       FIELD_TYPE       Character         1
    3       FIELD_LEN        Numeric           3
    4       FIELD_DEC        Numeric           3
** Total **                                   18
```

Each record contains information about one field in the currently open .dbf file when the COPY STRUCTURE EXTENDED command was issued. In conjunction with the CREATE FROM command, the structure of a .dbf file can be modified under program control.

COPY TO <*file*> [FOR <*expression*>] The inverse of the APPEND FROM command. It copies the contents of the currently open .dbf file in the selected area to another file. A FOR clause can be used to selectively copy only records that meet a specified condition.

COPY TO <*file*> Copies the currently open .dbf file in the selected area to another .dbf file of the specified name.

The following conventions apply for deleted records. If SET DELETED

ON, deleted records are not copied. If SET DELETED OFF, deleted records are copied and are still flagged for deletion

COPY TO <*file*> SDF Copies the contents of the currently open .dbf file to an ASCII file with fixed length fields as in the following format.

```
Mary Anderson        123 Main      Berkeley     CA94704
John Jones           2345 Third    Oakland      CA94700
```

COPY TO <*file*> DELIMITED Copies the contents of the currently open .dbf file to an ASCII file with delimiters between fields in the following format.

```
"Mary","Anderson","123 Main","Berkeley","CA","94704"
"John","Jones","2345 Third","Oakland","CA","94700"
```

COUNT [<*scope*>] [<*expression list*>] [FOR <*condition*>] [WHILE <*condition*>] [TO <*memvar list*>] Most frequently used to count the number of records that meet a given condition.

```
COUNT FOR DELETED() TO numdel
COUNT FOR ZIP='94704' TO numzip
```

Each time the COUNT command is executed a separate pass is made through the file.

CREATE <*file name*> Puts the user into a full screen editing mode for creation of a file structure.

CREATE <*newfile*> FROM <*structure extended file*> The inverse of the COPY TO STRUCTURE EXTENDED command described above. It takes a file with the structure of the structure extended file and creates a new file from it. The steps for changing a file structure under program control are

1. USE file
2. COPY TO tempfile STRUCTURE EXTENDED
3. USE tempfile
4. change the contents of the records in tempfile to reflect the new field structure
5. CREATE newfile FROM tempfile

CREATE LABEL <*label name*> Creates a mailing label format in the interactive mode.

CREATE REPORT <*report name*> Creates a report format in the interactive mode.

CTOD() Converts a date in the form mm/dd/yy to a date type memory variable or field. Expressions can be used as part of the argument. CTOD(' ') creates a *blank date.*

```
mfyr='1986/87'
? CTOD('07/01/'+SUBSTR(mfyr,3,2))
07/01/86
```

Current work area The current work area is the area that is chosen by use of the SELECT command. When a USE <*file name*> is executed, the file is opened in the currently selected work area identified with the most recent SELECT statement.

DATE() When used as part of an output expression, returns the system date.

```
? DATE()
```

DAY(<*date*>) Returns the numeric day represented by the specified date.

```
. ? DAY(CTOD('01/01/88'))
  1
```

DBF() Returns the name of the .dbf file that is open in the currently selected work area.

DELETE [<*scope*>] [FOR <*condition*>] [WHILE <*condition*>] DELETE with no modifiers, flags the current record for deletion. The record is not physically removed from the file until a PACK is executed. Records flagged for deletion can be made seemingly to disappear by using SET DELETED ON. DELETE can be used also to delete multiple records.

```
DELETE FOR zip = '94704'
DELETE NEXT 20
```

DELETED() Returns a logical True if the current record is flagged for deletion, otherwise it returns a logical False. If the record pointer were positioned at a record flagged for deletion, this expression returns a .T.

```
? DELETED()
```

DELETE FILE <*file name*> Deletes the specified file name. The full file name including the extension, as .dbf or .ndx, must be used.

DIR Displays the names, numbers of records, and date of last update for all .dbf files in the currently logged subdirectory.

DIR *.* Displays the names of all files in the currently selected subdirectory. However, it doesn't display the amount of space used by each file. By contrast, RUN DIR accesses the DOS DIR command that displays the amount of space used by each file.

DISKSPACE() Returns the amount of space left on the currently selected drive.

```
IF DISKSPACE() < 500000
    ? 'Disk is almost full'
ENDIF
```

DISPLAY [<*scope*>] [<*expression list*>] [FOR <*condition*>] [WHILE <*condition*>] [TO PRINT] [OFF] DISPLAY by itself shows the contents of the record in a file at which the record pointer is positioned.

DISPLAY ALL is similar to LIST except the listing pauses at the end of each screen. Selected records can be displayed such as

```
DISPLAY FOR zip='94704'
```

The output of the DISPLAY command can be directed to the printer using the TO PRINT modifier. The OFF modifier suppresses the display of the record number.

DISPLAY HISTORY [TO PRINT] Displays commands previously entered at the dot prompt from the history buffer. The default number of commands is the last 20 commands that have been entered at the dot prompt. This setting can be changed with SET HISTORY TO.

DISPLAY MEMORY [TO PRINT] Displays memory variables. Variables that are created in a lower level subroutine will not be displayed unless they have been declared public. *See* PUBLIC.

DISPLAY STATUS [TO PRINT] Displays the names of all .dbf and .ndx files that are currently in use. Also displays information about various environmental parameters that are changed by use of SET commands.

DISPLAY STRUCTURE [TO PRINT] Displays the field structure, number of records, and date of last update of the open file in the currently selected area.

DISPLAY USERS Lists the users currently logged onto the system in a networked environment.

DO *<program name>* [WITH *<parameters>*] Causes execution of the specified program or procedure and passes the optional parameters specified.

DO CASE A program control structure that allows branching based on the value of a variable. One common use for branching is based on a menu choice.

```
DO CASE
    CASE menu='1'
        DO prog1

    CASE menu='2'
        DO prog2

    CASE menu='3'
        DO prog3

    OTHERWISE
        ? 'Invalid selection'
        WAIT
ENDCASE
```

The first true CASE is executed. All the instructions after the true CASE statement are executed until the next CASE statement is entered. Then control goes to the instruction after the ENDCASE.

The OTHERWISE is optional. If the OTHERWISE is included, and if none of the other CASE statements are true, the instructions between the OTHERWISE and the ENDCASE are executed.

DO WHILE *<condition>* A program control structure used for repetitive operations. The structure is terminated by an ENDDO statement. All of the instructions between the DO WHILE and ENDDO are executed as long as the condition is true. When control returns to the DO WHILE and the condition is false, the instruction after the ENDDO is executed. Otherwise, the loop is re-executed. After execution of the instructions within the DO WHILE loop begins, the condition is only checked when an ENDDO or LOOP is encountered.

DOW(*<date>*) Returns a numeric value corresponding to the day of the week with Sunday=1.

```
. ? DOW(CTOD('01/01/88'))
  6
```

DTOC(<*date*>) Converts a date type variable to a character string in the format corresponding to the format established with the SET DATE command.

EDIT A command used at the dot prompt to change the contents of a record. It is not useful in programs generally because it does not allow the programmer enough control over the way in which data is changed.

EJECT Causes a form feed to be executed by the printer. It is useful after some printing has been accomplished to flush out any data that may be *stuck* in the print buffer, and to position the paper at top of form for the next print job.

CAUTION: This command sends a form feed to the printer even if DEVICE is set to screen and PRINT is set OFF. Trying to execute an EJECT command when the printer is off-line can cause the computer to freeze up.

EOF() Tests for end of file. EOF() is only true when an attempt is made to skip past the last record in a file, not when the record pointer is positioned at the last record. It is often used as the condition for a DO WHILE loop when looking at every record in a file. For example,

```
DO WHILE .NOT. EOF().
```

ERASE <*file name*> Deletes a file. If a .dbf file is being erased, the .dbf extension must be stated explicitly. The syntax to erase a .dbf file named test is the following:

```
ERASE test.dbf
```

ERROR() Returns the number of the current error. The function is intended to be used in routines called with ON ERROR DO <*program name*>.

EXIT Used to exit a DO WHILE loop. When the EXIT command is encountered, control goes to the instruction after the ENDDO.

FIELD(<*n*>) Returns the name of the indicated field. FIELD(1) returns the name of the first field in the currently open .dbf file.

NOTE: In a loop checking for FIELD() equal to a null string cannot be used as a test for the last field because FIELD(<expr>)="" is always true. This can be overcome by testing for LEN(FIELD(i))=0.

Rather incredibly, FIELD() cannot be used as part of a macro. To use the FIELD() function for accessing the contents of a field, a memory variable such as mfield1=FIELD(1) must be defined, and then the macro of the memory variable can be used to access the field contents. This code fragment can be used to determine the number of fields in a file.

```
USE <file name>
numfields=1
DO WHILE LEN(FIELD(numfields)) <> 0
     numfields=numfields+1
ENDDO
numfields=numfields-1
```

FILE(<*file name*>) Returns a logical True if the file exists and a logical False if it does not. The file function is useful for checking whether or not files exist such as checking if index files exist and if not recreating them.

```
IF .NOT. FILE("name.ndx")
     ? 'Indexing—Please wait'
     USE address
     INDEX ON lname+fname TO name
ENDIF
```

FKLABEL(*n*) Evaluates to the name of the function key referenced. In this arcane scheme of things, since F1 is help and cannot be reassigned, FKLABEL(1) returns F2.

```
. ? FKLABEL(1)
F2
. ? FKLABEL(2)
F3
```

FKMAX() Returns the number of programmable function keys for the given computer, either 9 or 11 for an IBM PC compatible. F1, the Help key, cannot be programmed and therefore is not counted.

FLOCK() Used in a networked environment and returns a True if it possible to lock the .dbf file open in the currently selected work area. If the file is already locked, a False is returned.

FIND An earlier version of the SEEK command that is included for compatibility with dBASE II. The FIND command is used to find a record based on the value of its key field for the index that is open currently. It can only be used when an appropriate index is open. The FIND command expects a literal argument corresponding to the key field in the index. For example, an appropriate FIND command for a last name index is

```
FIND Smith
```

Quotes can be used around the argument if desired, such as when leading spaces are present. The FIND command can be used with a memory variable and a macro using the syntax

```
mlname='Smith'
FIND &mlname
```

A FIND command should always be followed by a test to see if the FIND was successful.

```
IF EOF()
    ? 'No records found that match condition'
ENDIF
```

FOR FOR clauses indicate sequential access of a file. FOR clauses such as FOR zip='94704' can be used to modify the commands

```
LIST
DISPLAY
REPORT FORM
LABEL FORM
COPY TO
APPEND FROM
```

With a FOR clause, unless a REST modifier is used, the command being modified always starts with the top of the file (the first logical record in an indexed file or the first physical record in a nonindexed file) and checks each record to see if the FOR clause is true. Execution of commands modified by a FOR clause are relatively slow but useful when no appropriate indexes are present.

FOUND() Used after a FIND or SEEK to test if the search was successful.

```
IF .NOT. FOUND()
    ? 'Record not found'
ENDIF
```

GET *See @.*

GETENV(<*DOS environmental variable*>) Returns the status of various environmental variables from the operating system.

```
. ? GETENV('path')
\DB3
. ? GETENV('comspec')
C:\COMMAND.COM
```

GO Positions the record pointer.

GO BOTT Positions the record pointer at the last record in the file—the last physical record if no index is in use or the last logical record if an index is in use.

NOTE: EOF() is not true when the record pointer is positioned at the last record. EOF() is only true when an attempt is made to skip past the last record. Thus this sequence of commands will make EOF() true.

```
GO BOTT
SKIP
```

GO TOP Positions the record pointer at the first record in the file—the first physical record if no index is in use or the first logical record if an index is in use.

GOTO *n* Positions the record pointer at the physical record numbered *n*.

NOTE: There must be no space between the *GO* and the *TO*. The command GOTO is optional: a number can be typed and the record pointer will be moved to the physical record with that number if one exists.

HELP Calls up dBASE's online help facility.

IF...ELSE...ENDIF A program control structure that causes various instructions to be executed based on whether the IF clause is True or False. The ELSE is optional.

```
IF <logical expression>
   <program instructions>
ELSE
   <program instructions>
ENDIF
```

This program control structure is appropriate for situations involving two-valued logic that must be checked only once. For conditions that must be checked more than once, see DO WHILE. For conditions involving more than two possible values, see DO CASE.

IIF(condition,true,false) The inline or immediate IF is a function that can be used as the argument for an output function to return a value based on whether a condition is True or False. It is something like a spreadsheet IF statement.

```
LIST IIF(amt>0,STR(Amt),'Overdrawn')
```

This expression assumes a numeric field named *amt*. If *amt* is greater than zero, its value is converted to a string and output; otherwise the word *Overdrawn* is output. The STR function is necessary because both the expression to be output (if the condition is true) and the expression to be output (if the expression is false) must be of the same type. IIFs can be nested

```
LIST IIF(amt>0,STR(amt),IIF(amt=0,'Zero balance','Overdrawn'))
```

INDEX ON <*key expression*> TO <*file*> Creates an index based on the key expression. After the index is created, it is in effect as the master index until a USE, SET INDEX TO, INDEX ON, or similar command is executed. The INDEX expression can be up to 100 characters long. If various fields are included in the index expression, they must all be converted to the same type.

INKEY() Traps keyboard input one keystroke at a time. This program can be used to display the value returned for each key pressed. The INKEY() function works sporadically with the *left arrow* key.

```
SET TALK OFF
CLEAR
i=0
DO WHILE .NOT. i=27
    i=0
    @ ROW(),26 SAY 'INKEY() = '
    DO WHILE i=0
        i=INKEY()
    ENDDO
    ?? STR(i,3)
ENDDO
```

INT(*n*) Returns the integer portion of the number indicated.

```
. ? INT(1223.45)
    1223
```

ISALPHA(<*string expression*>) Returns a logical True if the first character of the string expression is alphabetic.

```
. ? ISALPHA('mnum')
.T.
```

ISCOLOR() Determines whether the system has a color or monochrome display so that screen attributes can be set under program control. ISCOLOR() returns a True if the system has a color monitor and a False if it doesn't.

ISLOWER(<*character string*>) Returns a True if the first character of the string is a lowercase alphabetic character and a False if it is not.

```
. ? ISLOWER('ABC')
.F.
```

ISUPPER(<*character string*>) Returns a True if the first character of the string is an uppercase alpha character and a False if it is not.

```
. ? ISUPPER('ABC')
.T.
```

JOIN WITH <*alias*> TO <*file name*> FOR <*condition*> Joins two physical .dbf files based on a common key field. In practice this command is rarely, if ever, used. Some people speculate that it was included just to enable dBASE to be called a relational data base system. When it is necessary to do a JOIN, a virtual JOIN is much more efficient using some variant of SET RELATION TO and various output commands.

LABEL FORM <*name of label form file*> [TO PRINT] Executes a label form file that was previously defined with the command CREATE LABEL <*file name*>. Adding TO PRINT causes output to be directed to the printer.

LEFT(<*string name*>,*n*) Returns the *n* leftmost characters of the specified string. It is equivalent to SUBSTR(<*string name*>,1,*n*).

LEN(<*string*>) Returns the length in characters of the specified string including blanks.

LIST [<*scope*>] [<*expression list*>] [FOR <*condition*>] [WHILE <*condition*>] [TO PRINT] [OFF] Defaults to showing the contents of all fields in all of the records in a file. The fields to be listed can be specified in the expression list. In addition, a FOR clause can be used to list only selected records that meet a given condition. For example,

```
LIST name,address,zip FOR zip='94706'
```

The LIST command is much more versatile than it appears at first and is discussed in chapter 5. If TO PRINT is specified, the output is directed to the printer.

LIST HISTORY/MEMORY/STATUS/STRUCTURE <TO PRINT> *See* each of the above under DISPLAY. When used with the LIST command verb, the listing is continuous, whereas with DISPLAY it is paged on the screen.

LOAD <*file name*> LOADs a binary file into memory for execution by using the CALL command.

LOCATE [<*scope*>] FOR <*expression*> Finds a record based on the contents of specified fields when an index is not present. Any combination of field contents can be specified. Some uses of the LOCATE command are

```
LOCATE FOR lname='Smith'
LOCATE FOR lname='Smith' .AND. zip='94704'
LOCATE FOR DELETED()
```

The LOCATE command finds the first occurrence of a record meeting a condition. To see subsequent occurrences, *see* CONTINUE. A LOCATE command always should be followed by a test to see if the LOCATE was successful.

```
IF EOF()
    ? 'No records found that meet condition'
ENDIF
```

LOCK() or RLOCK() In a multi-user environment, returns a logical True if it is possible to lock the current record in the .dbf file open in the currently selected work area and locks the record.

LOG(*n*) Returns the natural logarithm of the number specified.

LOOP Checks whether a DO WHILE condition is still true while inside a DO WHILE loop. When the LOOP command is encountered, control returns to the DO WHILE statement above the LOOP statement. If the DO WHILE statement is true, the instruction after the DO WHILE is executed. Otherwise, the instruction after the ENDDO is executed.

Lotus *See* APPEND FROM WKS and COPY TO WKS.

LOWER(<*character string*>) Returns a string with all upper case characters in the original string converted to lower case.

LTRIM(<*string*>) Returns a string that removes the leading blanks from the specified string.

LUPDATE() Returns the date when the .dbf file in the current work area was last updated, assuming that the system clock is set correctly.

Macros MACRO substitution is a form of string substitution in which one value is substituted for another. *See* &.

```
. mname='Smith'
Smith
. ? '&mname'
Smith
```

CAUTION: Be careful about changing the value of a macro within a DO WHILE loop when the value is in the DO WHILE condition. Amazingly, dBASE does not allow this.

Master Index The index that is used as the basis for ordering the file. If multiple indexes are open, the one that is listed first is the master index. In the following example, ind1 is the master index.

```
USE <file> INDEX <ind1>,<ind2>,...<ind7>
```

The master index can be changed most effectively by using the SET ORDER TO command. SET ORDER TO 2 would make ind2 the master index because it is the second index listed.

MESSAGE() Returns the message associated with the current error condition. It is designed for use in ON ERROR routines. *See also* ERROR().

MIN(<*numeric expression1*>,<*numeric expression2*>) Compares two numbers and returns the smaller of the two. The arguments can be numeric fields or memory variables.

MOD(<*n1*>,<*n2*>) Returns the remainder from dividing *n1* by *n2*.

```
. ? MOD(7,3)
  1
```

MODIFY COMMAND Calls up dBASE III PLUS's default text editor that should be avoided in serious programming because of limitations including a maximum file size of 5K. Another word processor, such as WordStar, can be used by including the tedit=WS command in the config.db file. If this is done, WordStar will be loaded when MODIFY COMMAND is typed. A better approach is to use a RAM resident word processor such as SideKick notepad.

CAUTION: If using WordStar as a text editor be sure to use the non-document mode. If using Sidekick, turn of word wrap with Ctrl-O R 250.

MODIFY LABEL <*file name*> Modifies a label form created with CREATE LABEL.

MODIFY REPORT ***<file name>*** Modifies a report form created with CREATE REPORT.

MODIFY STRUCTURE Modifies the structure of the currently open .dbf file. The structure of the file appears so that field names, types, and lengths can be changed or added. dBASE then attempts to append the records into the new file structure. However, in some cases data can be lost. The best approach is not to change both field names and field lengths in the same modify structure operation. Always be sure to have backup copies of the files before a modify structure operation is undertaken. If a backup copy is maintained in the same subdirectory, make sure that it has an extension other than .bak because dBASE creates its own backup file with that extension.

MONTH(*<date>*) Returns the numeric value of the month represented by the specified date.

```
. ? MONTH(CTOD('09/19/88'))
   9
```

NDX(*<n>*) Returns the name of the index associated with the specified number. Index 1 is the first index name listed after the INDEX keyword; Index 2 is the second one listed, etc.

```
. USE vendor INDEX vendno, name
. ? NDX(1)
C:vendno.ndx
. ? NDX(2)
C:name.ndx
```

ON ERROR DO ***<file name>*** Allows programmers to write their own error-trapping routines by specifying a program to be executed if an error occurs. If such a file is executed, it should trap the error in some way and not just resume program execution as if the error had never occurred.

NOTE: A problem with the ON ERROR command that limits its usefulness is that system errors such as *printer not ready* are not trapped.

ON ESCAPE DO ***<file name>*** As long as SET ESCAPE OFF has not been executed, this command will cause the specified command file to be executed when the Escape key is pressed.

ON KEY DO ***<file name>*** Causes the specified command file to be executed when any key is pressed. This would be useful to halt a print operation, for example.

OS() Returns a character string identifying the operating system running on the computer.

```
. ? OS()
DOS 3.00
```

PACK Physically and irrevocably removes records that have been flagged for deletion from the file. Generally it is not necessary to use the PACK command. The PACK command removes the deleted records but does not reduce the size of the file. In many cases a better way to remove deleted records from the file is the following:

```
USE file
SET DELETED OFF
COPY TO purges FOR DELETED()
COPY TO new FOR .NOT. DELETED()
USE
RENAME file.dbf TO old.dbf
RENAME new.dbf TO file.dbf
```

This approach has the advantage of putting the deleted and nondeleted records in separate files that are the size of the actual number of records that they hold.

PARAMETERS When parameters are being passed to a program file, a PARAMETERS statement must be the first noncomment line in the program except in a procedure file where the PARAMETERS statement must follow the PROCEDURE statement. The parameters must be listed in the same order as after the WITH statement that called the program

```
PROCEDURE test
PARAMETERS q1,q2,q3
q3=q2*q1
RETURN
```

PCOL() Returns a number representing what dBASE thinks is the current column to which the printer print head is positioned.

PROW() Returns a number representing what dBASE thinks is the current row to which the printer print head is positioned.

PICTURE Used after an @...SAY or @...GET to format the input or output of a variable by using a template or function. The syntax requires that there must be a space between the word *PICTURE* and the template. PICTURE'!' will generate a syntax error because there is no space between the word *PICTURE* and the apostrophe.

When used with a GET, the PICTURE clause actually changes the value of the variable to fit the template. When used with a SAY it only formats the output and does not change the underlying value. Commonly used PICTURE template symbols include

! force capitals

9 force numeric values into a character variable

PRIVATE A declaration for memory variables that hides the variables being defined from higher level definitions using the same name:

```
PRIVATE memvar1,memvar2
```

PROCEDURE A declaration used to identify each individual PROCEDURE within a PROCEDURE file.

PUBLIC A declaration for memory variables that makes the variables so defined accessible to higher level routines.

```
PUBLIC memvar1,memvar2
```

QUIT Closes all open files and exits from dBASE.

READ Activates a series of GETs starting with the first GET after the previous READ.

READKEY() Used to determine how a user exited from a READ or a full screen editing command. For programming purposes, the function is most useful in determining what happened during a READ. For example, if a series of GETs are being edited with a READ, it is useful to know whether any of the values were changed so that a series of REPLACEs can be done. READKEY() returns rather arcane values. The most important ones are

12	exiting from a READ using escape
0–36	no changes made to data
>256	changes made

RECALL The inverse of DELETE. *RECALL* will remove the deletion flag from the current record if one exists. RECALL ALL will remove all deletion flags for records in the currently selected file with SET DELETED OFF.

RECCOUNT() Returns the number of records in the .dbf file that is currently open in the selected work area.

RECNO() Returns the physical record number of the record at which the record pointer is positioned.

Record Pointer The record pointer is dBASE's internal pointer that identifies the current record. When DISPLAY is executed, the record to which the record pointer is pointing is displayed. The number of the physical record to which the record pointer is pointing can be identified with ? RECNO().

RECSIZE() Returns the size in bytes of each record in the .dbf file open in the selected work area.

REINDEX Recreates all currently open indexes for the current .dbf file. It eliminates retyping the full index key each time.

RELEASE ALL Releases all memory variables created within a given program.

RELEASE MODULE <*module name*> Unloads a binary file loaded with the LOAD command.

RENAME <*file*> TO <*newname*> Renames the specified file to a new name. If a .dbf file is to be renamed, the .dbf extender must be stated explicitly. If the .dbf file has memo fields, the corresponding .dbt file must be renamed also or error messages will be generated when an attempt is made to use the file under the new name.

REPLACE [<*scope*>] <*field name*> WITH <*expression*> [,<*field2*) WITH <*expression2*>..] [FOR <*condition*>] [WHILE <*condition*>] Changes the contents of fields under program control.

```
REPLACE lname WITH 'Smith'
REPLACE lname WITH mlname
```

The REPLACE command defaults to changing fields in the current record only. The ALL modifier can be used to replace all records, or a FOR clause can be used to only replace certain records:

```
REPLACE ALL pdate WITH DATE()
REPLACE pdate WITH DATE() FOR pdate>DATE()
```

REPLICATE(<*char*>,*n*) Returns the specified character *n* times.

```
. ? REPLICATE('-',20)
--------------------
```

REPORT FORM <***file name***> **[**<***scope***>**] [FOR** <***condition***>**] [WHILE** <***condition***>**] [TO PRINT] [TO FILE** <***file name***>**]** Executes a report previously defined using CREATE REPORT. TO PRINT directs the output to the printer. TO FILE <*file name*> directs the output to the designated file.

RESTORE FROM <***memfile***> **[ADDITIVE]** Restores memory variable from the contents of a .mem file created with the SAVE TO command. If the ADDITIVE switch is used, the memory variables are added to the memory variables already in memory.

RESUME Continues program execution after it has been SUSPENDed.

RETRY Used in network applications. It is similar to RETURN in that it returns control to the calling program except that it tries to re-execute the command that called the program instead of the command *after* the command that called the program.

RETURN Closes a program file and returns control to the instruction after the DO that called it. If a RETURN is not present at the end of the program, the end of file marker is interpreted as a RETURN. RETURN has no effect on the .dbf files that were opened in the program, but it does wipe out all private memory variables created in the program.

RIGHT(<***string***>**,*n*)** Returns the rightmost *n* characters of the string specified.

```
. ? RIGHT('dBASE',4)
BASE
```

RLOCK() OR LOCK() In a multi-user environment, returns a logical True if it is possible to lock the current record in the .dbf file open in the currently selected work area and it locks the record.

ROUND(<***n***>**,**<***number of decimals***>**)** Rounds off a number to the number of decimals specified.

```
. ? ROUND(123.456,2)
123.460
```

ROW() Returns the current row position on the screen. The following expression would cause output at the next row and column on the screen.

```
@ ROW()+1,COL()+1 SAY message
```

RTRIM(<***string***>**)** The same as TRIM() and removes the trailing blanks from the specified string.

RUN Executes a DOS .exe or .com program from within dBASE by loading a second version of command.com into memory. The following command would run a DOS directory of all *.prg files in the current subdirectory.

```
RUN DIR *.PRG
```

SAVE TO <*file name*> Saves memory variables to a disk file with a .mem extender so that they can later be RESTORed.

SEEK Finds a record based on the value of its key field for the index that is currently open. It can only be used when an appropriate index is open. The SEEK command expects a memory variable or expression corresponding to the key expression in the index. For example, an appropriate SEEK command for a last name index is

```
SEEK "Smith"
    or
mlname = 'Smith'
SEEK mlname
```

A SEEK command should always be followed by a test to see if the SEEK was successful.

```
IF EOF()
    ? 'No records found that meet condition'
ENDIF
```

If a SEEK command does not successfully find a record, try TRIMming the value being sought.

```
SEEK TRIM(mlname)
```

SELECT Selects a work area. There are 10 possible work areas identified by the numbers *1–10*, the letters *a–j*, or the name of the file currently open in the work area.

If the file names were open in work area 2, any of the following constructs would select that work area.

```
SELECT 2
SELECT B
SELECT names
```

SET Invokes a menu-driven full screen option that shows the status of many of the SET options and allows them to be changed.

The SET commands allow various environmental variables to be switched on and off or to be changed. Some SET commands set a condition on or off. Others set a condition to a number or other value. Most SET commands that set a value to something can be reset by typing them with no argument. When a condition is set ON or OFF, the default is shown in upper case.

SET ALTERNATE on/OFF; SET ALTERNATE TO <***file name***> Traps screen output, with the exception of @...SAYs, to a disk file. Several steps are required.

```
SET ALTERNATE TO test.txt
SET ALTERNATE ON
LIST
SET ALTERNATE OFF
SET ALTERNATE TO
```

SET ALTERNATE TO test.txt identifies test.txt as the alternate file. .txt is the default extension for alternate files. SET ALTERNATE ON then directs any subsequent screen output, with the exception of @...SAYs, to the alternate file. In this example LIST is used as the command that is used so that its output can be trapped. SET ALTERNATE OFF turns off ALTERNATE so that screen output is no longer trapped. SET ALTERNATE TO cancels the designation of test.txt as the alternate file and closes the file.

NOTE: Some commands such as REPORT have a TO FILE option that allows the output of the report to be sent to a file by using the following syntax.

```
REPORT FORM rep1 TO FILE test.txt
```

SET BELL ON/off Turns the beep off and on, which occurs after the last character in a field is entered with a GET.

SET CENTURY on/OFF Determines whether or not the first two digits of the year are displayed when dates are displayed on the screen. If SET CENTURY OFF has been executed, the first two digits of the year are assumed to be *19* and are not displayed.

SET COLOR TO [<*standard foreground/standard background*>] [,<*enhanced foreground/enhanced background*>][,<*border*>] Controls screen attributes including foreground, background, and border. Different screen attributes have different meanings with different types of monitors.

These are selected SET COLOR TO parameters for monochrome monitors

i	reverse video
n	invisible
u	underline
x	invisible
*	invisible

SET COLOR TO can be used to change how GETs appear. For example, SET COLOR TO b,u results in GETs being displayed as underlines on a monochrome monitor instead of the default of reverse video. Simply typing SET COLOR TO defaults to the normal screen attributes.

SET COLOR ON/OFF Switches between two monitors if they are present. The default value is based on the monitor in use when dBASE was started.

SET CONFIRM on/OFF Forces the user to press Return at the end of each GET.

SET DATE AMERICAN/ansi Switches between various date formats. For domestic applications the most useful are the following:

AMERICAN	mm/dd/yy
ANSI	yy.mm.dd

SET DEBUG on/OFF Used in conjunction with SET ECHO ON. If both are set on, program instructions are echoed to the printer rather than to the screen as they are executed.

SET DECIMALS TO <*n*> Determines the number of decimal places that are displayed in the result of certain mathematical operations such as division and SQRT. If SET FIXED ON has been executed, the number of decimals specified with SET DECIMALS TO will apply to the display of all numeric data. SET DECIMALS TO and SET FIXED ON do not apply to GETs. To input decimal places to memory variables, they must be initialized with the appropriate number of decimal places.

SET DEFAULT TO <*drive name*> Specifies the dBASE default drive—the drive on which dBASE will look for files unless the name of the drive is explicitly included in the file name. SET DEFAULT TO has no impact on the DOS default drive.

SET DELETED on/OFF Makes all records flagged for deletion with the

DELETE command appear to be invisible. SET DELETED OFF allows records that are flagged for deletion to be seen.

SET DELIMITERS on/OFF

SET DELIMITERS TO '<*character*>' Refers to which characters are used to delimit variables input with a GET. The default is displaying no delimiters. If SET DELIMITERS ON is executed, the default delimiter is a colon (:). That default delimiter can be changed by executing SET DELIMITERS TO followed by the new delimiter character enclosed in quotes.

SET DEVICE TO print/SCREEN Directs the output of all @...SAYs to the printer or screen. When directing @...SAYs to the printer, make sure that all @...SAY coordinates are sequential in order to avoid extraneous page ejects.

At the end of a print job, before issuing SET DEVICE TO SCREEN, it is useful to issue an EJECT command to position the print head at the beginning of the next page.

CAUTION: If a program aborts abnormally while device is set to print, all @...SAY and GET commands will continue to be directed to the printer, including menus that are generated with @...SAY commands. To avoid this problem, it is useful to include a SET DEVICE TO SCREEN command within the menu loop.

SET DOHISTORY on/OFF Traps commands to a memory buffer as they are executed in a program file. This setting is used as a debugging aid. The commands trapped in history can be accessed using LIST HISTORY or DISPLAY HISTORY. The default number of commands that can be displayed in the history buffer is 20. This number can be increased by executing SET HISTORY TO <*n*>.

SET ECHO on/OFF Echoes command lines to the screen as they are executed. It is a useful tool to see how a program is executing or to determine the speed at which each line is being executed. The drawback of using this setting is that command lines are echoed all over the screen making user screens practically unreadable. When used with SET DEBUG ON, the command lines are echoed to the printer rather than to the screen.

SET ENCRYPTION ON/off When the protect security system is in effect, determines whether files created by copying other .dbf files are encrypted.

SET ESCAPE on/OFF Disables the Escape key. This command should be used sparingly, such as when an operation in progress must not be interrupted. Examples of such commands include PACK or REINDEX. Termination of these commands in midstream may result in some type of file corruption. If Escape is set OFF, the user cannot terminate the program without rebooting.

SET EXACT on/OFF Applies to certain equality tests such as equality between two variables and equality with an index key as accessed with FIND or SEEK. If EXACT is off, only the leftmost characters must match. If exact is set ON, all characters must match

```
. m1='test'
test
. m2='te'
te
. ? m1=m2
.T.
. SET EXACT ON
. ? m2=m1
.F.
```

Typically this setting is most critical when doing SEEKs or FINDs with index keys. If exact is set off and an index is open involving last names, the following command

```
SEEK "S"
```

will find the first occurrence of a last name beginning with S.

When memory variables are compared with SET EXACT OFF, the value on the right side of the equal sign must be contained in the value on the left side for an equality to be true.

```
. ? 'vv'='vvv'
.F.
. ? 'vvv'='vv'
.T.
```

SET EXCLUSIVE ON/off In a network environment, determines whether files are open in exclusive or shared modes.

SET FIELDS on/OFF Makes dBASE temporarily forget which fields have been set until a SET FIELDS ON is executed. When a SET FIELDS TO <field expression) is executed, fields are set on.

SET FIELDS TO ***<field list>*** Causes dBASE to act as if only certain fields exist. If the following command is entered

```
SET FIELDS TO name,city,zip
```

dBASE will act as if only the three named fields exist. The SET FIELDS command also assures that the fields will be displayed in the order specified with the SET FIELDS command. If a SET FIELDS statement is in effect, the DISPLAY STRUCTURE output will show greater than signs in front of the fields that have been designated with the SET FIELDS command.

The SET FIELDS command can be canceled by the command

```
SET FIELDS TO
```

See also SET FIELDS ON/OFF.

SET FILTER TO [<***expression***>] Causes dBASE to "remember" a FOR clause. If a filter is set, such as SET FILTER TO zip='94706', dBASE will act as if only records that meet this condition exist.

The filter can be canceled by one of these methods:

1. Closing the file
2. SET FILTER TO

A filter can be used for other than a field condition, such as SET FILTER TO DELETED() to see deleted records only.

SET FILTER TO has no effect on the creation of an index, however, it has an effect on whether or not a find is successful.

```
USE address INDEX city
SET FILTER TO zip ='94704'
SEEK "Berkeley"
```

Both the filter must be true and the SEEK condition must be met for the SEEK to be successful. If no Berkeley record is found with zip equal to 94704, EOF() will be true. The SEEK will be successful only if a record exists with city=Berkeley and zip code 94704.

To check whether a filter is in effect, use DISPLAY STATUS.

CAUTION: After invoking SET FILTER TO <*expression*>, always do a record positioning command such as GO TOP to position the record pointer to the first record in the file that meets the filter condition. SET FILTER does not move the record pointer. If a record positioning command is not issued after FILTER is set, the record pointer will remain pointing at the same record whether or not that record meets the FILTER condition.

To test whether any records exists that meet the filter condition,

```
USE file
SET FILTER TO <condition>
GO TOP
IF EOF()
    ? 'No records exist that meet condition'
    WAIT
ENDIF
```

See FOR for commands effected by SET FILTER TO.

SET FIXED on/OFF SET FIXED ON makes dBASE display all numbers as if they had the number of decimal places specified with SET DECIMALS TO. These commands can produce somewhat misleading results because variables only have as many places as they are initialized to have. The precision of fields is determined by using the CREATE command. The precision of memory variables is determined by the assignment statement with which they are defined. Using SET DECIMALS TO <*n*> to show a greater number of decimal places than are actually there may provide misleading results. For example, mcost is defined as mcost=0.00. If SET FIXED ON and SET DECIMALS TO 3 are executed, mcost will be shown with three decimal places. However, the third decimal place is meaningless because it cannot be input to and it implies a degree of precision that is not there.

SET FORMAT TO <*file name*> Activates the designated format files. Format files are special cases of command files that contain only @...SAY and GET statements. They are occasionally useful if a program contains a big chunk of code containing only @...SAY and GETs. That chunk of code could be put into a separate file with an .fmt extension and called a format file. The code could then be activated using the sequence of commands

```
SET FORMAT TO <file name>
READ
```

The problem with this approach is that for input validation purposes, it is rare to have a large chunk of code with just @...SAYs and GETs since DO WHILE loops are frequently needed for input validation. This limitation of format files makes them marginally useful.

Format files can also be used to change the appearance of the default APPEND and EDIT screens when used at the dot prompt. A format file is designed using @...SAYs for the proper field positioning. The following sequence of commands will cause the APPEND command to be executed with the new format.

```
SET FORMAT TO <file name>
APPEND
```

However, this approach is generally not used in programming.

SET FUNCTION <*n*> TO <*expression*> Resets the assigned values of the function keys. All keys may be reassigned with the exception of function key F1, which is permanently assigned to Help. At the beginning of a program it is useful to either reassign or unassign all function keys. Ashton-Tate assumes that function keys will be used for various commands at the dot prompt. While this may be fine in certain circumstances, if a user is executing a program and accidentally hits function key F9 for APPEND, problems could be caused. For this reason it is best to reset function keys to blanks if they are not going to be used otherwise. This is accomplished with

```
SET FUNCTION 2 TO ' '
etc.
```

Contrary to Ashton-Tate's approach of assigning commands to function keys, it is often advantageous to use function keys to aid in input by assigning certain commonly used string values to function keys so that a function key can be hit in response to a GET rather than by typing in the complete string each time.

```
SET FUNCTION 3 TO 'Net 30 days'
```

This function key assignment can be used to put a common value into a payment terms field. A semicolon (;) in a function key assignment is interpreted as a Carriage Return.

SET HEADING ON/off Toggles on and off field name headings which commands such as LIST, DISPLAY, SUM, COUNT, and AVERAGE display. The width of each column displayed is the greater of the field width or the heading width if HEADING is set ON. If an expression is used in the field expression, that expression is displayed in the heading.

SET HELP ON/off SET HELP OFF can be executed to get rid of the message *Do you want some help?* (*Y/N*), which is displayed whenever a typo is made in a command.

SET HISTORY ON/off Toggles the capability of dBASE to store commands entered at the dot prompt into a history buffer that can be accessed later using the command LIST HISTORY.

SET HISTORY TO <*n*> Sets the number of commands that can be stored in the buffer. The default number of commands is 20. *See also* SET DOHISTORY, which stores command executed in program files.

SET INDEX TO <*index file list*> Used to open new indexes for a currently open .dbf file. When SET INDEX TO is executed, the currently open index files are closed and the new index files are opened. SET INDEX TO without an index list, closes all existing indexes in the currently selected work area. SET ORDER TO is often a more efficient way of changing the master index without the overhead of file openings and closings.

SET MARGIN TO <*n*> Sets the left margin for printed output generated with @...SAYs, LIST, or REPORT. SET MARGIN TO 10 would move all printed output 10 places to the right. This command is useful when an application for a client is being developed on the programmer's printer where the client's printer assumes a different margin. The SET MARGIN TO command can be inserted into the client's program to move everything to the right without changing the absolute positions of the @...SAY coordinates.

SET MEMOWIDTH TO <*n*> Sets the display width for memo fields output with the LIST, DISPLAY, or ? commands.

SET MENUS ON/off Turns off the menus in full screen editing modes such as APPEND or EDIT. Even if the menu is off, it can still be accessed by pressing the F1 key.

SET MESSAGE TO <*string*> Resets the message that will appear at the bottom of the screen when STATUS is set ON.

SET ORDER TO <*n*> Changes which index is the master or controlling index after a series of indexes have been opened. The beauty of SET ORDER TO is that it changes the order of the indexes without physically opening or closing files. A typical example might be

```
USE address INDEX zip,name,state
```

After this command is executed, zip is the master index based on which records will be found. To make name into the master index, use the following command

```
SET ORDER TO 2
```

After this command is executed, name will be the master index because it is the second index listed. The other indexes will still be open in case records are appended to the file. To make dBASE act as if no indexes are open, the command is SET ORDER TO 0.

SET PATH TO <*path name*> Defines a directory search path from within dBASE. SET PATH works in a similar fashion to the DOS path in that if a file is not found in the current directory, the search path is checked. The SET PATH command sets a search path within dBASE that does not effect the DOS search path.

SET PRINT on/OFF Directs the output of ?, DISPLAY, LIST, and REPORT to the printer. The output is also echoed to the screen.

SET PRINTER TO <*device name*> Redirects printer output in a manner similar to the DOS mode command. For example to redirect printed output to the serial port, the command would be SET PRINTER TO com1. To set the baud rate and other communications parameters, the DOS mode command must be used.

SET PROCEDURE TO <*file name*> Opens a procedure file containing up to 32 separate procedures. The advantage of aggregating command files into a single physical procedure file is that the file does not have to be physically opened each time a procedure is called with the DO command.

SET RELATION TO <*key expression*> INTO <*alias*> Links two .dbf files based on a common key field. It is best used for many-to-one or one-to-one relations. The same results can often be achieved somewhat more efficiently with some programming, as described in the chapter on SET RELATION TO.

SET SAFETY ON/off Allows overwriting existing files without getting the prompt asking if it is ok to overwrite the file. However, even if SAFETY is off, an error message will appear if an attempt is made to rename a file to a file name that already exists.

SET SCOREBOARD ON/off Turns off the display at the top of the screen indicating whether or not the Caps Lock, Insert, or Num Lock is on and displays certain error messages. If STATUS is set ON, these messages are displayed at the bottom of the screen. If both SCOREBOARD and STATUS are set OFF, certain error messages will not be displayed.

SET STATUS ON/off Toggles the status display at the bottom of the screen that shows which .dbf file is currently open and the number of the record to which the record pointer is pointing.

SET STEP ON/off One of the most useful debugging features of dBASE III PLUS when combined with SET ECHO ON. SET STEP ON allows a programmer to step through each instruction in a program. After each instruction is executed, a prompt appears to press the spacebar to execute the next instruction, *S* to suspend, or *E*scape to cancel. If *S* is pressed to suspend program execution, the dot prompt appears and commands can be entered to check the status of memory variables and fields. Execution of the program can then be continued by typing RESUME.

CAUTION: When you enter commands while a program is suspended, it is important not to enter commands that will move the record pointer if the intention is to resume program execution.

SET TALK ON/off Displays certain information on the screen as commands are executed. This information includes the value of a memory variable after an assignment statement, the position of the record pointer after a command that moves it is executed, and the status messages that monitor the progress of commands such as INDEX and APPEND FROM.

SET TYPEAHEAD TO <*n*> Defines the size of the typeahead buffer for storing keystrokes. The default size is 20. SET TYPEAHEAD TO 0 disables the typeahead buffer, but commands such as INKEY() and ON KEY, which depend on the typeahead buffer, will no longer work.

SET UNIQUE on/OFF Determines whether an index can have duplicate key values. It is best to leave SET UNIQUE OFF and check for duplicates at the time of input.

SKIP <*n*> Moves the record pointer in the currently open file by the specified number of records, including negative numbers. SKIP by itself will move the record pointer forward one record. Whether or not an index is open determines if the file is in physical or logical order and thus whether SKIP will move the record pointer to the next physical record or the next logical record as determined by the index.

If an attempt is made to SKIP past end of file, EOF() becomes true and dBASE appears to add a blank record to the file, but it is not added physically.

SORT Physically rearranges a .dbf file into the specified order. It is not generally necessary or desirable to use SORT in programs.

SPACE(*n*) Returns the number of spaces specified. It is most useful for initializing memory variables to a precise number of spaces.

```
lname=SPACE(15)
```

SQRT(*n*) Returns the square root of the number specified.

STORE <*expression*> TO <*memvar list*> One form of an assignment statement. STORE 0 to mtotal is the same as *mtotal=0*. The only advantage is that multiple memory variables can be created on a single line, for example,

```
STORE 0.00 to msub1, msub2, mtotal
```

STR(<*numeric expression*>,*length*,*decimals*) Converts a number to a string and rounds it off at the same time. The length and decimals specifiers are optional.

```
. memvar=12.8
12.8
. ? STR(memvar)
         13
. ? STR(memvar,10,2)
         12.8
```

SUBSTR(<*string*>,*start*,*length*) Returns another string that is part of the original string. The starting position of the new string and its length are specified. If the length parameter is not specified, SUBSTR() returns the remainder of the string from the specified start position.

```
. ? SUBSTR('dBASE',2,4)
BASE
```

NOTE: When SUBSTR() is used as part of an index key, the length parameter must be specified.

SUM <*field list*> TO <*memvar list*> [FOR <*condition*>] [WHILE <*condition*>] Sums a single numeric field or list of fields separated by commas to a single memory variable or to separate memory variables separated by commas.

```
SUM amt1,amt2,amt3 TO mtot1,mtot2,mtot3
```

SUSPEND Temporarily suspends execution of a program so that commands can be entered at the dot prompt to check the values of memory variables and the position of the record pointer. Program execution can be resumed with the RESUME statement.

TEXT...ENDTEXT Outputs information to the screen. All text included between these two statements is output to the screen if SET PRINT OFF is in effect, or to the printer if SET PRINT ON has been executed.

TIME() Returns the system time as a character string.

TOTAL ON <*key field*> TO <*file name*> [FIELDS <*fields list*>] [FOR <*condition*>] [WHILE <*condition*>] Creates a new summary file. The new file has the same structure as the file being totaled and contains a single record for each unique occurrence of the key field in the currently open file, assuming that the currently open file is indexed on that key field or physically in that order.

All numeric fields are subtotaled for that key expression. For example, if an address file that is indexed on zip is *totaled* on zip, a new file is created with one record for each unique zip code that appears in the main file. All the numeric fields are subtotaled by zip unless only certain numeric fields are specified with the FIELDS expression. The TOTAL command behaves something like the subtotal feature in the Report Generator.

TRANSFORM(<*expression*>,<*picture clause*>) Allows the use of PICTURE clauses to format output generated by ?, LIST/DISPLAY, or in the REPORT FORM. It is useful to such purposes as inserting commas in numbers.

```
. ? TRANSFORM(123456789.11,'999,999,999.99')
123,456,789.11
```

TRIM(<*string*>) Removes the trailing blanks from the specified string.

```
. mstring='Hello   world
Hello world
. ? LEN(mstring)
        18
. ? LEN(TRIM(mstring))
        12
```

TYPE <*file name*> [TO PRINT] Displays the contents of an ASCII file in a manner similar to the DOS type command. If TO PRINT is specified, the output is directed to the printer.

UNLOCK In a networked environment, UNLOCK releases the most recent lock placed on the file in the current work area.

UPDATE ON <*key field*> FROM <*alias*> REPLACE <*field1*> WITH <*exp1*> [,<*field2*> WITH <*exp2*>...] [RANDOM] Posts the contents of one .dbf file to another based on a common key field. Field contents of one file can be added to or subtracted from the field contents of the other file. One example is posting the contents of a temporary file containing accounting data to the general ledger accounts in the master file.

```
SELECT A
USE transac
INDEX ON acctnum TO acct
TOTAL ON acctnum TO transactot
USE transactot
SELECT B
```

```
USE gl
UPDATE ON acctnum FROM transactot;
REPLACE dbbal WITH dbbal+a->dbamt, ;
    crbal WITH crbal+a->cramt
```

UPPER(<*string*>) Converts all alphabetic characters in the specified string to upper case. If UPPER() is used in an output statement, the contents of the original string are not changed. If used in a REPLACE or STORE statement, the contents of the specified variable are changed.

USE <*file name*> INDEX <*index file list*> Opens .dbf and index files that have already been created. USE by itself closes the .dbf and index files in the currently selected area. Up to seven indexes can be opened at once with the first index listed as the master index that is checked to implement SEEKs or FINDs.

VAL(<*string*>) Converts a string to a numeric value if the string contains numbers. If the first character in the string is not a number, VAL() returns a 0.

```
. ? VAL('1234')
1234.00
. ? VAL('abc')
    0.00
```

VAL() performs an LTRIM() automatically

```
. ? VAL(' 123')
  123.00
```

VERSION() Returns the version of dBASE being run.

```
. ? VERSION()
dBASE III PLUS Version 1.1
```

WAIT "prompt" [TO <*memvar*>] WAIT by itself pauses the screen display with the prompt *Press any key to continue* until a key is pressed. Optionally a prompt can be specified in quotes. WAIT can also be used to store the keystroke to a character type memory variable:

```
WAIT "Is printer ready? (Y/N)" TO mprint
IF UPPER(mprint) <> "Y"
    RETURN
ENDIF
```

WHILE <***condition***> Can be used with such commands as LIST, DISPLAY, AVERAGE, SUM, REPORT, and COUNT. Unlike using these commands with a FOR clause, the record pointer is not positioned to the beginning of the file. Rather, the WHILE clause is evaluated against the current record. If the WHILE clause is true, the command executes, otherwise it does not. As soon as a record is encountered where the WHILE clause is not true, the command stops executing. The WHILE clause is best used in conjunction with an indexed file after a SEEK to make the WHILE clause true. For example,

```
SEEK 'Smith'
LIST WHILE lname='Smith'
```

A WHILE clause can be used in conjunction with a FOR clause to selectively look at certain records meeting the WHILE clause.

```
SEEK 'Smith'
LIST WHILE lname='Smith' FOR state ='CA'
```

This approach, using only an index on last name, will go immediately to the first Smith record and then selectively list all Smith records where the state='CA'. This example is one of the few cases in dBASE where indexed and sequential access can be combined for effective results.

YEAR(<***date***>) Returns the numeric value of the year represented by the specified date.

```
. ? YEAR(CTOD('09/19/88'))
  1988
```

ZAP Equivalent to DELETE ALL and PACK. It irrevocably gets rid of all records in the currently selected data base.

Appendix 2

HIGHLIGHTS OF dBASE IV MODIFICATIONS OF COMMANDS

The following is a summary of new and enhanced commands that are of most interest to dBASE programmers and power users. This section does not include SQL commands.

One feature that is useful when working at the dot prompt and that has been added to commands that accept a file name as an argument, is the ability to enter a *?* in place of the file name to display a menu of available files. Selection can be made from the menu based on pointing and shooting. For example, the USE ? command will display a menu of all .dbf files in the current directory and allow selecting the desired file.

Note that dBASE command lines can now be up to 1024 characters long. When you type a command line greater than 254 characters at the dot prompt, press Ctrl-Home to enter the Editor. When the full line has been entered, press Ctrl-End to save it.

?/?? <*expression 1*> [PICTURE <*clause*>] [FUNCTION <*function list*>] [AT <*expression*>] [STYLE] [<*font number*>] [,<*expression 2*> ...] This simple output command has been enhanced with bells and whistles, including optional switches that can customize the appearance of the output.

PICTURE uses the same template characters allowed for @...SAYs, using the *?* command plus some additional templates.

FUNCTION allows use of the functions associated with @...SAYs plus some additional functions.

@B	Left aligns text within field
@I	Centers text within a field
@J	Right aligns text within a field
@T	Trims leading and trailing blanks

These functions work in conjunction with a PICTURE template such as the following, where the width of the output field is defined with the X template character, and the @I causes centering within that field.

```
. memvar='Hi'
Hi
. ? memvar picture '@I XXXXXXXXXXXXXXXX'
      Hi
```

AT specifies the column at which the output will appear. This example displays the memory variable starting at column 10.

```
. ? memvar AT 10
         Hi
```

STYLE can include a combination of letters and numbers. Numbers refer to fonts defined in config.db. Letters refer to the following attributes.

B	Bold
I	Italic
U	Underline
R	Raised
L	Lowered

NOTE: Not all monitors or printers will display all of these attributes.

??? [<*expression*>] The three-question-mark command sends output directly to the printer, bypassing the installed printer driver and without changing the printer row and column positions. This command is useful to send printer control codes to the printer. No SET PRINT ON is needed as the output is sent directly to the printer. In order to support sending printer control codes, an escape code can be sent using the syntax

```
??? "{ESC}"
```

Thus, if for a given printer, escape *E* turns on emphasized printing, the following command would send the printer control code for emphasized printing.

```
. ??? "{ESC}E"
```

@ *r,c* [SAY <*expression*> [PICTURE <*clause*>] [FUNCTION <*function list*>]; @ *r,c* [GET <*variable*> [[OPEN] WINDOW <*window name*>] [PICTURE <*clause*>] [FUNCTION '<*function list*>] [RANGE <*low,high*>] [VALID <*condition*>] [ERROR <*error message*>]]; [WHEN <*condition*>] [DEFAULT <*expression*>] [MESSAGE <*expression*>] [COLOR [<*standard*>][,<*enhanced*>]]] For printed output the row range has been increased from 255 to 32,767. If a window has been ACTIVATEd, @...SAY coordinates must be relative to the window. For example, if a window is defined from 17,1 to 23,79, row 18 becomes row 0 for that window. Row 19 becomes row 1, etc.

The **RANGE** clause now supports character variables as well as numbers and dates. RANGE supports entering only a lower bound that will force input to be greater than the lowest amount entered. This forces an entry that is greater than or equal to one.

```
mage=0
@ 2,1 GET mage RANGE 1
```

The VALID clause has been added to allow specifying a logical condition that must be true. The ERROR switch specifies the error message that will be displayed if the VALID clause is not satisfied. If no ERROR value is specified, a general error message will be displayed saying *Editing condition not satisfied (press SPACE)*.

This displays an error message if all five characters of the zip code have not been entered.

```
mzip=SPACE(5)
@ 2,1 SAY 'zip code ' GET mzip VALID .NOT. ' ' $ MZIP;
      ERROR 'Enter all 5 characters of zip code'
READ
```

The optional COLOR switch allows specifying the screen attributes that will be set for SAYs and GETs. The <*standard*> COLOR will be used for SAYs and the <*enhanced*> COLOR for GETs.

DEFAULT can assign a default value to the variable being "gotten."

MESSAGE can specify a prompt that appears at the bottom of the screen when control moves into the variable being "gotten."

WINDOW allows specifying a window for editing of memo fields when Ctrl-Home is pressed. If OPEN is specified, the memo field is automatically loaded into the Editor when the GET is executed.

PICTURE and FUNCTION are basically unchanged from dBASE III PLUS except for the support of new picture functions:

^	displays numbers in scientific notation
I	Centers text within a field
J	Right align text within field
M	Allows list of choices for GET variable
T	Trims leading and trailing blanks from a field

Finally, the output of @...SAY statements can be directed to a file, using SET DEVICE TO FILE <*file name*>

@ *r1,c2* FILL TO *r2,c2* COLOR <*color attribute*> Fills a rectangular region of the screen with a specified color attribute.

@ *r1,c1* TO *r2,c2* [DOUBLE/PANEL <*border definition string*>] [COLOR <*color attribute*>] Draws a box on the screen. This fills a box with inverse video on a monochrome monitor.

```
@ 1,1 FILL TO 3,20 COLOR i
```

See SET BORDER TO.

ACCESS() Used in multi-user mode to return the user's access level (1–8).

ACOS(*n*) The arccosine function. It returns the angle size (in radians) that produces a trigonometric cosine equal to *n*.

ACTIVATE MENU <*menu name*> [PAD <*pad name*>] Activates a previously defined bar menu and displays it on the screen. If the pad name is specified, the highlight bar appears on the specified pad of the menu.

ACTIVATE POPUP <*POPUP name*> Activates a previously defined pop-up menu.

ACTIVATE SCREEN Restores access to the full screen, canceling an ACTIVATE WINDOW command but leaving the window displayed on the screen.

ACTIVATE WINDOW Activates and displays a previously defined window and directs all screen output to that window.

ALIAS(<*expression*>) Returns the alias name of the work area referenced. Either the letter (*a–j*) in quotes or numbers (*1–10*) can be used to identify the work area.

APPEND FROM <*file name*> [[TYPE] <*file type*>] [FOR <*condition*>] Enhanced to allow appending from these types of foreign files in addition to the file types already supported in III PLUS.

FW2	Framework II
RPD	RapidFile
DBASEII	dBASE II

APPEND FROM ARRAY <*array name*> [FOR <*condition*>] Appends the contents of an array to the currently open .dbf files. The contents of each row in the array become a new record in the .dbf file.

APPEND MEMO <*memo field name*> FROM <*file name*> [OVERWRITE] Appends the contents of a text file to the named memo field in the current record. If the OVERWRITE switch is specified, the current contents of the memo field are erased prior to appending, otherwise the contents of the file are appended to the current contents of the memo field.

ASIN(*n*) The arcsine function that returns the angle size (in radians) that has a trigonometric sine of *n*.

AT(<*str1*>,<*str2*>/<*memo field name*>) Now supports memo fields that are string searchable to see if <*str1*> is contained in a memo field.

ATAN(*n*) The arctangent function that returns the angle size (in radians) with the trigonometric tangent equal to *n*.

ATN2(<*n1,n2*>) Returns the angle size (in radians) of an angle with the sine equal to *n1* and the cosine equal to *n2*.

AVERAGE TO ARRAY <*array name*> The results of the AVERAGE command can now be stored to a one-dimensional array.

```
DECLARE av[4]
AVERAGE field1,field2,field3,field4 TO ARRAY av
```

This command assumes field one, two, three, and four are all numeric. It averages field1 to array element av[1], field2 to array element av[2], etc.

AVG(<*field expression*>) The new AVG() function works as part of a CALCULATE statement.

```
CALCULATE AVG(contrib) FOR zip='94704'
```

BAR() Returns the selected bar number of the most recently selected pop-up menu.

BEGIN TRANSACTION Tells dBASE to record subsequent modification of data and index files in a .log file until an END TRANSACTION statement is encountered. This approach allows using the ROLLBACK command to roll-back all modifications made since BEGIN TRANSACTION. Commands that erase or overwrite files are not allowed in a BEGIN TRANSACTION...END TRANSACTION structure. The function COMPLETED() tests whether or not the transactions have been completed.

BROWSE Various switches have been added. Browse now allows toggling between a default table view and a form view that displays only the highlighted record on the screen in a display similar to the default EDIT mode. Some of the more useful new switches include

NOEDIT. Makes all fields read only. This approach allows the user only to look at the data and not to change it.

NODELETE. Prevents the user from deleting records when in BROWSE.

NOCLEAR. Leaves the browse display on the screen after BROWSE is exited.

COMPRESS. Slightly compresses the table format to allow two more lines of data to appear on the screen.

FORMAT. Allows using the VALID and other clauses attached to @...SAYs in a FORMAT file but ignores the row and column coordinates.

LOCK <*n*>. Locks the *n* fields at the left of the screen.

WIDTH. Sets a maximum column width for all fields in the BROWSE table.

WINDOW. Activates a window to contain the BROWSE table.

FIELDS. Allows specification of the fields to be displayed and the order in which they are to appear. Fields can be designated as read only by typing */r* after the field name.

BUILD A utility included in the developer's release that allows BUILDing an entire application for distribution with the run-time version of dBASE.

CALCULATE [<*scope*>] <*option list*> [FOR <*condition*>] [WHILE <*condition*>] [TO <*memvar list*>/TO ARRAY <*array name*>] Extracts summary statistics from a file with only a single pass through the file. The functions that can be used with CALCULATE include NPV(),STD(),VAR(),MIN(), MAX(),AVG(),SUM(),CNT(). More than one of these functions can be used with the CALCULATE verb to extract statistics from a file with one pass through the file.

```
CALCULATE SUM(sales),AVG(sales) TO msum,mavg
```

CEILING(*n*) Returns the smallest integer greater than or equal to *n*.

CHANGE() Works in networked environments on files that have been CONVERTed to add a _dbaselock field. CHANGE() returns a logical True if the contents of the current record in the open .dbf file in the currently selected area have been changed since they were read from disk.

CLEAR MENUS Erases all horizontal bar menus from the screen and releases them from memory.

CLEAR POPUPS Erases all pop-up menus from the screen and releases them from memory.

CLEAR WINDOW Deactivates all windows, erases them from the screen, and releases them from memory.

COMPILE <*program name*> Checks for a .prg or .prs program source file and generates a program object file (.dbo) with the same file name.

COMPLETED() Used in conjunction with a BEGIN TRANSACTION...END TRANSACTION construct to test whether a transaction has been successfully completed.

CONVERT Adds a field named _dbaselock to the structure of the currently open .dbf file that contains information required to do multi-user lock identification. Information stored in the field includes the time and date when the record was locked and the name of the user who locked it (if the lock is still in effect). A backup of the original .dbf file is created with a .cvt extension.

COPY INDEXES/TAG <*file list*> TO <*mdx file name*> Allows copying .ndx file or tags to another .mdx file.

COPY MEMO <*memo field name*> TO <*file name*> [ADDITIVE] Copies the specified memo field from the current record in the currently open .dbf file to a text file. The contents of the memo field can be added to an existing file if the ADDITIVE keyword is specified.

COPY STRUCTURE EXTENDED TO <*file name*> Now includes a field in the target file that indicates whether or not the field is an index key field.

COPY TAG <*mdxtag*> [OF <*mdx name*>] TO <*ndx file name*> Allows creating an .ndx file based on one of the tags from an mdx file.

COPY TO <*file name*> [SDF/DIF/SYLK/WKS/FW2/RPD/DBASEII/DELI] Now supports copying open .dbf file in the currently selected work area to a Framework II file, RapidFile, or dBASE II file. *See* APPEND FROM.

COPY TO ARRAY <*array name*> FIELDS <*fields list*>] [<*scope*>] [FOR <*condition*>] [WHILE <*condition*>] Transfers the contents of fields in a .dbf file to a previously created array. The array must be created first by using the DECLARE statement. This syntax assumes that the open file has 10 fields.

```
USE <file name>
DECLARE edit[10]
COPY NEXT 1 TO ARRAY edit
```

COS(*n*) Returns the trigonometric cosine of an angle of *n* radians.

CREATE <*file name*> A floating point field type has been added as well as flags for which fields are key fields.

DBLINK <*file name*> A stand-alone program used for linking together multiple .dbo files into a single .dbo file for faster execution. This utility is only available in the developer's edition.

DEACTIVATE MENU Deactivates the active horizontal bar menu and erases it from the screen. It is not released from memory, however.

DEACTIVATE POPUP Deactivates the active pop-up menu and erases it from the screen without releasing it from memory.

DEACTIVATE WINDOW <*window name*>/ALL Deactivates and clears the named windows from the screen. Any previously activated window is reactivated. The window is not cleared from memory.

DEBUG <*file name*> Activates the full screen debugger on the named file.

DECLARE <*arrayname* [*r,c*]> Creates an array of *r* rows and *c* columns and sets aside memory variables for each element in the array. Array elements are initialized as logical False until an assignment statement is used to make them equal to a value. The maximum number of elements in an array is 1170.

DEFINE BAR <*exp*> OF <*pop-up name*> PROMPT <*string*> MESSAGE <*string*> [SKIP [FOR <*condition*>]] Specifies a single menu choice in a pop-up menu. The PROMPT or how it will appear on the menu can be specified as well as the MESSAGE that will appear at the bottom of the screen. The optional SKIP switch allows the specified bar to not be displayed if a specified FOR condition is true.

DEFINE BOX FROM *c* TO *c1* HEIGHT <*exp*> [AT LINE <*exp*>] [SINGLE/DOUBLE/<*border definition string*>] Defines parameters for drawing a graphic box on the printer.

DEFINE MENU <*menu name*> [MESSAGE <*string*>] Defines a horizontal bar menu.

DEFINE PAD <*pad name*> OF <*menu name*> PROMPT <*string*> [AT *r,c*] MESSAGE <*string*> Defines a single option for a horizontal bar menu by identifying the menu PROMPT and the optional MESSAGE to appear at the bottom of the screen.

DEFINE POPUP <*pop-up name*> FROM *r,c* TO *r1,c1* [PROMPT FIELD <*field name*>/FILES [LIKE <*skeleton*>]/STRUCTURE] [MESSAGE <*string*>] Creates pop-up menus under program control by specifying the menu PROMPT and the optional MESSAGE to appear at the bottom of the screen.

DEFINE WINDOW <*window name*> FROM *r1,c1* TO *r1,c2* [DOUBLE/PANEL/NONE /<*border definition string*>] [COLOR [<*standard*>][<*enhanced*>] [<*frame*>]] Defines a window by specifying its name, size, colors, and, border pattern of the window and its location on the screen.

DELETE TAG <*mdx tag*> [OF <*mdx name*>]/[<*ndx file name*>].... Removes the specified index tag from the specified .mdx file or closes the specified .ndx file.

DIFFERENCE(<*str1*>,<*str2*>) Returns a number (0–4) indicating how similar two strings are to each other using the soundex code of each. A *4* means that the two strings are perfectly matched.

```
. ? DIFFERENCE('high','hi')
        3
```

DISPLAY [[FIELDS] <*expression list*>] [OFF] [<*scope*>] [FOR <*condition*>] [WHILE <*condition*>] [TO PRINTER/TO FILE <*file name*>] Enhanced to include a TO FILE switch so that output can be directed to a file. For redirecting output to a file, the LIST syntax is superior because it does not require pressing a key at the end of each screen.

DISPLAY HISTORY [LAST <*n*>] [TO PRINTER/TO FILE <*file name*>] Enhanced to allow direction of the commands stored in the history buffer to a file. This feature is useful for experimenting with various sequences of commands at the dot prompt and then saving them to a file so that they can be incorporated into a program. For redirecting output to a file, the LIST syntax is superior because it does not require pressing a key at the end of each screen.

DISPLAY MEMORY [TO PRINTER/TO FILE <*file name*>] Enhanced to include window names, menu names, and the amount of memory consumed by each. The output of display memory can be directed to a file as well as to the printer. For redirecting output to a file, the LIST syntax is superior because it does not require pressing a key at the end of each screen.

DISPLAY STATUS [TO PRINTER/TO FILE <*file name*>] Now shows both MDX and NDX information, supports redirection to a file as well as to the printer, and shows the number of files open.

DISPLAY STRUCTURE [IN <*alias*>] [TO PRINTER/TO FILE <*file name*>] Enhanced to display a data base structure in a work area other than the one currently selected using the IN clause and allows redirection to a file as well as to the printer.

DMY(<*date expression*>) Returns a character representation of the date in dd month yy format.

```
. ? DMY(DATE())
24 December 88
```

SET CENTURY ON causes 19 to be displayed as part of the year.

DO <*program file name*>/<*procedure name*> [WITH <*parameter list*>] Looks for the program or procedure being called in the sequence

1. As a separate procedure in the current .dbo file
2. As a procedure in a file identified with SET PROCEDURE TO <*file name*>
3. A procedure in another open .dbo file
4. A .dbo file that has not yet been opened
5. As a separate .prg file that has not yet been compiled
6. A .prs file containing SQL commands

DTOR(*n*) Converts degrees to radians.

DTOS(<*date expression*>) Used when indexing on a date field plus a field of another type. When you index on a date field only, index on that field without any type conversion. To index on ssn plus date, the following could be used

```
INDEX ON ssn+DTOS(date) TAG ssndate
```

EDIT Now supports the features discussed under BROWSE, but still is not useful for programming purposes because it does not give programmers enough control over how data is accessed and changed.

ENDPRINTJOB Terminates a print job by sending the ending codes defined by the *_pecodes* memory variable and loops back to PRINTJOB to check the number of copies remaining to print based on the *_pcopies* system memory variable.

END TRANSACTION The end of the program control statement initiated by BEGIN TRANSACTION.

ENDSCAN Terminates the program control statement started by SCAN.

EXPORT TO <*file name*> [FIELDS <*field list*>] [<*scope*>] FOR <*condition*>] [WHILE <*CONDITION*>] [TYPE] [PFS/FW2/ RPD/DBASEII] The EXPORT command has been expanded to allow exporting .dbf files to Framework II, RapidFile, and dBASE II type files as well as to PFS files. *See* APPEND FROM for the codes for each of these new types of files supported.

FIXED(float expression) Converts a floating point value to a fixed data type N binary coded value.

FLOAT(fixed expression) Converts a data type N number to a floating point number.

FLOOR(*n*) Returns the largest integer that is less than or equal to *n*.

FUNCTION <*function name*> Defines a user-defined function (UDF). User-defined functions are special types of procedures. Because many commands cannot be used in a UDF, they are of limited value.

FV(<*payment*>,<*rate*>,<*periods*>] Returns the future value of the specified payment over the specified number of periods at the rate indicated.

The following shows the future value of 60 payments of $100 at a 12% annual interest rate.

```
? FV(100,.12/12,60)
    8166.97
```

Note that the interest rate must be the interest rate per period. In this case the annual interest rate of 12% is divided by 12 months, assuming that payments are made once a month.

GO/GOTO BOTTOM/[RECORD] <*n*>/TOP [IN <*alias name*}. Enhanced to allow moving the record pointer in a nonselected area by specifying the alias name with the IN switch.

GO TOP IN A would move the record pointer to the top record in work area A regardless of the currently selected work area.

IMPORT FROM <*file name*> [TYPE] PFS/FW2/RPD/WK1/DBASEII] Expanded to allow IMPORTing files from Framework II, RapidFile, dBASE II, and PFS files to .dbf files. IMPORT creates an entirely new .dbf file with the same name as the file being imported.

INDEX ON <*key expression*> TO <*index file*]/TAG <*MDX tag*> [OF <*MDX name*>] [UNIQUE] [DESCENDING] Enhanced to allow indexing to tags in .mdx files. The DESCENDING switch now allows creation of index tags in descending order. Using the dBASE III format will allow creating a dBASE III PLUS .ndx file. However, the DESCENDING switch can be used for .mdx tags only, not for stand-alone .ndx files.

```
INDEX ON field1 TO file1 &&creates an .ndx file
INDEX ON field1 TAG tag1 &&creates a tag in .mdx file
```

INKEY([<*n*>]) Modified to accept an argument of *n* seconds that defines the number of seconds to pause before program execution is resumed.

ISMARKED([*alias*]) Works in conjunction with the BEGIN TRANSACTION...END TRANSACTION program control structure to see if a transaction is in progress. If ISMARKED() returns a True, a transaction is in progress. It can be used in the following way

```
USE <file name>
IF ISMARKED()
    ? 'File was closed with transaction in progress'
    ? 'Execute either a ROLLBACK or a RESET'
    WAIT
ENDIF
```

KEY([<*mdxfile*>,] <*n*> [,<*alias*>]) Returns the key expression for the *n*th .ndx file or index tag. For example '? KEY(1)' would return the key field or fields for the first index tag in an open .mdx file.

LABEL FORM <*label name*> [<*scope*>] [FOR <*condition*>] [WHILE <*condition*>] [SAMPLE] [TO PRINTER/TO FILE <*file name*>] Enhanced to allow direction of output to a named text file.

LASTKEY() Returns the decimal ASCII value of the last key pressed.

LEFT(<*string*>/<*memofield name*>,<*n*>) Now takes the *n* leftmost characters from a memo field as well as from a character string.

LEN(<*string*>/<*memo field name*>) Now returns the length in characters of a memo field as well as a character string.

LIKE(<*pattern*>,<*string*>) Returns a logical True if the specified pattern with wild-card characters such as * and ? matches the specified string.

```
. ? LIKE('n*','neil')
.T.
. ? LIKE('n??l','neil')
.T.
```

LINENO() Returns the line number of the current command. LINENO() is best used in ON ERROR routines to record the line number in which the error occurred.

LIST ....[TO PRINT/TO FILE] Enhanced to allow redirection of output to a named text file.

LIST MEMORY [TO PRINT/TO FILE] Same as DISPLAY MEMORY except that it does not pause for a keystroke after each screen. It has been enhanced in dBASE IV to allow redirection of output to a named text file.

LKSYS(<*n*>) Works with .dbf files that have been CONVERTed in a multi-user environment. It returns the time of the record lock, the date of lock, or the ID of the user who last locked the record or file. The values of *n* can be

0	time the lock was placed
1	date the lock was placed
2	name of the user who placed the lock

LOCK([<*record number list*>][,<*alias*>]) LOCK() is used in multi-user environments and now allows locking multiple records with a single line command. Fifty simultaneous locks are possible now. LOCK() does not prevent a locked record from being read while locked. If a record number list is not specified, then an attempt is made to lock the current record.

LOG10(*n*) Returns the logarithm base 10 of *n*.

LOGOUT Clears memory variables, closes .dbf files, and resets other internal dBASE IV parameters in both single- and multi-user modes.

LOOKUP(<*return field*>,<*look-for exp*>,<*look in field*>) A function that works in a similar manner to the LOCATE command: no index is required.

```
? LOOKUP(lname,'123456789',ssn)
```

This command looks for a record in which ssn='123456789'. If a match is found, the lname field from that record is returned. If a match is not found, blanks are returned.

MDX(<*n*> [,<*alias*>]) Returns the name of the *n*th .mdx file open in the specified work area.

MDY(date) Returns the date in its spelled-out form.

```
. ? MDY(DATE())
December 26, 88
```

To see the first two digits of the year, SET CENTURY ON must be executed.

MEMLINES(<*memo field name*>) Returns the number of lines that a memo field will occupy based on the line length determined with SET MEMOWIDTH TO <*n*>.

MEMORY() Returns the number of kilobytes of available RAM.

MENU() Returns the name of the most recently ACTIVATEd horizontal bar menu.

MLINE(<*memo field name*>,*n*) Returns the *n*th line of the specified memo field based on the line length set with SET MEMOWIDTH TO <*n*>.

MODIFY COMMAND/FILE <*file name*> [WINDOW <*window name*>] Now invokes a real text editor that allows editing up to 32,000 lines of code. When a .prg file is edited and saved with MODIFY COMMAND, the old .dbo file will be deleted forcing dBASE to recompile the program. The WINDOW switch can be used to force editing to take place in a specified window.

MODIFY STRUCTURE Now supports the new floating point field type and the flag for whether or not each field is an index key field.

MOVE WINDOW TO *r,c*/BY <*delta row,delta col*> Moves a predefined window to a new screen position specified by either the absolute row and column coordinates or by a change in the row and column coordinates.

NDX(<*n*> [,<*alias*>]) Returns the name of the *n*th index in the index list for the specified work area.

NETWORK() Returns a logical True if dBASE is currently running on a network and a logical False if it is not.

ON ERROR <*command*> Specifies the program to be executed when an error occurs, but it still does not trap system-level errors such as *Printer not ready*.

ON KEY [LABEL<*key label name*>] [<*command*] ON KEY has been enhanced to allow for a *hot key* by trapping specific keystrokes while waiting for input with a READ. Keys that can be used as hot keys include the normal, shifted, alt, and ctrl values of function keys.

ON KEY LABEL F2 DO test Causes a program or procedure named test to be executed when F2 is pressed during a READ. Note that the procedure specified must be a procedure in the current .dbo file or a procedure in a file identified with SET PROCEDURE TO. To cancel key trapping, enter the ON KEY command with no argument. Note that commands that are not allowed in UDFs are also not allowed in procedures called by ON KEY LABEL.

ON PAD *<pad name>* **OF** *<menu name>* **[ACTIVATE POPUP** *<pop-up name>*] Defines which pop-up menu will be activated when the selection bar is positioned to the prompt pad of the specified menu.

ON PAGE [AT LINE *<n>*] *<command>* Allows a procedure to be executed when a page break occurs during printing.

ON READERROR [*<command>*] Specifies a command to be executed when variables are entered that violate the RANGE or VALID conditions of the @...SAY...GET or when an invalid date is entered into a date variable. ON READERROR with no argument disables range and valid checking.

ON SELECTION PAD *<pad name>* **OF** *<menu name>* [*<command>*] Indicates the action to be taken when a selection is made from a horizontal bar menu previously DEFINEd and ACTIVATEd.

ON SELECTION POPUP *<pop-up name>*/**ALL** [*<command>*] Indicates the action to be taken when a selection is made from a pop-up menu previously DEFINEd and ACTIVATEd.

ORDER([*<alias>*] With no argument, returns the master tag or index in the currently selected work area. If an alias is specified, it returns the name of the master tag or index in the alias specified.

PAD() Returns the name of the most recently chosen option from a horizontal bar menu.

PAYMENT(*<principal>*,*<rate>*,*<periods>*) Calculates the payment for a given principal, rate, and number of periods.

```
. ? PAYMENT(12000,.12/12,60)
        266.93
```

Note that the annual rate of 12% is divided by 12 to give the monthly interest because it is amortized over 60 months.

PI() Returns the floating point value of pi with precision based on SET DECIMALS TO

```
3.1415926535897...
```

PLAY MACRO *<macro name>* Replays the designated keyboard macro. Using keyboard macros as part of a program is not a good idea generally.

POPUP() Returns the name of the most recently ACTIVATEd pop-up menu.

PRINTJOB A program control statement that begins the sending of a print job. When PRINTJOB is encountered the starting printer codes (defined by the _pscodes system memory variable) are sent to the printer.

PRINTSTATUS() Returns a logical True if the printer is ready and a logical False if it is not.

PROGRAM() Returns the name of the program or procedure being executed. It is most useful for inclusion in ON ERROR routines to flag where an error occurred.

PROMPT() Returns the prompt string of the most recently selected menu option of a horizontal bar menu or pop-up menu.

PV(<*payment*>,<*rate*>,<*periods*>) Calculates the present value of a flow of payments at a specified interest rate for a number of periods

```
. ? PV(100,.12/12,60)
     4495.50
```

The present value of $100 received once a month for 60 months at a 12% opportunity cost is $4495.

PROTECT No longer an external utility. It is immediately available from the dot prompt and the Control Center in both single- and multi-user application to password protect and encrypt .dbf files.

PUBLIC <*memory variable list*>/[ARRAY <*array definition list*>] Now can declare both named memory variables and arrays to be public. PUBLIC still requires explicitly listing the names of all memory variables to be declared public—it does not allow using wild cards.

RAND([<*n*>]) Returns a random number between 0 and 1. If an argument *n* is specified, *n* is used as the seed value. If not specified, the seed value is based on the system clock.

REINDEX Now includes support for .mdx files. It rebuilds the indexes for all open .mdx and .ndx files in the current work area.

RELEASE MENUS [<*menu name list*>] Releases the named horizontal bar menus and any associated ON PAD and ON SELECTION commands.

RELEASE POPUPS [<*popup name list*>] Releases the named pop-up menus and any associated ON SELECTION commands from memory.

RELEASE WINDOWS [<*window name list*>] Deactivates the specified windows, restores any text obscured by the window, and releases the window definition from memory.

REPLACE [<*scope*>][FOR <*condition*>] [WHILE <*condition*>] <*field*> WITH <*exp*>[ADDITIVE] [,<*field*> WITH <*exp*>[ADDITIVE]] Modified to automatically convert between memo fields and character strings. If the ADDITIVE switch is specified, character or memo text will be added to the memo field specified.

REPORT FORM <*report form file name*>...[TO PRINTER/TO FILE <*file name*> Generates an .frg file instead of its own proprietary format. The .frg file can be edited to effect the appearance of the report. However, once it is edited, it can't be modified in the Report Generator mode.

RESET [IN <*alias name*>] Resets the integrity flag for a transaction in progress in the specified database header. The integrity flag indicates that a transaction initiated with BEGIN TRANSACTION has not been completed as determined by ISMARKED() returning a True.

RESTORE WINDOW <*window name list*>/ALL FROM <*window file*> Restores the specified window or all window definitions saved with the SAVE WINDOW command.

RETURN [TO MASTER]/ [<*exp*>] Enhanced to allow returning an expression when used in a user-defined function.

RIGHT(<*string*>/<*memo field*>,*n*) Returns the *n* rightmost characters from a memo field as well as a string.

RLOCK() *See* LOCK()

ROLLBACK [<*data base file name*>] Attempts to restore each data base and index file in the current transaction (bracketed between a BEGIN TRANSACTION...END TRANSACTION program control statement) to its condition prior to the initiation of the transaction.

ROLLBACK() The ROLLBACK() function returns a logical True if the last ROLLBACK command was successful.

RTOD(*n*) Converts radians to degrees.

SAVE WINDOW <*window name list*>/ALL TO <*window file*> Saves either all of the named window definitions or the named window to a specified window file.

SCAN [<*scope*>] [FOR <*condition*>] [WHILE <*condition*>][<*commands*>] [LOOP] [EXIT] ENDSCAN A program control statement that initiates a loop ended by ENDSCAN. The loop is similar to a DO WHILE with an embedded SKIP. If SCAN WHILE <*condition*> is used, the WHILE condition must first be made true with a SEEK or other record positioning command, or the loop will not execute.

SEEK(<*key values*>,[*alias*]) The SEEK() function, as opposed to the SEEK command, returns a logical True or False based on whether the key value specified is found in the file with the specified alias. If no alias is specified, the currently open file in the selected work area is assumed. Note that the file must be indexed for the SEEK function to work.

SELECT() Returns the number of the highest unused work area available for opening a .dbf file.

SET(<*character expression*>) SET() is used to determine the status of certain environmental variables. For environmental variables that can be set on or off, an *ON* or *OFF* is returned. For certain SET variables that are set to an integer value, the integer is returned. This function is useful at the beginning of a general-purpose subroutine so that the current setting of the environmental variables can be stored and reset at the end of subroutine execution.

```
. ? SET('talk')
OFF
. ? SET('echo')
OFF
. ? SET('history')
ON
```

SET ALTERNATE TO <*file name*> [ADDITIVE] Enhanced with an ADDITIVE switch to allow appending the data trapped with a SET ALTERNATE ON command to the end of an existing text file rather than overwriting the file as in previous versions of dBASE.

SET AUTOSAVE on/OFF Controls when the contents of memory buffers are saved to disk. When AUTOSAVE is set OFF, changes made to records in .dbf files are only saved to disk when the file is physically closed. If AUTOSAVE is on, changes are saved automatically to disk before the file is closed. Generally, for programming purposes, it is better to have AUTOSAVE OFF so that the programmer can control when data is written to disk.

SET BELL TO [<*frequency*>,<*duration*>] Modifies the frequency and duration of the bell tone. Frequency can be 19–10,000 cycles/second. Duration can be 2–19 ticks. The default is 2 ticks of 512 cycles/second.

SET BLOCKSIZE TO <*n*> Determines the blocksize of newly created .mdx and .dbt files as a multiple of 512. The range is 1–32. The default block size is one. This feature would be useful if you are working with very large memo fields.

SET BORDER TO [SINGLE/DOUBLE/PANEL/NONE/<*definition string*>] Changes the characters used in the borders of windows, boxes, pop-up menus, and lines.

SET CLOCK on/OFF Determines whether or not the system clock is displayed on the screen. It is automatically displayed when using BROWSE or the Control Center. This feature is most useful for displaying the clock as part of menu screens with developed applications.

SET CLOCK TO [*r,c*] Defines the row and columns coordinates at which the clock will be displayed if SET CLOCK is on.

SET COLOR OF NORMAL/MESSAGES/TITLES/BOX/HIGHLIGHT/INFORMATION/FIELDS TO [<*color attribute*>] Selects the colors used in text, headings, boxes, etc. The colors available will depend on the display adapter.

SET CURRENCY LEFT/right Determines whether the currency symbol appears on the left or right of numbers.

SET CURRENCY TO [<*exp*>] Determines the character that will be used for the currency symbol. The default is the dollar sign.

SET DATE [TO] AMERICAN/*ansi/british/french/german/italian/japan/usa/mdy/dmy/ymd* Expanded to include USA and JAPAN formats as well as mdy, dmy, and ymd. SET DATE only effects how dates are displayed, not how they are stored.

SET DESIGN ON/off Intended to allow developers to use the Control Center as a front end for applications by allowing them to keep end users from entering data base, form, label, program, or report design modes. Perhaps they should have included a command called SET CONTROL CENTER OFF.

SET DEVELOPMENT ON/off Determines whether or not dBASE will compare the creation date and time of an existing .dbo file with its related source file to determine if the program should be recompiled.

SET DEVICE TO SCREEN/PRINTER/FILE <*file name*> Allows redirection of @...SAY output to screen, printer, or file. The ability to direct the output of @...SAYs to a file is a major enhancement that has been lacking in earlier versions of dBASE. The following syntax would cause all subsequent @...SAY output to be trapped to a text file called trap.txt.

```
SET DEVICE TO FILE trap.txt
```

SET DISPLAY TO MONO/COLOR/EGA25/EGA43/MONO43 Allows specifying the type of display adapter that is being used. *See* the ISCOLOR() function under dBASE III PLUS.

SET DOHISTORY on/OFF SET DOHISTORY was retained for compatibility with dBASE III PLUS but performs no function in dBASE IV. Ashton-Tate states that DOHISTORY, which traps command lines to a memory buffer as they are executed, is no longer necessary because of the new debugger.

SET FIELDS TO <*field*>[/R/*calculated field id*>..]/ALL [LIKE/EXCEPT <*skeleton*>] Enhanced in a number of ways. /R after a field makes it read only. Calculated fields can be defined with the SET FIELDS statement:

```
SET FIELDS TO item,extprice=price*qty
```

In this example *item*, *price*, and *qty* are fields. *extprice* is a calculated field identifier that is defined as being equal to the product of the *price* and *qty* fields.

Also, wild-card skeletons can be used to select fields.

SET FIELDS TO ALL LIKE C*

This command sets fields to all fields in which the field name begins with a C.

SET FIXED ON/off Retained for compatibility with dBASE III PLUS but does not really do anything in dBASE IV.

SET FUNCTION <*n*> TO <*character expression*> Resets the function keys to a string value. In dBASE IV the controlled and shifted values of the function keys can be defined.

SET HOURS TO [12/24] Sets the system clock to a 12- or 24-hour clock.

SET INDEX TO <*list of ndx* or *mdx file names*>/? [ORDER <*ndx file*>/ TAG <*MDX tag*> [OF <*mdx NAME*>]] Enhanced to support .ndx and .mdx files. If an .mdx file is specified, the TAG switch must be used to specify which tag in the .mdx file to make the master index. If a production .mdx file exists, it is opened automatically when the .dbf file is opened.

SET INDEX TO ? displays a list of .ndx files in the currently selected subdirectory. However, it is not smart enough to know which indexes go with which .dbf files.

SET INSTRUCT ON/off Causes Help windows to be displayed after a full screen editing command is issued.

SET LOCK ON/off Controls whether or not dBASE will perform automatic file and record locking before commands such as AVERAGE, CALCULATE, and REPORT are executed in a multi-user environment. The idea is that if one user is changing a record in the file, the results of AVERAGE, CALCULATE, or REPORT won't be accurate unless all users are locked out from making changes while the report is being generated.

SET MARK TO <*character expression*> Changes the delimiter that is used to separate month, day, and year when dates are displayed.

SET MENUS ON/off Retained for compatibility with dBASE III PLUS but performs no function.

SET NEAR on/OFF Determines the position of the record pointer in a file after an unsuccessful SEEK or FIND. If NEAR is set OFF, an unsuccessful SEEK will result in the record pointer being positioned at end of file. If NEAR is set ON, the record pointer will be positioned at the record following where the record being sought would be in the index.

For example, if SEEK '94704' is executed with SET NEAR ON to find a zip code of 94704 when there are no 94704 records, but there are 94705 records, the record pointer will be positioned at the first 94705 record.

SET ORDER TO [<*n*>]/[TAG <*mdx tag*> [OF <*mdx name*>]] Supports tags as well as .ndx files.

SET POINT TO [<*character expression*>] Defines the symbol displayed as the decimal point character. The default is a period.

SET PRECISION TO <*n*> Determines the precision of type *n* numbers. The number specified must include the decimal point and the sign. The range is 10–20 and the default is 16.

SET PRINTER TO <*DOS device*>; SET PRINTER TO \\<*computer name*>\<*printer name*> = <*destination*>; SET PRINTER TO \\SPOOLER; SET PRINTER TO \\CAPTURE; SET PRINTER TO FILE <*file name*> Redirects printer output.

SET REFRESH TO <*n*> Works with the BROWSE and EDIT commands in multi-user mode. One user can be BROWSEing records while another user is changing records. SET REFRESH TO specifies the number of seconds between checks to see if data has been changed. The range is 1–3600 seconds and the default is 0.

SET RELATION TO <*exp*> INTO <*alias*> [,<*expN*> INTO <*alias*>]... Enhanced to support multiple relations out of an area.

SET REPROCESS TO <*n*> Works in multi-user mode and allows setting the number of retries when attempting to lock a record that has been locked previously. The maximum value is 32,000 and the default is 0.

SET SEPARATOR TO <*character*> Changes the symbol displayed between thousands in a numeric expression. The default is a comma.

SET SKIP TO [<*alias*> [,<*alias*>]..] Works with the SET RELATION TO command to allow support for one-to-many relations.

SET SPACE ON/off Determines whether or not a space is placed between fields separated by a comma in the ? and ?? commands.

SET SQL on/OFF Allows accessing SQL mode at the dot prompt. When SQL mode is on, many normal dBASE commands are not available.

SET TRAP on/OFF Determines whether the debugger is invoked when an error occurs or the Escape key is pressed during program execution as long as ON ESCAPE has not been used to define another action to be taken when the Escape key is pressed.

SET WINDOW OF MEMO TO <*window name*> Defines a default window for editing memo fields with the BROWSE or EDIT commands.

SHOW MENU <*menu name*> [PAD <*pad name*>] Displays a defined horizontal bar menu on the screen without activating it.

SHOW POPUP <*pop-up name*> Displays a defined pop-up menu on the screen without activating it.

SIGN(*n*) Returns a 1 if *n* is positive, 0 if *n* equals 0, and −1 if *n* is negative.

SIN(*n*) Returns the trigonometric sine of an angle of *n* radians.

SKIP <*n*> [IN <*alias name*>] Enhanced to allow skipping in a nonselected work area by specifying the alias with the IN clause.

```
SKIP IN A
```

This command moves the record pointer by one record in the file open in work area A.

SORT TO <*file name*> ON <*field1*> [/A] [/C] [/D] [,<*field2*> [/A] [/C] [/D] ...] [ASCENDING/DESCENDING] [<*scope*>] [FOR <*condition*>] [WHILE <*condition*>] Not useful in programming applications generally. It is usually more efficient to use indexes.

SOUNDEX(<*character expression*>) Returns a phonetic character string code based on the sound of the specified character string.

```
. ? SOUNDEX('high')
H200
. ? SOUNDEX('hi')
H000
```

SUBSTR(<*string name*>, *start*, *len*) Now can be used to extract a string from a memo field as well as from a character field or memory variable.

SUM [<*expN list*>] [TO <*memvar list*>/TO ARRAY <*array name*>] [<*scope*>] [FOR <*condition*>] [WHILE <*condition*>] Enhanced to allow summing to an array.

TAG([<*mdxfile*>,] <*n*> [,<*alias*>]) Returns the name of the *n*th TAG in the currently selected work area. If an alias is specified, it returns the name of the *n*th TAG in that work area.

TAN(*n*) Returns the trigonometric tangent of an angle with *n* radians.

TYPE <*file name*> [TO PRINTER/TO FILE <*file name*>] [NUMBER] Enhanced to direct output to a file as well as to the printer or the screen. The NUMBER switch can be used to generate line numbers.

UNLOCK [ALL] [IN <*alias name*>] Enhanced to allow releasing records or file locks in a work area other than the currently selected work area by using the alias name.

USE [<*.dbf file*>]/?] [IN <*work area number*>] [[INDEX <*.ndx file1*>/ <*.mdx file1*> [,<*.ndx file2*>/<*.mdx file2*>...]] [ORDER <*tag name*>] [OF {*.mdx name*.]]] [ALIAS <*alias name*>] [EXCLUSIVE] [AGAIN] [NOUPDATE] The venerable USE command has been enhanced in a number of ways.

- **USE ?** displays a listing of .dbf files in a pop-up menu format and allows a file to be selected using the point-and-shoot method. The subdirectory can be changed by selecting the desired subdirectory and pressing Enter.
- **USE** <***file name***> **IN** <***n***> opens a file in a nonselected work area by specifying the number (1–10) or letter (a–j) of the work area as part of the IN clause.
- The **ORDER** clause is used to select an index tag as the master index.
- The **AGAIN** switch allows the .dbf file to be opened in more than one work area. Note that when you open a file in more than one work area, it should be opened as read only by using the NOUPDATE switch in at least one of them.
- **NOUPDATE** opens the file as read only when it is desirable to have the user look at data but not change it.

USER() Returns the name of the user logged into PROTECT.

VARREAD() Returns the name of the field or memory variable currently being edited.

INDEX

SAMPLE PROGRAMS AVAILABLE ON DISK

Save the time it would take to type in the sample programs in this book. To order a disk containing all of the sample programs, send a check or money order for $30 with the completed form below. California residents add 7% sales tax.

NHD Software
P.O. Box 61
Berkeley, California 94701

Name ____

Company ______________________________________

Address ______________________________________

City __________________________ State ______ Zip ______

___ 5¼″ disk　　　　___ 3½″ disk

dBASE for Professionals

Make check payable to NHD Software

Van Nostrand Reinhold is not affiliated with NHD Software and assumes no responsibility for any defect in the disk or program.